My
Digital Entertainment
for Seniors

Jason R. Rich

que®

800 East 96th Street,
Indianapolis, Indiana 46240 USA

AARP®
Real Possibilities

My Digital Entertainment for Seniors

Copyright © 2016 by Pearson Education, Inc. All rights reserved.

ISBN-13: 978-0-7897-5660-2

ISBN-10: 0-7897-5660-9

Library of Congress Control Number: 2016930331

First Printing March 2016

Trademarks

All terms mentioned in this book that are known to be trademarks or service marks have been appropriately capitalized. Que Publishing cannot attest to the accuracy of this information. Use of a term in this book should not be regarded as affecting the validity of any trademark or service mark.

Warning and Disclaimer

Special Sales

For information about buying this title in bulk quantities, or for special sales opportunities (which may include electronic versions; custom cover designs; and content particular to your business, training goals, marketing focus, or branding interests), please contact our corporate sales department at corpsales@pearsoned.com or (800) 382-3419.

For government sales inquiries, please contact governmentsales@pearsoned.com.

For questions about sales outside the U.S., please contact intlcs@pearson.com.

Editor-in-Chief
Greg Wiegand

Senior Acquisitions Editor
Laura Norman

Development Editor
Charlotte Kughen

Marketing
Dan Powell

Director, AARP Books
Jodi Lipson

Managing Editor
Sandra Schroeder

Project Editor
Seth Kerney

Copy Editor
Barbara Hacha

Senior Indexer
Cheryl Lenser

Proofreader
Kathy Ruiz

Technical Editor
Greg Kettell

Editorial Assistant
Kristen Watterson

Book Designer
Mark Shirar

Compositor
Bronkella Publishing

Contents at a Glance

Table of Contents

6 Streaming Video with YouTube and Other Services 153

7 The Evolution of Radio: Beyond AM and FM 175

About the Author

Jason R. Rich (www.jasonrich.com) is an accomplished author, journalist, and photographer. Some of his recently published books include *iPad and iPhone Tips and Tricks,* Fifth Edition (Que), *My Digital Photography for Seniors* (Que), *Apple Watch and iPhone Fitness Tips and Tricks* (Que), and *My GoPro Hero Camera* (Que).

As a photographer, Jason's work continues to appear in conjunction with his articles published in major daily newspapers, national magazines, and online, as well as in his various books. He also works with professional actors, models, and recording artists to develop their portfolios and take their headshots, and continues to pursue travel and animal photography.

Through his work as an enrichment lecturer, he often offers digital photography workshops and technology-related classes aboard cruise ships operated by Royal Caribbean, Princess Cruises Lines, Carnival Cruise Lines, and Celebrity Cruise Lines, as well as through adult education programs in the New England area. Please follow Jason R. Rich on Twitter (@JasonRich7) and Instagram (@JasonRich7).

About AARP and AARP TEK

AARP is a nonprofit, nonpartisan organization, with a membership of nearly 38 million, that helps people turn their goals and dreams into *real possibilities*™, strengthens communities, and fights for the issues that matter most to families such as healthcare, employment and income security, retirement planning, affordable utilities, and protection from financial abuse. Learn more at aarp.org.

The AARP TEK (Technology Education & Knowledge) program aims to accelerate AARP's mission of turning dreams into *real possibilities*™ by providing step-by-step lessons in a variety of formats to accommodate different learning styles, levels of experience, and interests. Expertly guided hands-on workshops delivered in communities nationwide help instill confidence and enrich lives of the 50+ by equipping them with skills for staying connected to the people and passions in their lives. Lessons are taught on touchscreen tablets and smartphones—common tools for connection, education, entertainment, and productivity. For self-paced lessons, videos, articles, and other resources, visit aarptek.org.

Dedication

This book is dedicated to my family and friends, including my niece, Natalie, my nephew, Parker, and my Yorkshire Terrier, named Rusty, who is always by my side as I'm writing.

Acknowledgments

Thanks again to Laura Norman and Greg Wiegand at Que for inviting me to work on this project, and for their ongoing support. I would also like to thank everyone at AARP, including Kimberly Haslam and Anne Jacoby, for their support.

Over at Que, my gratitude goes out to Todd Brakke, Charlotte Kughen, Cindy Teeters, Kristen Watterson, Seth Kerney, and everyone else whose talents and hard work helped to make this book a reality.

Finally, thanks to you, the reader. It is my greatest hope that this book allows you to develop a clearer understanding of the technology that's available in your everyday life, and that it encourages you to utilize this technology so you can access the vast and ever-growing collection of digital entertainment that's readily available to you.

We Want to Hear from You!

As the reader of this book, *you* are our most important critic and commentator. We value your opinion and want to know what we're doing right, what we could do better, what areas you'd like to see us publish in, and any other words of wisdom you're willing to pass our way.

We welcome your comments. You can email or write to let us know what you did or didn't like about this book—as well as what we can do to make our books better.

Please note that we cannot help you with technical problems related to the topic of this book.

When you write, please be sure to include this book's title and author as well as your name and email address. We will carefully review your comments and share them with the author and editors who worked on the book.

Email: feedback@quepublishing.com

Mail: Que Publishing
ATTN: Reader Feedback
800 East 96th Street
Indianapolis, IN 46240 USA

Reader Services

Register your copy of *My Digital Entertainment for Seniors* at quepublishing.com for convenient access to downloads, updates, and corrections as they become available. To start the registration process, go to quepublishing.com/register and log in or create an account*. Enter the product ISBN (9780789756602) and click Submit. After the process is complete, you will find any available bonus content under Registered Products.

*Be sure to check the box that you would like to hear from us to receive exclusive discounts on future editions of this product.

Subscribe to and read digital
editions of magazines on
your smartphone or tablet.

In this chapter, you'll discover how technology has changed the ways we enjoy our entertainment. You'll learn

→ What forms of digital entertainment are available
→ Some basic terminology related to digital entertainment
→ How technology is quickly changing the ways we enjoy various forms of entertainment

The Changing World of Digital Entertainment

Thanks to the Internet—as well as technology that is built in to today's television sets, cable boxes, digital video recorders (DVRs), smartphones, and tablets—how we experience many forms of entertainment has changed forever. However, unless you understand what's available and how and where to access it, it's easy to miss out on the vast assortment of digital entertainment that's readily available to you—24 hours per day, 7 days per week.

My Digital Entertainment for Seniors is all about teaching you how to experience television, radio, music, movies, books, audiobooks, newspapers, and magazines in the digital age, and it introduces you to the vast assortment of content you can begin enjoying immediately.

Defining Digital Entertainment

Digital entertainment refers to accessing and experiencing your favorite entertainment—TV shows, movies, books, music, radio broadcasts, newspapers, magazines, and audiobooks—using the Internet and technology that's available to you. For example, instead of turning on your television set to watch your favorite show on a specific night, at a predetermined time, on a particular channel, there are now many other ways to access and watch that same TV show "on-demand" from your television set at home.

"On-Demand" Means When and Where You Want It

The phrase *on-demand* will be used often throughout this book. When content is offered on-demand, you can access and experience it when and where you want it.

When you watch traditional television, a specific TV show may air once per week at a particular time, on a particular channel. When that same show is offered "on-demand," either by your cable TV provider or via the Internet, you can start watching it whenever you want. You can also pause it, do something else, and then return to watching the show from where you left off, at your convenience.

In addition, it's possible to stream the current (or a past) episode of a TV show from the Internet to your computer or mobile device and watch it right away, or you can download the show to your computer or mobile device (so you can later watch it later, without an Internet connection). Shown here is a purchased episode of a television show playing on an iPad, using the Videos app that comes preinstalled on the tablet.

Watch a TV show on your tablet's screen.

Watching television programs isn't the only thing you can do to enjoy digital entertainment. You can also use a computer, smartphone, tablet, or even a television set to read a newspaper or magazine, listen to the radio, enjoy almost any movie, or listen to any music—anytime and from almost anywhere. For example, you might be used to reading a hard copy of your daily newspaper or favorite magazine, but printed newspapers and magazines are quickly becoming a thing of the past. Fortunately, the same content you'd read in any popular major newspaper or magazine can now be accessed by using the Internet web browser on your computer or with special apps on your smartphone or tablet. The figures show *The New York Times* being accessed from the publisher's website at www. nytimes.com and from the publication's mobile app on the iPad.

The New York Times website   *The New York Times* on an iPad's screen

One wonderful aspect of digital entertainment is that you can customize the experience to your liking. It's possible to read the digital editions of newspapers or magazines from cover to cover to access the same information that's featured within the printed publications, but you can also customize what your digital devices offer so only the information that's directly of interest to you is presented. Also, in many cases, as new information becomes available, it's updated in real-time, so you always have access to the most up-to-date information.

Digital Publications Are Often Interactive

Instead of just reading what's on the printed page and looking at still images, many digital editions of newspapers and magazines offer interactive elements.

For example, if you click or tap a photo, you can view an entire collection of related images, or even a video clip. In some cases, when you click or tap a keyword within an article, you're redirected to additional articles or websites with more relevant information. This is functionality that's not possible in the printed editions of publications.

With digital entertainment, you can experience what you want, when and where you want it, in a cost-effective and easy way. You just need to know how to do it. An iPad, iPad mini, iPad Pro, or any Android-based tablet, for example, can become your gateway to virtually unlimited digital entertainment that's available literally at your fingertips. This book tells you all the ins and outs of getting the most out of your digital entertainment experience.

Understanding the New Terminology

As you discover how to tap into this digital revolution, you need to become familiar with a lot of terminology. For example, when you watch live television, that television signal is broadcast over the airwaves and retrieved and displayed by your television set. How it works is not really important, as long as you understand that when you turn on your television set and set it to the appropriate channel, the TV show you want to watch is displayed.

However, if you're a cable TV subscriber, that same television show is transferred to your television set using a different delivery method, such as through fiber optic cables that connect your television set to the cable TV service provider, via your cable box.

Thanks to today's technology, you can also watch that same television show via the Internet. By visiting a website operated by a television network, cable TV provider, or a subscription-based online streaming service (such as Netflix, Amazon Prime, or Hulu), it's possible to use your computer to stream TV shows (or movies) from the Internet and view them on your computer screen.

Streaming Is Different From Downloading

When you *stream* audio or video from the Internet, that content is sent from a particular website or online service and is viewed and/or heard on your computer, smartphone, tablet, or television set. The program, however, is not recorded and saved. When you're streaming content from the Internet, you must have a continuous Internet connection for the device you're using to stream that programming.

However, when you *download* content, such as a TV show or movie, from the Internet, that content is stored as a digital file within your computer or mobile device. Then, after it's saved, you can watch it later, whether or not an Internet connection is available.

>>>Go Further

MANY SUBSCRIPTION-BASED STREAMING SERVICES ARE AVAILABLE

For a flat monthly fee of less than $10.00, you can subscribe to a streaming service, such as Netflix (www.netflix.com), Amazon Prime (www.amazon.com/Prime), or Hulu (www.hulu.com), and then have unlimited access to that service's vast library of past and current television shows, as well as thousands of on-demand movies.

Each of these services also offers some original and exclusive programming. For example, Netflix offers the award-winning *Orange Is the New Black* and *House of Cards* television series.

From your computer's web browser, after signing into the service you subscribe to, visit the service's website, select the programming you want to watch, and then it will stream from the Internet and be shown on your computer screen, within your web browser window.

From your smartphone, tablet, or the streaming device (or cable box) that connects to your television set (including Apple TV, TiVo, Roku, or Google Chromecast), launch the app for the streaming service you subscribe to, select the programming you want to watch, and then enjoy it on the screen of your mobile device or television set.

Meanwhile, if you're watching television of a "smart television" that connects directly to the Internet, as long as an Internet connection is available, you're able to stream programming from services like Netflix or Amazon Prime Video, without connecting additional equipment to that television set.

Step-by-step directions for using these services can be found in Chapter 3, "Television in the 21st Century."

As you discover how to access different forms of digital entertainment, you'll learn relevant new terminology. At the same time, you'll discover that when it comes to accessing and enjoying each form of digital entertainment, you always have multiple options—some are available for free, whereas others cost money.

Free Is a Relative Term

When content is offered for free, as you enjoy it, you're typically exposed to advertising, which can take up screen space, require time to watch, or be otherwise distracting. So although you aren't paying money for the service or content, there is a cost in terms of the quality of the experience. In most cases, if you pay for content, it is presented ad free.

Types of Digital Entertainment

Digital entertainment is a very broad term. It basically refers to accessing any form of entertainment-related content that's available to you via the Internet, from your cable TV provider, from a satellite TV provider, or by utilizing a computer, smartphone, or tablet.

This book covers how to access and enjoy many forms of digital entertainment and explains the various ways each is available to you. Some of the more popular forms of digital entertainment are covered in the following sections.

Audiobooks

Some book publishers offer audiobooks, which you can listen to. An audiobook is typically a book that's read, word-for-word, by an actor. Depending on the book, an abridged or unabridged version may be available. Most fiction bestsellers, as well as some nonfiction bestsellers, and many other titles are offered as audiobooks you can listen to. In the past, audiobooks were distributed on cassette tapes or audio CDs.

These days, an audiobook can be purchased and downloaded as a digital audio file via the Internet, and saved to and played using a computer, smartphone, tablet, or digital audio player. The figure shows the iPad playing an audiobook using the Audible mobile app.

Play audiobooks on your smartphone or tablet.

Audiobooks Are Available from Multiple Sources

As explained in Chapter 12, "Listening to Audiobooks," there are several services, such as Audible.com and iBook Store, from which you can purchase and download audiobooks to enjoy listening on your computer, mobile device, or digital music player.

Computer and Video Games

There are many ways to experience computer and video games. For example, you can use a Nintendo Wii, Microsoft Xbox, or Sony PlayStation video game system. It's also possible to download and install game software on your computer, or install game-related mobile apps on your smartphone or tablet.

You can also experience online-based games via the Internet using a computer's web browser. Many games allow you to play alone, against computer-controlled opponents, or in real-time competition against other human players.

You can choose from all sorts of interactive computer and video games, ranging from arcade-style games to digital versions of popular board games, card games, or casino games. You learn more about these options in Chapter 9, "Having Fun with Games and Interactive Entertainment."

eBooks

Once upon a time, books were printed on paper and nicely bound, and you held them in your hands and manually turned the pages as you read them. An eBook offers the same content as a printed book, but it's available in digital form. All the book's text and graphics are displayed on your digital device's screen in a format that replicates a printed book page.

You can acquire and download eBooks from the Internet, and, as you discover in Chapter 11, "Reading eBooks," almost any book that's published in printed form is also made available in eBook form. The figure shows an eBook as it appears on the iBooks app on an iPad.

Book Publishers Now Publish eBook Versions of Their Latest Titles

Almost every major book publisher now offers an eBook version of every new fiction or nonfiction book it publishes. In addition, self-published eBooks are made available from aspiring or up-and-coming authors. Classic and otherwise out-of-print books have also been adapted into eBook form and are readily available.

Although you might often purchase printed books from brick-and-mortar retail bookstores, eBooks are acquired from online-based booksellers, such as Apple's iBook Store, Amazon.com, or barnesandnoble.com, and then downloaded from the Internet to the device they'll be read on, such as an eBook reader, smartphone, tablet, or computer.

What Do You Need to Read an eBook?

To read an eBook, you need to use a dedicated eBook reader, such as a Kindle eBook reader from Amazon.com or a Nook eBook reader from Barnes and Noble. Alternatively, you can use eBook reader software on your PC or Mac computer, or you can use an eBook reader mobile app on your smartphone or tablet.

An eBook reader, any computer, or a mobile device is capable of simultaneously storing hundreds, or even thousands, of full-length eBook titles. Thus, you can literally carry around an entire library with you on your mobile device or notebook computer.

Movies

Movies are aired on television and on premium cable TV networks, such as HBO, Showtime, and Cinemax. You can also purchase digital editions of movies, own them, and watch them as often as you'd like via your cable TV provider. Yet another option from your television set is to watch available movies *on-demand*, which means you decide what to watch and when to watch it.

In some cases, on-demand movies are offered for free from your cable or satellite TV provider, or you can rent them (and watch within a predetermined time period). You can also stream digital movies from the Internet via a streaming service or purchase them, in which case you download the movie file to your computer or mobile device so that you can watch it at any time. Another option, if you're a paid subscriber, is to use a mobile app from a premium cable service, such as HBO or Showtime, to watch programming and on-demand movies from these networks.

For example, you can use the iTunes software on your PC or Mac, Apple TV, or the iTunes mobile app on your iPhone or iPad (shown in the figure) to purchase (or rent) thousands of popular movies from the iTunes Store.

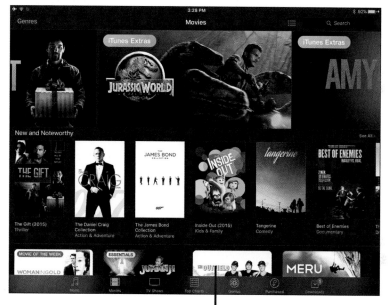

Choose from thousands of movies to watch or rent via the iTunes Store.

Movies Are Available in Many Ways

In addition to gaining access to countless movies from your television set (via your cable or satellite service provider), movies are available for purchase or rent via your computer, smartphone, or tablet.

Chapter 5, "On-Demand Movies at Your Fingertips," explains how you can stream movies from the Internet or, in many cases, download, save, and view them using your computer, smartphone, or tablet.

Movies are also available using Internet-enabled streaming devices that connect directly to your HD television set using a supplied cable. These devices include Apple TV, Amazon Fire TV, Roku, and Google Chromecast, which you also learn more about shortly.

Music

What do 8-track tapes, cassette tapes, vinyl records, and CDs have in common? They're all outdated ways of storing and listing to music. Today, music can be acquired, stored, and experienced in digital form, using a standalone digital music player (such as an iPod), using digital music player software on a PC or Mac (such as Apple iTunes), or a digital music player mobile app that's built in to any smartphone or tablet.

You can also stream music from the Internet via a music service such as Apple Music, Pandora, or Spotify. The focus of Chapter 8, "Digital Music: No More Records, Tapes, or CDs," covers all aspects of acquiring, streaming, and enjoying digital music.

Using the Music apps that come preinstalled on the iPhone (shown in the figure), the iPad, and all Android-based smartphones and tablets, you can store a vast personal digital music collection within your mobile device and have it accessible to you anywhere.

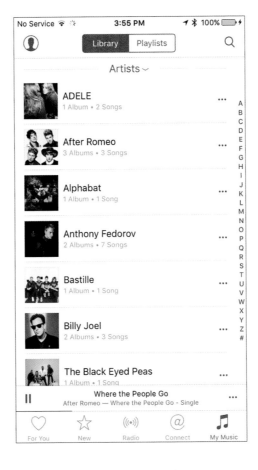

Newspapers and Magazines

For many people, gone are the days of having a printed newspaper delivered to their doorstep every morning, and then sitting down to read that newspaper, cover to cover, over morning coffee or during their commute to work. Likewise, few people have the time or inclination these days to sit down and read printed magazines.

As a result, virtually every newspaper and magazine that's published in printed form is now also available in digital form so that you can read it on a computer, an eBook reader, or a mobile device's screen.

However, as you discover in Chapter 10, "Reading Digital Newspapers and Magazines," you can also use your web browser or a specialized mobile app to easily read articles published by your favorite newspaper(s) and/or magazine(s). In other words, you have several digital alternatives to reading your favorite traditionally printed publications.

What's a Mobile Device?

Throughout this book, references are often made to various mobile devices. A *mobile device* is a smartphone, tablet, or potentially an eBook reader or digital music player, that allows you to experience one or more forms of digital entertainment. Most mobile devices offer Internet connectivity and utilize apps that give them additional functionality. They're also battery powered and extremely lightweight and portable, so you can use them almost anywhere.

The Apple iPhone, iPad, or an Android-based smartphone or tablet are examples of popular mobile devices.

Radio Programming

For decades, you needed an AM/FM radio to be able to listen to the radio. The problem was that as soon as you traveled outside of a station's signal radius, all you heard was static. Next came Sirius/XM satellite radio. With a specialized receiver, you can listen to any satellite radio station from coast-to-coast.

These days, instead of using a traditional radio receiver to listen to a radio station, that same programming can be streamed from the Internet and enjoyed from your computer, smartphone, or tablet. In addition to streaming traditional AM, FM, or satellite radio stations, you can choose from thousands of Internet-based radio stations.

Thanks to the Internet and many radio network or radio station–specific mobile apps, it's possible to listen to any radio station, from anywhere in the world, for free, and in some cases, access on-demand radio programming.

Most Radio Stations Now Simultaneously Broadcast Over the Internet

Chapter 7, "The Evolution of Radio: Beyond AM and FM," covers all the ways to experience your favorite radio stations and programs via the Internet, using your computer or a mobile device.

For example, if you install the free NPR (National Public Radio) app onto your smartphone or tablet, it's possible to listen to the live broadcast of any NPR station in America, and listen to many popular public radio programs on-demand, for free.

Television Shows

As with movies, you're no longer limited to watching TV shows on your television set only when a TV network or cable TV channel decides to air what you want to watch. It's now possible to watch episodes of many current or past television series, on an on-demand basis, from your television set (that's connected to a cable TV box or satellite TV receiver) or by using a streaming device, smartphone, or tablet. In some cases, you can acquire, download, and view shows; in other cases you stream them from the Internet to your compatible computer, TV, or mobile device.

As you'll discover shortly, for the most recently aired shows, there are sometimes limitations as to when episodes become available, how long they're available, and how many episodes from a current season are offered at once for streaming or download. What's available and when it's available often depends on the method you're using to access or acquire the programming.

Another option is to connect an optional DVR to your television set. This device allows you to record your favorite shows as you would with a VCR (but without using videocassette tapes), and then play them back at your leisure. DVR technology is built in to some cable boxes and satellite receivers. In addition, a company called TiVo offers standalone, programmable DVRs that are covered in Chapter 3.

There Are Many Ways to Watch TV Shows in This Digital Era

In Chapter 3, you discover how watching TV has changed, thanks to cable and satellite TV service providers, when a cable box, digital video recorder, or streaming device is used. The chapter explains what equipment you need, how much it costs, and how to use this equipment.

Then Chapter 4, "Watching TV on Your Devices," describes how to watch any episode or almost any TV series, on-demand, from your computer, smartphone, or tablet (without needing a TV set or cable TV subscription, for example).

World Wide Web

A wide range of online services, video streaming services, and social media services provide an ever-growing selection of multimedia entertainment that's available to you from any Internet-connected computer, television set, smartphone, or tablet. For example, YouTube (www.youtube.com) offers millions of hours of original video programming, which you can stream from the Internet for free. Chapter 6, "Streaming Video with YouTube," explains all the ins and outs of using YouTube.

Considering Compatibility Issues

The digital content you'll ultimately want to access is typically available to you in a variety of ways. Just like anything else having to do with technology, the equipment you need to access specific types of entertainment content varies. It's important to understand that the equipment you'll be using must be compatible with the file format of the digital content you're trying to enjoy.

When content is distributed in a specific digital file format, you need specific equipment to acquire, access, or experience that entertainment-oriented content.

Chances are, you already have access to some or all of the equipment you need to begin enjoying various forms of digital entertainment. However, if there's equipment that you don't yet possess, this book will help you develop an understanding of what you need and what options are available for accessing specific types of digital entertainment.

For example, if you already have an Apple iPhone or iPad, or an Android-based smartphone or tablet (that has Internet access via a cellular or Wi-Fi data connection), you're already in possession of a key piece of equipment for acquiring, accessing, and enjoying many forms of digital entertainment.

>>>Go Further
SOME MOBILE DEVICES OFFER TWO INTERNET CONNECTION OPTIONS

Depending on the mobile device you'll be using, chances are it offers Internet connectivity via a Wi-Fi Internet connection. This means that for the device to access the Internet, you must be within the signal radius of your wireless home network or a public Wi-Fi hotspot.

Some mobile devices also offer cellular Internet connectivity via a 3G or 4G (LTE) connection. This means that the device connects to a service provider's cellular signal to access the Internet. When it comes to cellular Internet, the terms 3G or 4G (LTE) refer to the speed of the connection. 4G (LTE) is currently the fastest cellular Internet available, although within the next year or two, 5G will be introduced in the United States.

To use a cellular data connection, a month-to-month or ongoing subscription fee is required, and in some cases, the service provider limits your monthly access, or after a certain amount of data usage, throttles down the speed of your connection.

If your cellular data service provider offers you a monthly data allocation, such as 5GB, and you use it up by streaming a lot of video or music, for example, you will often be charged for additional cellular data usage. Ideally, you want a cellular data plan that offers unlimited data (with no monthly allocation). Be sure to check with your cellular service provider so you understand what limitations, if any, you have when it comes to using cellular data (a 3G, 4G, LTE cellular data connection).

Typically, a Wi-Fi Internet connection is faster, but the signal radius is fewer than 200 feet from the wireless router/modem. When you travel beyond the signal radius, the Internet connection drops. A cellular data signal is available anywhere there is cellular service from the service provider you subscribe to.

Likewise, if you already have an HD television set, and subscribe to a cable or satellite TV service, you already have access to a vast selection of television programming, as well as on-demand viewing capabilities.

Meanwhile, if your have a DVR connected to your cable box (or satellite TV receiver), or DVR technology is built in to your cable box or satellite receiver, you have the capability to record your favorite shows and movies and watch them at your leisure on your television set, and potentially use other devices as well.

>>>Go Further

WATCH IN ANY ROOM FROM ONE TV

In the past, if you wanted to watch TV in the living room, dining room, and/or your bedroom, you needed to set up a separate television set (with a cable box or satellite TV receiver connected to each TV) within each room. This is no longer the case.

Most cable and satellite TV services now offer a free mobile app that allows you to stream programming from a single cable box, satellite TV receiver, or DVR directly to the screen of your computer, smartphone, or tablet.

This means you can watch your favorite live or recorded shows from anywhere within the signal radius of your home wireless network (and in some cases, while you're away from home as well). Chapter 4 explains more about this option for watching television.

By connecting a streaming device to your television set, that's also connected to the Internet, it's possible to stream TV programming and/or music, and experience a vast selection of on-demand programming. This type of programming is available in three ways:

- It's free and available to you anytime, on an unlimited basis.

- Content can be purchased or rented. You pay a one-time fee for each TV show or movie you want to watch on-demand. You can either purchase this content outright and own it, so you can watch it as often as you'd like in the future, or, in the case of movies, you can rent them and watch them as much as you'd like within a 24-hour period, for example.

- Pay a flat monthly fee for a subscription to a streaming TV/movie service, such as Amazon Prime, Netflix, or Hulu, and watch as much on-demand programming as you'd like.

Specialized Equipment May Be Required

When you subscribe to a streaming TV/movie service, such as Amazon Prime, Netflix, or Hulu, you are required to connect specialized equipment to your HD television set. However, what's required is currently built in to many cable boxes and satellite TV receivers, as well as DVRs (like TiVo).

Streaming devices (Apple TV, Amazon Fire TV, or Google Chromecast, for example) that connect to your HD television set and the Internet can also be used with services such as Amazon Prime, Netflix, or Hulu.

You can use your smartphone or tablet to install the Amazon Prime, Netflix, or Hulu app needed to access these streaming services. From your computer's web browser, visit the respective website for the streaming service you subscribe to in order to watch available content on-demand, on your screen.

It's Not All Good

A High-Definition Television Set Is Required

To have the most access to digital entertainment from your television set, you need to have a high-definition (HD) television set. The latest HD televisions are able to display video content at up to 4K resolution, which is significantly higher quality than the now-outdated standard television sets. These 4K resolution television sets also offer better resolution than 720p or 1080p resolution high-definition television sets.

A television's picture quality is measured by its resolution. In other words, a television set's resolution determines how many individual colored dots (called pixels) are used to compose a single video image on the screen. A 720p "Standard HD" television set, for example, displays video images at 1280 by 720 pixels.

The most common "Full HD" television sets utilize 1080p resolution, which displays images at 1920 by 1080 pixels. However, the latest 4K ("Ultra HD" or "UHD") resolution television sets display video images at 3840 by 2160 pixels.

As of early 2016, however, programming designed to be seen on 4K resolution television sets is very limited because the television networks currently offer most of their programming in 1080p Full HD resolution. Thus, for at least the next several years, you'll find that a Full HD, 1080p resolution television set will be more than adequate when it comes to watching your favorite TV shows.

Standard HD, Full HD, and Ultra HD television sets are now widely available wherever televisions are sold, such as at Best Buy, Costco, Walmart, and Target. In recent years, prices for these high-definition television sets have dropped significantly, and they're available in a wide range of screen sizes, ranging from 19 inches (diagonal) to well over 70 inches (diagonal).

In addition to offering a much clearer picture that displays more detail and more vibrant colors (compared to outdated standard TVs), these HD television sets also have HDMI ports, which enable you to connect the latest accessories, such as a DVR, DVD player, Blu-Ray player, cable box, satellite TV receiver, or streaming device—all of which allow you to access and watch HD programming.

Thus, if you haven't already done so, it will be necessary for you to upgrade your standard television set(s) to high-definition television sets, which range in price from around $100.00 to several thousand dollars, depending on their resolution and screen size.

One benefit to high-definition televisions is that they're much thinner than standard television sets, and most can easily be mounted on a wall.

Don't Be Afraid!

As you begin to delve into the world of digital entertainment, you'll quickly discover that an unprecedented amount of content is available to you. The trick is to figure out what content you want or need access to, and then determine the easiest and most cost-effective way(s) to access that content.

My Digital Entertainment for Seniors offers a comprehensive, easy-to-understand introduction to all aspects of digital entertainment. If you already have access to an HD television set with cable or satellite service, or have a computer, smartphone, or tablet with Internet access, you already have most (if not all) of the equipment you'll need to get started.

Start Off Slowly, and Proceed at Your Own Pace

If you find the digital world to be a bit overwhelming, you're certainly not alone. However, by following the directions offered within this book and then focusing on just one aspect of digital entertainment at a time, you too will soon be saying goodbye to reading printed newspapers, magazines, and books and will no longer have a need for your record player (turntable), CD player, or AM/FM radio. Plus, when you sit in front of your HD television set, you'll soon be able to watch the show or movie you want, exactly when you want to watch it. Or, using your smartphone or tablet, you'll be able to access all of this available content from home, while on the go, or from just about anywhere.

Remember, you can adopt this technology into your life at your own pace, and utilize it in only the ways you feel comfortable. Keep in mind, however, that there will definitely be a short adjustment period as you learn new skills and adjust your habits for consuming media.

What You'll Need To Get Started

In addition to the specific equipment you need to access various forms of digital entertainment (all of which will be explained, in detail, throughout this book), you also need curiosity and a willingness to experiment with and embrace the technology that's available to you.

Whether you lead an active and very hectic lifestyle and want to make maximum use of your media consumption when and where it's convenient; whether you're constantly on-the-go, but want to stay informed and entertained; or if you want to experience more ways to stay entertained and informed using technology, chances are you'll benefit from utilizing digital entertainment.

The equipment you need to access various forms of digital entertainment varies depending on what devices you're most comfortable using and how many devices you're willing to have. For example, to read the digital version of a book, which is called an eBook, you can use a dedicated eBook reader (such as a Kindle or Nook). However, you can also use eBook reading software on your computer or an eBook reader mobile app on your smartphone or tablet.

The figure shows a dedicated eBook reader, called the Kindle Paperwhite ($119.99), which is available from Amazon.com. It's one of many such devices available, although you can read eBooks formatted for Kindle eBook readers on virtually any tablet by using the Kindle app that's available from the app store associated with your mobile device.

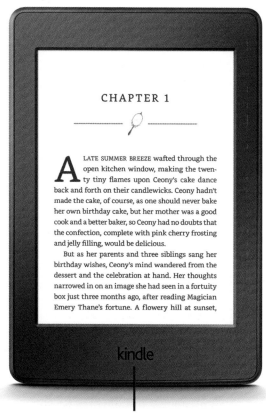

Kindle Paperwhite eBook reader from Amazon.com

In general, to access almost any form of digital entertainment (from your computer, television set, smartphone, or tablet, for example), Internet access is required. The exception is when you're accessing content via your television set, and service is provided by your cable or satellite TV service provider.

Each chapter of this book focuses on accessing and experiencing a different form of digital entertainment and provides the step-by-step directions you'll need to get started.

Starting in Chapter 2, "Getting Started with Digital Entertainment," you learn more about the types of equipment you need and the services you may need to subscribe to in order to gain unfettered access to the entertainment-oriented content you want. The costs associated with accessing, acquiring, and/or utilizing digital entertainment are also covered.

It's Not All Good

Don't Pay For Services and Technology You Don't Need Or Want

One of the biggest challenges you may encounter is being sold equipment or services that you don't need or want. For example, if you subscribe to cable or satellite TV, the provider will offer many, and often confusing, plans or "packages," each of which will have multiple "hidden" charges associated with them. The same is true when signing up for home Internet service or a service plan for your smartphone or tablet.

Before subscribing to or signing up for any service, make sure you understand all the fees involved and which features, services, and/or programming options are included. Also, determine if you're making a one- or two-year commitment to that service, and whether there is a hefty early-termination fee associated with canceling or changing your service plan.

Although you can often save money by bundling cable TV, home Internet, and home telephone services through one service provider or by obtaining a comprehensive service plan for your smartphone (that includes unlimited calling, texting, and cellular data), make sure you're not acquiring services you don't want or need, and that you're not overpaying for what you sign up for.

After reading this book, you'll have a much better understanding of what's possible when it comes to experiencing all forms of digital entertainment. Using this knowledge, you'll have a much easier time determining your needs when it comes to services like cable or satellite TV, home Internet, and cellular service for your smartphone or tablet.

An HD television set is used to experience multiple forms of digital entertainment. (A Sharp AQUOS LED HD TV is shown here.)

Photo Credit: © Sharp

In this chapter, you discover what equipment you need to enjoy a wide range of digital entertainment, including

→ What equipment and services you need to watch television and movies on your television set
→ What equipment you need to enjoy various forms of digital entertainment on the go
→ What the equipment and various digital entertainment content services cost

2

Getting Started with Digital Entertainment

Once upon a time, if you wanted to watch television, all you needed to do was buy a basic television set, plug it in, adjust its rabbit-ear antenna, and then watch whatever programming happened to be airing at that time on the small handful of stations that were broadcasting. Recording a TV show required a video cassette recorder (VCR) and a blank video-cassette tape, and then you had to figure out how to adjust that annoying flashing clock that always appeared on the front of VCRs.

Today, almost all forms of entertainment are available in digital form, which means specific equipment is needed to experience that entertainment, and some type of service is required to acquire or stream the content.

In some ways, having many forms of digital entertainment available, as well as a vast and ever-growing selection of content, has made our lives richer, but it has also made things a bit complicated. Because consumer-oriented technologies are constantly evolving, it can be a challenge to figure out what equipment you actually need, and then what service(s) you need subscribe to so that you can enjoy various forms of digital entertainment.

It's Not All Good

Subscribe with Caution

With so many types of equipment available, as well as many service providers offering us various forms of digital entertainment for a fee, it has become commonplace for people to overpay for services and access to content they don't need or want, or wind up having to pay for multiple services with overlapping content in order to gain access to the specific selection of content they actually want.

Understanding what content is available, your options for accessing this content, and having the right equipment at your disposal will help prevent you from overpaying for unnecessary services and content.

Step one requires learning about what's possible and what's available to you in today's digital age. Step two involves determining your personal needs and wants when it comes to digital entertainment.

Step three involves gathering the right combination of equipment, products, and services to help you acquire, access, manage, and experience various forms of digital entertainment. Finally, step four requires you to become a savvy consumer to make sure you're not overpaying for digital entertainment content or subscribing to too many services that offer overlapping content (or content that you don't want or need).

To get started with digital entertainment, you need the required core equipment, such as an HD television set, desktop computer, notebook computer, and a smartphone or tablet. This is what you use to watch, listen to, read, interact with, and experience various forms of digital entertainment.

Next, you need an Internet connection, because that's the primary way you acquire, stream, or receive digital entertainment. It doesn't really matter what type of equipment you opt to use; you must have Internet access. As you'll discover shortly, you can obtain access to the Internet in a variety of ways, depending on the equipment you're using.

After your equipment is connected to the Internet, you need to acquire the digital content you want to experience. Thus, it will become necessary to subscribe to various types of service providers, or pay a per-use fee to access or acquire specific forms of digital entertainment content that is compatible with your equipment.

Confused? Don't worry. This chapter explains the types of equipment and services you'll ultimately need to experience various forms of digital entertainment. You'll also get a broad understanding of the initial and ongoing costs associated with each form of digital entertainment.

As you proceed through the rest of this book, you'll get more detail about each form of digital entertainment, as well as your options for acquiring and experiencing specific types of entertainment-related content. Then, after you understand what's possible, you can decide what forms of digital entertainment you want access to and how you want to access it. This determines how much you'll ultimately need to pay.

Saving Money When Shopping for Consumer Electronics

Some people enjoy the experience of shopping for consumer electronics by visiting a retail store and interacting with a salesperson who is able to answer questions on the spot. Others appreciate the benefits of shopping online, and are often able to save money in the process. When it comes to acquiring the equipment you need to enjoy digital entertainment, both shopping at retail stores and shopping online are viable options.

Shop at Retail Stores

When shopping at your favorite retail stores, follow these steps to become a savvy shopper and save money when purchasing any mid- to high-priced consumer electronics products, including most of the equipment discussed in this book:

1. Determine your needs, and see what's available by visiting several retail stores to learn about your various options firsthand and see the product(s) demonstrated. Determine exactly what you want to purchase (including the make, model, size, and so on). Try to obtain the 12-digit UPC barcode number for the desired product.

2. Perform online research about specific product(s) or product categories. Read independently published and unbiased product reviews from trusted sources, such as *Consumer Reports* and Reviewed.com, and pay attention to online customer reviews and star-based ratings. Visit a website, such as Reviewed.com, select a product category, or enter details about the product you're interested in within the Search field.

Search field   Product categories

2 Reviewed.com

Retailer-Specific Models

Keep in mind, some stores (including membership warehouse clubs, such as Costco or BJs Wholesale Club), often sell models of particular devices (from well known manufacturers) that are exclusive to them. Thus, a TV with very similar technical specifications may be sold at Costco and Best Buy, for example, but have different model numbers, which makes comparison shopping by product model number or UPC barcode a little trickier.

3 When you're ready to make a purchase, choose a retail store that offers a price match guarantee and has what you're looking for in stock.

4 Do research online or use a free mobile app on your smartphone or tablet to enter the details about what you want to purchase, being as specific as possible. Determine which nearby retailers and online merchants have the same product in stock, but at a lower price. Upon visiting www.nextag.com, PriceGrabber.com, Price.com (or a similar service), enter exactly what you're looking for within the Search field, then click any search result to visit that online vendor's website.

4 **Search field**

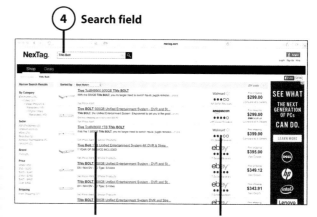

Vendor search result   Vendor's average star-based rating

Making Price Comparisons

Visit websites like Nextag.com, PriceGrabber.com, or Price.com, or use a mobile app, such as Red Laser, Shop Savvy, or Quick Scan, to compare prices for the equipment you want to purchase. When using these services, enter as many details as possible. You can use your mobile device's camera to capture the UPC bar-code number, for example.

5 Either visit the competing merchant offering the lower price to make your purchase, or ask the store you're currently in to match the competitor's price.

(6) Check the retailer's own website to see if an "online only" sale or promotion is being offered. If so, ask the retailer to match their online price at the retail store. Shown here, the price of the TiVo Bolt DVR is displayed on the BestBuy.com website.

(7) Consider waiting to make the purchase until the retailer holds a seasonal sale or promotion. Ask the salesperson when the desired product last went on sale, what the sale price was, and when it's expected to go on sale again. Shown here, the annual Black Friday Sale is promoted on the BestBuy.com website.

(8) Before making the purchase, determine if home delivery and installation (if applicable) is available, and what the additional cost will be.

(9) Determine the return policy for the product at the retail store, and ensure that no restocking fee will be charged. Do not assume that all retail stores offer a 30-day return policy, especially on open consumer electronics items such as TVs and computers. Be sure to save your receipt.

(10) For high-priced items, consider purchasing the optional insurance or extended warranty that's offered by the retailer, assuming the cost and length of coverage is reasonable.

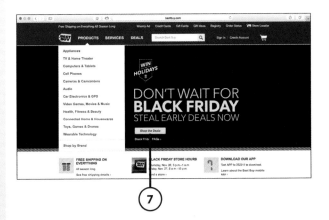

Shopping at Retail Stores Offers Some Benefits

Although you might wind up paying a bit more to shop at a local retail store (in contrast to online), some of the biggest benefits to shopping at retail are that you can speak with an often knowledgeable salesperson, see products demonstrated firsthand, and get all your questions answered. In a retail store, you can compare similar products, and more easily determine what features and functions you'll benefit from, based on seeing them demonstrated. Retail salespeople will typically take the time to educate you about various technologies and help you choose equipment that's most suited to your needs.

Shop Online

For many non-tech-savvy people, shopping online, especially for high-priced items, can be intimidating or confusing. However, by shopping online using your computer's web browser or a specialty shopping app on your mobile device, you're often able to save a lot of money, and get free shipping on your orders, when you shop around for the best deal.

(1) Determine your needs, and see what's available by visiting several retail stores to learn about your various options and see the product(s) demonstrated. Determine exactly what you want to purchase (including the make, model, size, and so on). Try to obtain the 12-digit UPC barcode number for the desired product.

(2) Perform online research about specific product(s) or product categories. Read independently published product reviews from trusted sources, such as *Consumer Reports* or Reviews.com, and pay attention to online customer reviews and star-based ratings associated with the product(s) you want to purchase.

3 Visit a popular and reputable online shopping service, such as Amazon.com, and check the price of your desired item. Do this by typing the exact name of the product (or its UPC code number) into the website's search field.

An Amazon.com Perk

If you subscribe to the Amazon Prime service ($99.00 per year), you can receive free, two-day shipping on all your orders of Prime-eligible products.

4 Visit one or two price comparison websites, such as Nextag.com, PriceGrabber.com, or Price.com, to determine what price a handful of other online merchants are selling the desired product for. Enter the product you're looking for into the Search field. Shown here, Nextag.com was used to research the price of the Bose Acoustimass 10 Series V home theater system.

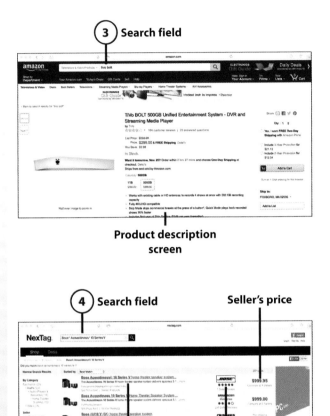

3 Search field

Product description screen

4 Search field

Seller's price

Desired product search result

Seller's star-based rating

(5) Visit the website(s) for your favorite retail stores, such as Target, Walmart, Best Buy, or Costco, and within the Search field, enter the product you're looking for. Determine the price each retailer is selling your desired product for, and determine if any online-only sales are being offered. Shown here, a listing for the TiVo Bolt DVR is displayed on Walmart.com.

(5) Search field

Save on Shipping

To avoid shipping charges, you can often make a purchase online from a major retailer's website, but pick up your item(s) at their local retail location.

(6) Shipping offer

Return policy

(6) Look for online merchants that offer free shipping and a no questions asked, 30- or 60-day return policy. Read the fine print carefully, to make sure the return period is 30 days (and not 7 or 10 days), and that there is no restocking fee.

Amazon.com Makes Product Returns Easy

One benefit to shopping online with Amazon.com is the company's easy, quick, and no-hassle return policy. If you receive an item that's defective, incorrect, or that you don't want for whatever reason, you can process a return (within 30 days) online in just minutes. The Amazon.com website generates a return shipping label and arranges for a courier to pick up the product from your home or office. In many cases, Amazon.com covers the return shipping and handling charges.

Amazon.com's return policy also applies to any third-party merchant that uses Amazon for order fulfillment.

(7) When using a price comparison website, read the customer
reviews for the online merchant
to make sure it's reputable. Shop
online only with merchants that
have hundreds or thousands of
positive customer reviews and
very few complaints (negative
reviews). When shopping online,
you can read reviews of both
the products you're considering
purchasing, as well as the online
merchants you want to do business with.

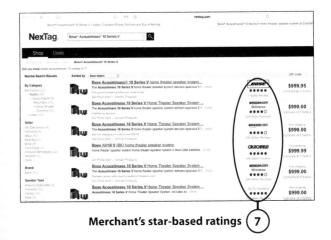

Merchant's star-based ratings (7)

(8) Before making a purchase from
a particular online merchant,
visit any Internet search engine
(such as Google.com, Yahoo.
com, or Bing.com), and within
the Search field, enter the phrase
"*[merchant's name]* discount
coupons" or "*[merchant's name]*
discount codes" to see if there is
a code you can enter at checkout
to receive an additional discount.
Shown here are websites that
offer free discount codes for Abe's
of Maine (www.abesofmaine.
com), a popular online-based
seller of consumer electronics.

9 Use a major credit card—not a debit card, prepaid credit card, or store-specific credit card. Later, if you have a problem with the merchant or the product, you can always contact your credit card issuer and file a dispute or request a chargeback, which is something you can't do if you made the purchase using a debit card. Shown here is the checkout and payment page of the Crutchfield.com website, also a popular online seller of consumer electronics.

10 For high-priced items, consider purchasing the optional insurance or extended warranty that's offered by the online merchant, assuming the cost and length of coverage is reasonable.

9 **Use a major credit card to make your online purchase.**

Paying with an Online Payment Service

Instead of providing individual online retailers with your credit card details, many allow you to make purchases using an online-based payment processing system, such as PayPal, Google Wallet, or Apple Pay.

To use a service such as PayPal, you must first set up a free account by visiting www.paypal.com. During the account creation process, you provide PayPal with your full name, credit card or debit card number, billing address, and shipping address, as well as a corresponding phone number and email address. You have to enter this information only once.

When you're ready to make an online purchase from a participating online vendor, enter the email address associated with your PayPal account and your PayPal password. PayPal charges your credit or debit card for the purchase and pays the vendor, which then receives your name and shipping address, as well as your payment, but not your credit or debit card details. Services like PayPal help to protect consumers from identity theft and becoming a victim of credit card fraud.

Be Savvy About Warranties

Make sure the extended warranty offers additional and better coverage than what's already offered by the manufacturer's standard warranty, and that you're not being charged for something you don't need or will never take advantage of.

It's Not All Good

The Drawbacks of Shopping Online

Although you can almost always save money shopping online, one drawback is that you can't see or test the product before it arrives at your door, and there is rarely someone available to answer your questions about a product prior to making your online purchase. When you shop online, it's generally assumed that you already know and understand exactly what you want, and you're looking for the least expensive way to acquire it.

Furthermore, few online merchants offer technical support if you have questions about setting up or installing your purchases. Instead, you have to contact the product manufacturer's customer service department.

Overview of Required Equipment

Let's begin by taking a look at the various types of equipment you need to get started in the world of digital entertainment. The following sections also estimate the cost associated with this equipment. Keep in mind, the options for the equipment outlined in this chapter are always expanding, and prices continue to drop.

HD Television Set

To experience many forms of digital entertainment at home, including television shows, movies, music, and some video games, the primary piece of technology you need is a high-definition (HD) television set. HD TVs are available with many screen sizes, and they utilize different technologies to showcase extremely high-resolution video images.

HD TVs Come in Many Screen Sizes

Here's an example of the different screen sizes for just one type of HD TV: The Samsung LED J6300 Series Smart TVs are available in 32", 50", 55", 60", 65", or 75" models. All offer full HD 1080p resolution. To learn more, visit www.samsung.com.

Plan to spend $150.00 to $400.00 for an HD television set with 1080p resolution and a screen that's 24" or smaller. Prices go up considerably—between $500 and $5,000 (or more)—for a state-of-the-art, 4K resolution, flat-screen TV, with a screen size that's between 40" and 70" (or larger).

Dozens of popular consumer electronics manufacturers sell HD televisions sets, including Emerson, Insignia, JVC, LG, RCA, Samsung, Sharp, Sony, Vizio, and Westinghouse.

Based on the room where you'll be installing the TV, figure out the optimal screen size, and then take a look at the different screen technologies and resolutions by visiting a retail store, like Best Buy, Costco, Walmart, Target, or anyplace else that offers a nice selection of HD TVs. Choose a model that offers the screen size, picture quality (resolution), and features you want.

From a technological standpoint, be sure to purchase an HD television set with at least 1080p resolution, and one that offers multiple HDMI ports on its side or back.

What's HDMI?

HDMI stands for High-Definition Multimedia Interface. You use the HDMI port(s) on your HD TV to connect other pieces of technology to your television set, such as your cable or satellite television receiver, DVR, streaming device, and/or video game console. When you buy one of these components, the appropriate HDMI cable might be included in the box so you can immediately connect the component to your TV; if the cable isn't included, you need to purchase the required HDMI cable separately.

It's Not All Good

Extra Expense for Sound and Mounting

Keep in mind that most HD television sets have built-in speakers, but the quality of these speakers is typically not too good. In particular, larger HD TVs are designed to be used in conjunction with an optional external speaker system, such as a digital surround sound (home theater) system, that's sold separately. To have the best-quality viewing experience possible, you should plan to spend at least several hundred dollars more for a home theater system with decent-quality speakers.

In addition, depending on the size of the HD TV, you might need to purchase an optional stand or wall mount. If you opt to mount the TV on a wall, consider hiring a professional installer, which will cost additional money.

Home Delivery May Be Required

Large screen televisions come packaged in large (padded) boxes. If you're shopping at a retail store, depending on the size of your vehicle and your ability to lift the oversize and heavy box, it may be necessary to have your new television set delivered to your home. An additional delivery fee, which may or may not include installation and setup, will typically apply.

Desktop and/or Notebook Computer

When it comes to shopping for a computer, begin by making two decisions. First, do you want a personal computer (PC) or Mac? Second, do you want a desktop, notebook/laptop, or two-in-one computer?

PCs are manufactured by any of a wide range of companies, such as Acer, Asus, Dell, HP, Lenovo, Microsoft, and Toshiba. The main distinguishing factor between PCs and Macs is that PCs are designed to run the Microsoft Windows operating system. Shown here is a desktop personal computer offered by Dell. Designed to be used while sitting at a desk or table, desktop computers need to be plugged into an electrical outlet. The computer includes a full-size monitor (screen), and a central processing unit (CPU), which contains the motherboard, microprocessor, sound card, graphics card, hard drive, RAM, and other components that allow the computer to function. There's also mouse and keyboard that connect to the computer.

©Dell

Don't Get Confused by Computer Technobabble

You don't need to understand how the CPU, microprocessor, hard drive, or other components of a computer work in order to use it effectively, just as you don't need to know how the transmission in your car works in order to drive it.

These days, most PCs and Macs are designed for use by average consumers, and include all the computing power that's needed, right out of the box. So, unless you'll be using the computer for a specialized task that requires a faster processor, additional RAM memory, or an extra-large hard drive, it's not necessary to bog yourself down trying to understand these technologies.

Windows PCs are also available as notebook/laptop computers or as two-in-one devices (which run Windows and are designed to serve as both a notebook computer and tablet in one device). Shown here is a two-in-one device from Dell.

©Dell

A notebook/laptop computer offers the same computer power as a desktop computer, but the notebook/laptop is battery powered and portable. Two-in-one devices have the same features and functions as a notebook/laptop computer, with the addition of a tablet-like touchscreen display.

Mac computers are manufactured by Apple. They run Apple's OS X operating system. There are several things that non-tech-savvy people like about Apple computers, starting with the fact that they are not susceptible to computer viruses. Apple also offers superior technical support through its AppleCare+ program, which is available in-person, at any Apple Store worldwide, online, or by calling (800) 275-2237 (for all Apple Products except iPhone), or (800) 694-7466 (for iPhone-related support). Macs also tend to be easier and more intuitive to use, which is very appealing to non-tech-savvy people.

The biggest benefits to Windows-based PCs are their price and the availability of a vast software library. You can typically purchase a Windows computer (with comparable computing power) for much less money than a Mac.

Desktop models of Macs are called iMacs. (The higher-end Mac desktop computer model is called Mac Pro). iMacs feature a large, flat-screen monitor with the computer's CPU built into it. Mac notebook/laptop models are named MacBook, MacBook Pro, or MacBook Air, depending on their configuration. The figure shows the iMac options listed on Apple's website (www.apple.com/mac).

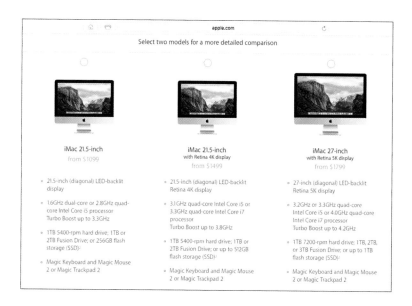

From a price standpoint, Windows PCs are typically cheaper than Macs. Prices vary greatly based on a wide range of factors, such as the size of the computer's screen, the size of RAM memory, and the capacity of the hard disk storage that is included, as well as the type and speed of the computer's microprocessor, for example.

For a Windows-based desktop or notebook/laptop computer, prices start around $300.00 and go up considerably. Meanwhile, iMacs start in price at $1,099.00 and go up to more than $2,000.00. The various MacBook models start at $899.00 and go up to more than $2,000.00.

All computers—regardless of manufacturer—can be easily connected to the Internet and have Wi-Fi (wireless) Internet capabilities built in. Some also allow you to easily connect to your Internet's modem or router via an optional Ethernet cable.

In addition to the operating system that comes preinstalled, all computers also come with a core collection of applications designed to handle the most common computing tasks, such as scheduling, email, web surfing, and contact management. You can download additional software and install it on any computer.

If you know little or nothing about computers, first figure out what you want to use the computer for, as well as how and where you'll be using it. This will help you define your needs. For example, after choosing between a desktop or notebook computer, if you plan to store thousands of digital photos, as well as many large size digital files for movies, television shows, music, and other content, how much hard drive storage space is available to you is an important factor.

Size Does Matter

Find a computer that's equipped with a 1TB or 2TB (terabyte) capacity hard drive. This will be more than adequate to handle all your storage needs for programs, data, documents, files, digital photos, and content. One terabyte (TB) is equivalent to approximately 1,000 gigabytes (GB).

Speak with computer experts, as well as the salespeople at computer stores, to help you determine your needs and define a budget. Then, after you choose between a desktop and notebook computer, and between a PC or Mac, take a look at what's offered. See which computer models and system configurations you like best.

Keep in mind, besides the price of the computer itself, you might need additional accessories and peripherals (such as a printer, an external hard drive, and/or a scanner), depending on how you plan to use the computer. All PC and Macs allow you to experience a wide range of digital entertainment using the computer's web browser, specialized software, its Internet connection, and, in some cases, optional equipment.

Smartphones and Tablets

Smartphones and tablets are battery-powered mobile devices that offer computing power on the go. They also serve as powerful information management, communication, organization, and web surfing tools, and they handle a wide range of tasks that allow you to experience many forms of digital entertainment from virtually anywhere.

Smartphones and tablets easily connect to the Internet using a Wi-Fi or cellular data connection, and they come with a wide range of apps installed to help you handle core tasks right out of the box. Smartphones and tablets also have access to an app store. From this online-based store, you can find and acquire optional apps that greatly expand the capabilities of your mobile device and open up even more digital entertainment–related options.

There are a few differences between a smartphone and tablet. First, a smartphone allows you to make and receive calls via a cellular service that you subscribe to. Second, smartphones are physically smaller than tablets. There is a significant amount of overlap and similarity, however, in terms of the other features, functions, and capabilities that both smartphones and tablets offer.

Like computers, smartphones and tablets run using a built-in operating system. The two most common mobile device operating systems are iOS, which is used by all Apple iPhones and iPads, and Android, which is used by smartphones and tablets manufactured by a handful of different companies, including Samsung, LG, HTC, Kyocera, and Motorola.

Microsoft Also Offers Windows Mobile Smartphones and Tablets

In addition to iOS and Android, a third, but significantly less popular, operating system for mobile devices is Windows Mobile from Microsoft. It runs on select smartphones and tablets. Lumia, which is a company owned by Microsoft, manufactures and sells Windows Mobile-based smartphones and tablets. The Microsoft Surface Pro 4, which is a Windows-based tablet that functions a lot like a notebook computer, runs Windows 10 rather than Windows Mobile.

Smartphones and tablets are powerful standalone devices unto themselves, but they're designed to sync data, documents, files, and content between your primary desktop and/or notebook computer(s) as well as your other mobile devices and the Internet, using software and technology that's built in to their operating system.

Syncing data has many benefits. For example, if you snap a digital photo on your smartphone, you can easily have things set up so that that image is uploaded to an online (cloud-based) account and then shared automatically with all of your other mobile devices and computers. Thus, within a few seconds, you will be able to view that newly shot digital image on your tablet or computer, for example, without manually having to do anything to copy the files. This same syncing functionality works with many types of content, data, documents, and files.

The iPhone smartphones are available in three screen sizes. The older iPhone 5s, for example, has a 4-inch (diagonal) display, whereas the iPhone 6 and iPhone 6s have 4.7-inch (diagonal) displays, and the iPhone 6 Plus and iPhone 6s Plus have 5.5-inch (diagonal) displays.

Android-based smartphones also come in a wide range of screen sizes and system configurations, based on the manufacturer. For example, the popular Samsung Galaxy S6 (and S6 Edge+) smartphone (shown in the figure on the Samsung.com website) has a 5.1-inch (diagonal) display.

Whether you want to watch television shows, movies, or other video content on the go, listen to music or audio programming, read eBooks or digital editions of newspapers and magazines, play interactive games, or experience other forms of digital entertainment, you can do it all using a smartphone and/or tablet. The main difference is that a tablet allows you to enjoy the experience on a larger size screen.

A basic Android-based tablet, like the Amazon Fire (with a 7-inch display) starts in price at $49.99. Depending on the screen size and amount of internal storage, as well as a few other factors, more powerful Android-based tablets cost anywhere from $100.00 to $800.00.

Priced at $49.99, the Amazon Fire is one of the least expensive tablets on the market.

iPad tablets from Apple also come in a wide range of system configurations and screen sizes, including 7.9 inches (iPad mini 4), 9.7 inches (iPad Air and iPad Air 2), and 12.9 inches (iPad Pro). Prices range from $269.00 to $1,079.00. Apple's website (www.apple.com/ipad) offers a price comparison chart related to the various iPad models. Click the Compare option that's displayed near the top of the web page.

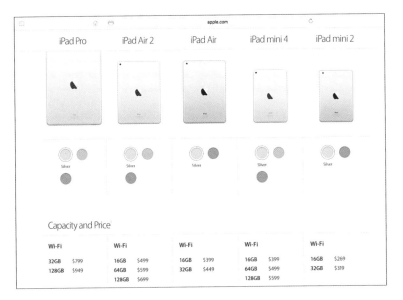

It's Not All Good

Most Mobile Devices Are Not Upgradable

When selecting a smartphone or tablet, keep in mind that the internal storage within these devices is not upgradable later. Thus, you want to select a device that will be able to store all your apps, data, digital photos, and content. Choose a smartphone or tablet with at least 64GB of internal storage space (although more storage space is typically better).

With some Android mobile devices you can insert an optional memory card to expand storage, but this option is not offered by the iPhones or iPads.

Also, new smartphone and tablet models are released every year. Although it's possible to subscribe to a cellular service provider that will automatically upgrade you to the newest smartphone model every year, most people will be able to use the same smartphone or tablet for at least two to three years (or longer) before needing to upgrade their device(s).

In addition to screen size, processor speed, and the amount of internal storage built in to tablets, one factor that impacts its price is how it connects to the Internet. All tablets come with Wi-Fi Internet connectivity built in, which means you need to be within the signal radius of a Wi-Fi hotspot or home wireless Internet network to access the Internet. For slightly more money, tablets can utilize a cellular data connection, which requires that it have access to a paid cellular data service, just like all smartphones.

A 3G/4G/LTE cellular data connection can be utilized anywhere a cellular signal is present, which includes coverage within most of the United States. What varies is the speed of the cellular data connection. These days, if you're going to pay for a cellular data connection, you want a 3G or considerably faster 4G LTE connection from your cellular data service provider.

When you start comparing smartphones, you'll discover that the various iPhone models (which all run the iOS 9 operating system) function pretty much the same way but offer different hardware configurations and screen sizes. The same is true with iPad tablets from Apple.

There are, however, many versions of the Android operating system used by the various smartphone and tablet manufacturers. All work pretty much the same way, but the appearance of certain icons, what options are included within menus, and which apps come preinstalled on each particular Android-based mobile device varies considerably.

Overall, all iOS and Android-based smartphones and tablets give you access to the same types of digital entertainment. What varies is the appearance of the device itself, and how apps and content appear on the screen. Thus, it's a matter of personal preference when choosing between an iOS (Apple) or Android-based device.

If you choose an iPhone, for example, and then opt to invest in a tablet, you'll have an easier time using the tablet if it's an iPad running the same version of the iOS operating system. The same is true for Android devices. When you're running the same app on multiple compatible devices, you can automatically sync your app-specific data, documents, files, and/or content between those devices as well. Thus, you will always have access to the information or content you want, regardless of which device you're using.

>>>Go Further

CHOOSING A CELLULAR SERVICE PLAN

All smartphones, as well as Wi-Fi + Cellular tablets, require that you subscribe to a cellular service plan. For a smartphone, this plan includes the capability to make and receive calls, send and receive text messages, and access the Internet. For a tablet, the cellular plan includes only the cellular data component.

To receive subsidized pricing on a smartphone, it is necessary to acquire a cellular service plan that has a two-year commitment. If you try to cancel the plan early, a hefty early termination fee will apply. Most smartphone plans these days include unlimited talk, unlimited texting, and a predetermined amount of cellular data usage per month (or unlimited data).

When you enroll in a subsidized smartphone plan, you can obtain a current model smartphone for less than $200.00, in contrast to paying the full price for the smartphone, which can be $600.00 to $1,000.00 (or more).

In 2016, many cellular service providers started moving away from offering subsidized smartphones with a two-year service contract, and instead allow customers to spread the cost of the phone into 12, 18, or 24 payments. After all payments are made, you own the phone outright. In the interim, you can trade your phone in for the latest model when it's released, but the payments begin again for the new phone. Thus, if you upgrade the phone before it's paid off, you're in essence renting the phone, as opposed to buying it.

After you've acquired the smartphone, plan to spend anywhere from $35.00 to $120.00 per month for a comprehensive cellular plan from a well-known, nationwide service provider, such as AT&T Wireless, Sprint, T-Mobile, or Verizon Wireless in the United States. Other smaller or regional cellular service providers offer lower-cost plans with a two-year commitment.

Another option, however, is to pay full price for your smartphone (or acquire a used or refurbished smartphone), and then sign up for a pay-as-you-go or month-to-month cellular service plan. This will cost anywhere from $35.00 to $120.00 per month, but there is no long-term commitment.

A cellular data plan for your tablet will cost anywhere from $10.00 to $50.00 per month, depending on the service provider and the cellular data usage allocation per month that's included with the plan. This can be anywhere from 512MG to 10GB, or unlimited.

Keep in mind, if you sign up for a limited cellular data plan for your smartphone or tablet and then exceed your data limit, the speed of the cellular data Internet connection will often automatically be throttled down and become much slower. The good thing about wireless data plans for tablets is that most are offered on a month-to-month basis and require no long-term commitment.

Choose a cellular service plan that offers the coverage you need, the services you want, and the highest possible cellular data connection speed at a monthly price you're willing to pay. This often means shopping around for the best deal.

Overview of Optional Equipment

Having access to an HD television set, computer, smartphone, and/or tablet gives you access to all the different forms of digital entertainment that are covered throughout this book. However, in some cases, to utilize functionality that's not built in to the equipment you have on hand, you might need some optional equipment.

This section outlines some of the more popular optional equipment that you might want to invest in, depending on the types of digital entertainment you want access to and how (and where) you want to access that content.

Cable or Satellite TV Receiver

In terms of using an HD television set to watch television programming, in most regions across the United States it is still possible to purchase a separate digital signal antenna and pull limited, local network affiliate station programming from the free airwaves. However, most people opt to subscribe to a cable or satellite TV service provider.

Even when you sign up for the most basic of cable or satellite television services, it can include hundreds of channels that broadcast in HD. This will include local affiliate stations for the main networks (ABC, CBS, FOX, NBC, and PBS), for example, as well as basic cable channels, such as AMC, Bravo, CNN, The Disney Channel, FOX News, Lifetime, SyFy, TNT, and The Weather Channel. For a slightly higher monthly fee, you can also sign up to receive premium cable channels, like Cinemax, HBO, and Showtime, as well as specialized sports programming packages. Some basic cable packages include just the main networks (ABC, CBS, FOX, NBC, and PBS), along with a few shopping and community access channels, but for a slightly higher monthly fee, many additional basic cable channels become accessible.

For your HD television set to receive cable or satellite television programming, you need a special receiver box (also called a cable box), which will be supplied by the cable or satellite service provider you sign up with. Companies such as Comcast/Xfinity, DirecTV, DISH, Time Warner Cable, and Verizon FIOS offer a variety of cable or satellite TV programming packages that have a monthly fee associated with them. Which specific cable or satellite service providers offer service in your city or region will vary, as will the monthly pricing you'll be charged for the programming package (channel lineup) you select.

The supplied cable or satellite receive box connects to your television set and allows you to receive television programming and view it on your HD television's screen. However, if you want to record your favorite shows and watch them at your convenience, you need either a cable or satellite receiver box with a built-in DVR (digital video recorder) functionality, or you'll need to invest in a separate DVR device that also connects to your HD television set and cable or satellite receiver box.

Many Cable or Satellite Receiver Boxes Also Allow You to Stream Programming

The cable or satellite receiver box you connect to your HD television set will receive programming from the cable or satellite service provider via a cable that runs into your home, or via a satellite signal. However, in many cases, the same cable or satellite receiver box also connects to your home's Internet service and allows you to stream TV shows, movies, music, and/or other content from the Internet.

In many cases, you can save money by subscribing to cable or satellite television service, home Internet service, and home phone service from the same company.

Digital Video Recorder (DVR)

A digital video recorder (DVR) is like a videocassette recorder (VCR) for the 21st century. All content you record, however, is stored digitally within the DVR's built-in hard drive. Thus, there is no need to tinker with videocassette tapes when recording or playing back recorded shows.

If your cable or satellite receiver box does not include DVR functionality, but you want to be able to record and play back your favorite shows at your leisure, you need an optional DVR. Chapter 3, "Television in the 21st Century," explains TiVo DVRs, including the TiVo Bolt.

DVD or Blu-ray Player

Over the next several years, all television and movie content will be made available to you exclusively on a digital, on-demand basis through your cable or satellite service provider, or from another streaming service, such as Netflix, Hulu, or Amazon Prime Video, which you'll soon be learning about.

Until this transition fully happens, TV shows and movies are still being made available on DVDs and Blu-ray discs, which require an optional DVD or Blu-Ray player to play them on your HD television set.

Video rental stores, like Blockbuster, are pretty much a thing of the past. However, you can still rent DVD and Blu-ray movies from Red Box vending machines that are found across the United States (www.redbox.com). You can also purchase DVDs and Blu-rays containing movies and individual seasons of TV series from many retail stores and online merchants.

It's important to understand, however, that DVD and Blu-ray technology is quickly being phased out and becoming outdated. Thus, it does not make a lot of sense to purchase a new DVD player to connect to your HD television set unless you already own a collection of DVDs that you want to be able to play on your TV.

As of 2016, adding a Blu-ray player to your home theater system is still a viable option, because it offers high-resolution audio and video, but this technology will also become outdated within the next few years.

These days, you can purchase a DVD or Blu-ray player that connects to your HD TV via an HDMI cable for well under $100.00.

Streaming Device for Your Television Set

As you'll learn from the next few chapters, in addition to watching TV shows and movies that are broadcast on various television and cable TV channels, or purchasing this content on DVD or Blu-ray discs, you can stream this content in a variety of ways from the Internet to your HD television set, computer, or mobile device.

If you don't have cable or satellite TV service for your HD TV, or your cable or satellite receiver box does not offer streaming capabilities from optional services like Netflix, Hulu, or Amazon Prime Video, you need to purchase and connect a streaming device to your television set.

These streaming devices cost between $30.00 and $200.00 and include Apple TV, Google Chromecast, Amazon FireTV Stick, and Roku Streaming Stick. Then, the ongoing subscription fee to access the programming offered by a streaming service costs less than $10.00 per month. You'll learn more about these devices, as well as the streaming services you can subscribe to, a bit later in this book.

Streaming Digital Entertainment Is Quickly Replacing DVDs and Blu-ray Discs

The capability to stream television shows, movies, and other content from the Internet directly to your television set, computer, smartphone, or tablet is quickly replacing DVD and Blu-ray disc technology. So, you're better off investing in a streaming device for your HD TV, for example, than in a DVD or Blu-ray player.

Home Theater System with Surround Sound Speakers

Most HD television sets include low-quality, not-too-powerful left and right stereo speakers built in. However, most HD television and movie programming is designed to be heard in digital stereo surround sound. As a result, you'll probably want to invest between $100.00 and $1,000.00 in a home theater system that connects to your HD television set and that allows you to experience crisp, clear, digital surround sound audio from your television set. Plan to spend around $400.00 for a good quality surround sound home theater system.

Many companies, such as Bose, Insignia, JBL, LG, Samsung, Sonos, Sony, VIZIO, and Yamaha, offer television surround sound systems (home theater systems) in a wide range of configurations, and that include vastly different quality speakers. They're available online, or from retail stores such as Best Buy, Walmart, Target, or Costco.

eBook Reader

All iPhones, iPads, and Android smartphones and tablets allow you to acquire, manage, and read eBooks and digital editions of newspapers and magazines. However, for less money than a full-featured tablet, standalone eBook readers are available from Amazon (Kindle) and Barnes and Noble (Nook).

Some of these eBook readers also allow you to connect headphones and listen to audiobooks or stream music from the Internet to the device, but their primary purpose is to display the pages of eBooks on their screens.

Amazon Kindle eBook readers range in price from $35.00 to about $200.00, depending on the type of screen, screen size, and the amount of internal storage that's offered. Some eBook readers offer a Wi-Fi-only Internet connection, whereas others also offer a cellular Internet connection for acquiring eBooks and content.

Barnes and Noble's Nook eBook readers range in price from around $100.00 to $350.00. It's important to understand that Kindle eBook readers allow you to acquire eBooks primarily from Amazon.com, whereas Nook eBook readers allow you to acquire eBooks primarily from barnesandnoble.com. The file formats used by each type of eBook reader is different. You'll learn more about this in Chapter 11, "Reading eBooks."

>>>Go Further

SMARTPHONES AND TABLETS OFFER EBOOK READING FUNCTIONALITY

The iPhone smartphones and iPad tablets all come with an app, called iBooks, that allows you to acquire eBooks and digital publications from Apple's online-based iBook Store and then read them on your iPhone or iPad. However, on your iOS mobile device, you can also download the free Kindle app and then acquire eBooks from Amazon.com that are otherwise formatted for Kindle eBook readers. You also have the capability to download the free Nook app and acquire eBooks from barnesandnoble.com that are formatted for Nook eBook readers.

Android mobile devices either come with the Kindle app preinstalled, or you can download and install the free Kindle and/or Nook app so that you can acquire, manage, and read eBooks and digital publications on your smartphone or tablet's screen.

To make things just a bit more confusing, some Amazon Kindle and Nook eBook readers offer a full-color touchscreen display, Internet connectivity, and much the same functionality as a full-featured tablet.

Unless you know that the only thing you want to do is read eBooks using a dedicated eBook reader, consider buying an inexpensive, full-featured tablet that can function as an eBook reader but can also easily handle many other tasks.

There are eBook distribution services that offer thousands of copyright-free eBook titles for free, or that offer an alternative to iBook Store, Amazon, or Barnes and Noble for acquiring and reading eBooks and digital publications. You learn about some of these services in Chapter 11.

Digital Music Player

HD television sets (with a streaming device or cable or satellite receiver connected), computers with Internet access, and all smartphones and tablets have the capability to play digital music.

However, there are also less-expensive, portable, battery-powered digital music players available that allow you to store and play digital music files while on the go or stream digital music from various services. Headphones or external speakers can be connected to a digital music player, based on the type of listening experience you desire.

The Apple iPods, such as the iPod nano (shown in the figure, www.apple.com/ipod), are the world's most popular digital music players, although other companies (such as Pono Music, www.ponomusic.com) offer similar devices. If you already have an iPhone or iPad, it comes with the Music app preinstalled. This app offers all the same functionality as an iPod digital music player. Android devices also offer apps that allow them to serve as full-featured digital music players.

Learn More About Digital Music

Chapter 7, "The Evolution of Radio: Beyond AM and FM," covers the various streaming digital music services available to you via the Internet, and Chapter 8, "Digital Music: No More Records, Tapes, or CDs," explains how to acquire, manage, and listen to digital music files on your HD TV, computer, smartphone, tablet, or digital music player.

Smartwatch

A smartwatch does a lot more than tell time. At this point in their evolution, though, you need a compatible smartphone to be able to effectively use a smart-watch. The watch serves as a second screen for your smartphone, allowing you to handle a wide range of tasks from your wrist.

The Apple Watch (shown in the figure, www.apple.com/watch) is currently the most popular smartwatch on the market. To use it, however, you must pair it with a current model iPhone, such as the iPhone 5s, iPhone 6, iPhone 6 Plus, iPhone

6s, or iPhone 6s Plus. Several models of the Apple Watch are available, starting in price at $349.00.

If you're an Android smartphone user, several Android-compatible smart watches are available from companies such as Samsung. The Samsung Gear S2 (www.samsung.com/us/mobile/wearable-tech/all-products), for example, ranges in price from $249.99 to $299.99. However, Pebble smartwatches (www.pebble.com/watches) are compatible with both iPhones and Android smartphones and range in price from $69.99 to $249.99.

All smartwatches have an ever-growing library of optional apps that allow you to further customize the devices and broaden their functionality. For example, there are apps that allow you to use the watch as a remote control for your television set or streaming device. Most also offer an assortment of games and other entertainment and personal fitness-related apps, as well as a selection of fashionable watchbands.

Console-Based Video Game Systems

You can play interactive video games on a computer, smartphone, or tablet using specialized software or mobile apps. These games allow you to play classic card games, board games, arcade-style games, first-person shooting games, role-playing adventure games, trivia games, and driving simulations. You can also experience a wide range of other interactive entertainment experiences against computer-controlled opponents or other human players.

A console-based video game system, such as the Microsoft Xbox One (shown here), the Nintendo Wii U, or the Sony PlayStation 4, connects to your HD television set, as well as the Internet, and allows you to experience vast libraries of video games that are suitable for all ages (or specific age groups). A console-based video game system costs between $199.00 and $599.00. However, in addition to the game system itself, you need to purchase individual games, which vary in price from around $10.00 to $70.00 each.

©Microsoft

Learn More About Video Games

Chapter 9, "Having Fun with Games and Interactive Entertainment," explains how to experience video and computer games using a console-based system that connects to your HD TV, as well as experience the latest and most popular computer games and games for your smartphone or tablet.

Internet Access Is Required

Regardless of what type of digital entertainment you want to experience, some type of Internet service is typically required. Within your home, you can pay a monthly fee for Internet service via your cable or satellite service provider. This involves the Internet service connecting to your home using a cable, FIOS (fiber optics), or a satellite signal.

After the Internet service reaches your home, you need a modem to accept the service so you can access it from your equipment. Some of the latest modems automatically offer an in-home network (via Wi-Fi) so all your equipment can connect to the Internet signal wirelessly.

If the modem your Internet Service Provider provides you with doesn't include wireless capabilities, you need to connect an external wireless router to your modem. The price for home Internet varies greatly, but averages between $30.00 and $60.00 per month, depending on the service provider and connection speed that's offered.

The company that offers your region cable or satellite service also offers Internet service. However, companies like Comcast/Xfinity, Time Warner Cable, and Verizon FIOS also offer standalone Internet service for a flat monthly fee. In most cases, you sign a one- or two-year service agreement, which includes a hefty early termination fee.

After you've set up a home wireless (Wi-Fi) network, you will be able to use it to connect your computer(s), HD TV(s), cable or satellite receiver box(es), DVR(s), console-based video game system(s), smartphone, and tablet to this wireless network to access the Internet.

However, if your smartphone or tablet is also able to connect to the Internet using a cellular data connection, you need to subscribe to a cellular data service plan from a cellular data service provider, which means you incur a separate monthly fee.

Overview of Content Service Providers and Suppliers

When you have the right equipment, and that equipment has access to the Internet, the various types of digital entertainment you want access to will come from various content providers—some of which will cost money, whereas others are offered for free. Throughout this book, you'll learn about the various content providers that offer specific forms of digital entertainment, such as TV shows, movies, music, videos, eBooks (and digital publications), audiobooks, or video games.

You'll download and save some of this content within the equipment you use to access it; in other cases, you stream content from the Internet and experience it using specific equipment—but you never save or store it. What you'll discover throughout this book is that various content service providers typically offer several forms of digital entertainment. However, you'll most likely need to utilize at least several content providers to have full access to all the different forms of digital entertainment you will ultimately want access to.

A streaming stick or device for streaming
content from the Internet to your television set.

Photo Credit: ©Amazon

This chapter covers the multiple options for watching TV shows and movies when they're aired by a television station or network or on an on-demand basis. Three of the popular ways to do this are covered in this chapter:

→ Subscribing to a cable or satellite television service and connecting a receiver box to your television set

→ Connecting a digital video recorder (DVR) to your television set and cable/satellite receiver TV box to record and play back your favorite shows

→ Attaching a streaming device to your television set that allows programming to be streamed from the Internet via a streaming service, or using a smart TV and the apps built into it (or downloaded to it)

Television in the 21st Century

It wasn't long ago that when you wanted to watch television, your options were limited to what was airing at any given time on one of the main TV networks, such as ABC, CBS, or NBC. Your television set pulled the network's broadcast signal from the airwaves and allowed you to watch your selected programming.

Although it's still possible for your television set to pull limited programming from the airwaves using an antenna, most people now subscribe to a cable television, fiber optic (FIOS), or satellite television service. The programming for hundreds of television stations and networks, which broadcast in high-definition, is delivered to your television set via cables or a satellite that sends the broadcast signal to a cable or satellite TV receiver box that is connected to your high-definition television set.

More Options for Watching Your Favorite Shows Exist

Another option for watching television shows and movies on-demand includes utilizing a mobile app offered by a cable television service or television network to stream shows via the Internet to your mobile device. How to do this is covered in Chapter 4, "Watching TV on Your Devices."

Recording Your Favorite Shows

In addition to being able to watch any of the hundreds of channels your cable or satellite TV box receives in real-time, you can use a digital video recorder (DVR) to record your favorite shows and watch them at your convenience. This process is similar to using a videocassette recorder (VCR), but without the hassle of having a bunch of videocassettes around!

With some DVRs, you have to connect a second device to your cable/satellite TV receiver box and your television set. In other cases, the DVR technology is built in to the cable or satellite receiver box that is provided by your cable or satellite television service provider.

Cable and Satellite TV Providers

Throughout the country, there are many cable TV service providers, such as AT&T U-Verse, Comcast/Xfinity, Time Warner Cable, Optimum, and Verizon FIOS. As for satellite TV service providers, two of the most popular companies are DIRECTV and Dish.

Each service provider offers different tiers of programming, which include a collection of basic and premium cable channels, as well as local network affiliate stations for ABC, CBS, FOX, NBC, and PBS, for example. These days, you'll want to watch television on an HD television set, which means you'll need to pay for HD programming from your cable or satellite service provider.

Most cable or satellite service providers require you to sign a two-year service agreement that includes a hefty early termination fee. These service providers offer discounts, however, if you bundle television, home telephone, and/or home Internet service together.

When signing up for cable or satellite TV, choose a channel lineup that you want, without paying extra for networks or channels you have no intention of ever watching. Having access to premium cable networks, like Cinemax, HBO, Showtime, and Starz, as well as specialty sports and/or adult channels, tends to cost extra.

Programming that's recorded using a DVR is stored as a digital file within the hard drive that's built into the DVR unit. Thus, how many hours of HD programming can be stored at any given time is determined by the storage capacity of the DVR (the size of its hard drive).

>>>Go Further

TIVO OFFERS A SELECTION OF POPULAR DVR DEVICES

If DVR technology is not already built in to your cable/satellite receiver box, an external DVR is required to digitally record your favorite shows.

TiVo (www.tivo.com) is a company that offers cutting-edge and versatile DVRs that make it easy to record your favorite shows and then watch them at your convenience on your television set. Or you can stream them from the TiVo (DVR) box to your mobile device or a separate TiVo receiver that's connected to another television set.

In addition to the TiVo DVR box itself, you have to have an ongoing subscription to the TiVo service. This service includes an interactive programming schedule for all channels you receive, and it enables you to easily record specific shows (or complete seasons of shows), even if you don't know on which network or on what date and time the desired show airs. The same TiVo box also serves as a streaming device and works in conjunction with several popular (and optional) video streaming services, including Netflix, Amazon Prime, Hulu, and Vudu.

The TiVo Bolt ($299.00 to $399.00) is among the company's latest DVR offerings. When you're watching shows in real-time, it allows you to pause programming and rewind. When you're watching recorded shows, you also have the capability to fast forward. The Skip feature allows you to press a single button on the remote control to skip through all commercials. The TiVo Bolt can replace a cable TV receiver box, and your HD television set will still receive all programming from your cable service provider (which you pay a monthly fee for).

Photo Credit: ©TiVo

Streaming Your Favorite Shows On-Demand

As a cable/satellite TV subscriber, one option that's offered to you is the capability to watch many of your favorite shows or movies on-demand. You do this by pressing the On Demand button on your cable or satellite receiver's remote control (when available), or by accessing your cable or satellite provider's On Demand menu that's then displayed on your TV screen. Typically, network television shows are offered on an on-demand basis, starting 24 hours after they originally air on their network.

When you select a particular show or movie to watch on-demand, that content is streamed from the cable or satellite service provider's system to your television set. The program is not recorded by your television set or DVR, but you can begin watching a selected show anytime, and you can pause the program or rewind it during the playback process.

Depending on your cable or satellite service provider, on-demand programming may be included with your monthly subscription fee, so you can use this functionality on an unlimited basis. In other cases, a fee applies for each TV show episode or movie you view on an on-demand basis.

To use the On-Demand feature offered by your cable or satellite service provider, you need only your HD television set and your cable or satellite receiver box—no additional equipment is required.

It's Not All Good

On-Demand Doesn't Mean Commercial-Free

When you watch on-demand programming for free, via your cable or satellite TV service provider, that program includes commercials that you will not be able to fast forward through. After you begin playing an on-demand show, you can pause or rewind the program, but not fast forward.

If you opt to rent a movie on an on-demand basis from your cable/satellite service provider, a rental fee may apply. That programming will not include commercials, and during the rental period (which is typically 24 or 48 hours), you can watch the movie as often as you're like, with the capability to pause, rewind, or fast forward using the cable box's remote control unit.

Finding On-Demand Shows and Movies

After you click the On Demand button found on the remote control (or access the On Demand menu) that's associated with your cable or satellite receiver, you can typically search for shows or movies by title, air date, popularity, or network.

Connecting a Streaming Device to Your TV

Yet another way to stream on-demand programming to your television set (via the Internet) is to purchase an optional streaming device, and then connect that device to your home's Internet service and your HD television set. Installation takes just minutes and can easily be done on your own, assuming you already have an HD television set and wireless home Internet.

You don't need cable or satellite television service to use a streaming device. However, you will most likely need to pay a low monthly fee (less than $10 per month per service) to subscribe to one or more streaming services, such as Amazon Prime Video, Hulu, or Netflix, for example. Streaming devices also include TV network-specific apps so you can stream some network programming for free, on an on-demand basis, and watch shows on your television set.

Several companies, including Amazon.com, Apple, Google, and Roku, offer streaming devices that are priced between $30.00 and $199.99. You can buy these devices from retail stores, such as Best Buy, Costco, Walmart, or Target, or purchase them online.

Double-Check Before Purchasing

Before you buy a standalone streaming device, make sure to check your cable or satellite receiver box, video game system, Smart TV, or DVR. Those pieces of equipment might have streaming capabilities similar to what's possible with an Amazon FireTV Stick, Apple TV, Google Chromecast, or Roku Streaming Stick. If you already have something that has streaming ability built in, you don't need one of these optional devices to stream on-demand programming from a streaming service or app.

>>>Go Further

FOCUS ON FEATURES WHEN CHOOSING A STREAMING DEVICE

Each popular streaming device offers its own set of features and functions, so although any of these devices easily connects to your HD television set and your home Internet service, the programming offered varies.

In addition to on-demand television shows and movies, most of these devices also allow you to stream music programming from the Internet. Using a service like Apple Music, Pandora, or Spotify, the music is broadcast through your television or home theater system's speakers.

As you're learning about the various streaming device options, pay attention to the features and functions each offers, as well as the selection of video and audio programming that is available using that device.

Apple TV

Apple TV has been around for several years now, but in late 2015, a fourth-generation version of the device was released. It includes a voice-controlled, handheld remote control, as well as new features and functions used for accessing and streaming audio and video programming (as well as your own photos and home videos).

The main component of the Apple TV device is a small black box, which is 1.4 inches high, 3.9 inches wide, and 3.9 inches deep. It weights just 15 ounces. On the back of this box are ports that enable you to connect it directly to your HD television set's High Definition Media Interface (HDMI) port via a cable. (See Chapter 2, "Getting Started with Digital Entertainment," for more information about HDMI ports.) It can also connect to your home's Internet via an ethernet cable or wirelessly (via Wi-Fi). A third port is used to connect a cable that plugs the box into an electrical outlet.

In addition to running Apple's proprietary tvOS operating system, this device has the capability to run many optional apps that grant you access to streaming programming from the Internet, as well as other functionality.

The Price of Apple TV

The Apple TV device is priced at $149.00 for the version of the device that includes 32GB of internal storage. For $199.00, the Apple TV box comes with a 64GB of internal storage. The internal storage space is used for storing third-party apps and content that you purchase and download.

If you'll be using Apple TV mainly to stream content from the Internet, via one of the device's preinstalled or optional apps, the 32GB version of Apple TV will be adequate.

Apple TV's Main Menu

Displayed along the top of Apple TV's Home screen (when the Movies icon is selected) is a Top Movies heading, along with thumbnails of popular movies currently available to purchase or rent via the iTunes Store. These movies can be downloaded to or streamed via your Apple TV device and watched on your television set.

App icons   Apple TV Home screen

Other Devices Work Similarly

Because Apple TV is one of the most popular streaming devices, its menu is described in detail, but the menus of other streaming devices work similarly.

All your previous iTunes Store purchases, including purchases made from your computer(s), iPhone, or iPad, are accessible from Apple TV, providing that you link your Apple TV device to your existing Apple ID/iCloud account. This content includes purchased TV show episodes, movie purchases, music videos, and music. Your single Apple ID account will have a credit or debit card linked with it, so when you purchase content, the charges are billed to that card without you having to reenter payment information. Prepaid iTunes gift cards are also available online or from retail stores, and you can redeem them online when acquiring content from the iTunes Store.

Immediately below the Top Movies heading are buttons for each of Apple TV's main menu options, including Movies (iTunes), TV Shows (iTunes), App Store, Photos, Music, Search, Computers, and Settings. After you start downloading and installing additional apps onto your Apple TV, app icons for them also appear on this main menu screen.

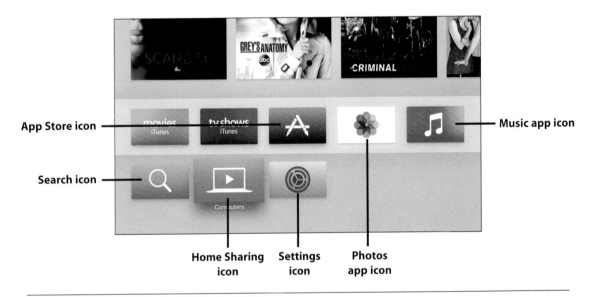

Accessing Music with Apple TV

Using the Music app that comes preinstalled on the Apple TV device, you have immediate access to all your previous music purchases made through the iTunes Store. If you're an Apple TV subscriber, Apple TV offers access to most of this service's features and functions. The Music app also gives you access to Apple Music, which is covered in Chapter 7, "The Evolution of Radio: Beyond AM and FM."

The Apple TV App Store

Your Apple TV has access to the Apple TV App Store, which offers a vast and ever-growing selection of optional apps that enable you to stream or acquire video or music content from a wide range of networks, services, and content providers. There are also third-party apps that allow you to view and showcase your digital photos or play exciting video games on your television screen.

Third-party apps from the App Store

The App Store offers apps that allow you to access popular streaming video and music services, some of which require a paid subscription. There are also apps from television and cable networks available that allow you to stream network-specific, on-demand programming.

Just like the App Store for the iPhone or iPad, some apps for Apple TV are offered for free. Others have a one-time purchase price associated with them. Some free and paid apps also require in-app purchases to unlock content as you're using the app.

The Apple TV App Store is divided into sections, including Featured, Top Charts, and Categories. Select the Featured option to see a listing of apps that Apple is showcasing and that are new or popular. Select the Top Charts option to see a listing of the most popular free, paid, and top grossing apps. Select the Categories option to view apps by category, such as Games or Entertainment.

App Stores for Other Devices

Similar apps can be added to some of the other streaming devices, or they already have the apps preinstalled that are needed to access various on-demand and streaming video and music services.

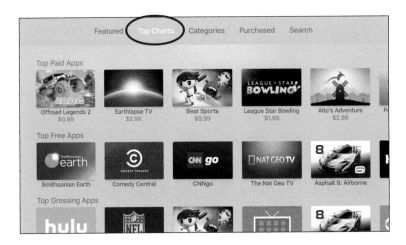

In terms of apps associated with streaming services and television networks, some of the optional and popular apps that are available via the Apple TV App Store include the following:

- **CNNGo**—Watch CNN news on an on-demand basis.

- **HBO Now**—If you're not already a paid subscriber to the HBO premium cable network, you can pay a flat fee ($14.99 per month) to access all HBO programming, on an on-demand basis, via this app running on your Apple TV. (A similar app is also available for your mobile device.) However, if you're already a paid subscriber to HBO through your cable or satellite TV provider, access to this app and HBO programming is free using the HBOGo app.

- **Hulu**—This streaming service is very similar to Netflix, but it offers its own collection of current and classic television shows and movies, as well as original programming that can be streamed, on an unlimited basis, to a television set, computer, smartphone, and/or tablet, for a flat monthly fee, starting at $7.99.

- **NBA.com League Pass**—Watch specialized programming from the NBA, including live and replay regular season games on an on-demand basis. Real-time scores, full-season stats, and video highlights are among this channel's other offerings. To access some programming, a monthly subscription fee applies.

- **Netflix**—The Netflix streaming service offers a vast collection of popular and classic television series, movies, and original programming that can be streamed to your television set, smartphone, tablet, or computer on an unlimited and on-demand basis, for a flat monthly fee of between $7.99 and $11.99 per month. The highest price plan includes access to HD and Ultra HD programming and the capability to view programming on up to four screens simultaneously.

- **Showtime**—Like HBO, subscribers to the Showtime premium cable channel can access all of this network's programming on an on-demand basis for free. Those who don't already subscribe to Showtime through their cable/satellite TV service provider can subscribe through this app for a monthly fee of $10.99, which grants unlimited access to all of Showtime's programming.

Watch Your Favorite Shows Without Commercials

Television programs watched on streaming services, like Netflix and Amazon Prime Video, are commercial free.

- **YouTube**—Stream free videos from YouTube, on an unlimited basis, using this app.

- **Network-specific apps**—In addition to premium cable television networks, Apple TV offers apps from most of the basic television and cable networks, including ABC, CBS, FOX, NBC, and PBS. These apps offer select current and past programming on an on-demand basis, but commercials are included within most of the programming. Access to these apps and their content is free of charge.

Beyond apps that offer on-demand access to television shows, movies, and special programming, you can use the App Store to get free and paid apps that offer additional functionality, as well as programming.

For example, it's possible to download and play games, and transform your television set into a video gaming system. There are apps that come preinstalled within Apple TV (or that can be added from the App Store) that grant you access to all iTunes Store television shows, movies, music, music videos, and audiobooks that you've purchased using your Apple ID/iCloud account. This content is readily available for streaming on your television set via Apple TV.

It's also possible to rent movies from the iTunes Store to watch on Apple TV. These movies typically cost $4.99 and can be viewed on an unlimited basis for 24 hours, starting the moment you begin playing the rented movie for the first time.

Meanwhile, if you're a Mac, iPhone, and/or iPad user, and you're using iCloud Photo Library to store and sync all your digital photos, those images (and the albums they're stored in) can be viewed on your television screen, via Apple TV, at no additional cost. A version of the Photos app that comes preinstalled on the Mac and all iOS mobile devices also comes preinstalled on Apple TV.

What Sets Apple TV Apart from Its Competition

Among the features that set Apple TV apart from other streaming devices include your ability to access and watch (or listen to) iTunes Store content you've purchased, rent movies via the iTunes Store, view your iCloud Photo Library photos, as well as download and experience games and other third-party apps from the Apple TV device.

Another useful feature of Apple TV is the Siri functionality that's built in to the wireless remote control. The remote has a series of buttons for navigating around Apple TV's onscreen menus and controlling the playback of the programming you choose to experience, but it also has Siri functionality built in. This means that instead of pressing buttons on the remote, you can press the single Siri button to activate this feature and then speak your requests or commands.

Set Up and Use Apple TV

When you purchase Apple TV, it comes with almost everything you need to connect it to your television set and begin using its built in features and functions. You need to purchase a standard HDMI cable to connect the Apple TV box to your television set.

There Are Two Ways to Connect Apple TV to Your Home's Internet

In order to function, Apple TV requires a continuous Internet connection. Using an optional ethernet cable, you can connect the Apple TV box directly to your modem or to a router within your home. However, if you have wireless Internet within your home already, Apple TV can wirelessly connect to your Wi-Fi network.

To initially set up your Apple TV, follow these steps:

1. Remove the Apple TV device and remote from the box and unwrap them.

2. Using the supplied Lightning to USB cable, plug the Lighting Port end of the cable into the bottom of the remote, and plug the opposite end into your computer's USB port (not shown). Alternatively, you can use an optional AC adapter to plug the remote into an external power source. The remote's battery should come partially charged, right out of the box.

(3) Connect one end of your HDMI cable (sold separately) to the back of the Apple TV box and the opposite end of the cable into an HDMI port of your television set.

(4) Plug one end of the Apple TV's power cord into the back of the Apple TV device and the opposite end into an electrical outlet.

(5) If you plan to connect your Apple TV to the Internet via an ethernet cable, plug one end of this cable into the back of your Apple TV device and the opposite end into your modem or router. Alternatively, if you plan to use a wireless Wi-Fi connection, make sure you set up the Apple TV within the radius of your home Internet's Wi-Fi signal (not shown).

(6) Turn on your television set and select the input setting that matches the HDMI port you've plugged Apple TV into. You do this by pressing the Source (or Input) button on the remote control that came with your television set, or by pressing the Source button on the set itself. If your TV has multiple HDMI ports, they'll be labeled HDMI 1, HDMI 2, and so on. The Apple logo, followed by the Apple TV introduction screen, will be displayed on your television set (not shown).

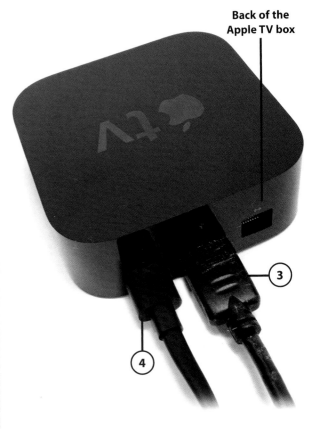

Back of the Apple TV box

Use the Apple TV Remote Control to Navigate

The Apple TV remote control is used to navigate your way around the Apple TV onscreen menus and then manage your experience by allowing you to play/pause, fast forward, or rewind as you're experiencing content. Alternatively, you can use the Remote app that's running on your iPhone or iPad to remotely control your Apple TV device that's connected to your television set.

(7) Follow the onscreen prompts to set up your Apple TV, and allow it to connect to your home's Internet. This process is easier if you hold your iPhone close to your Apple TV device and allow the smartphone to transfer information to your Apple TV via Bluetooth. However, you can manually enter the same information. Be sure to enter your Apple ID/iCloud account username and password into the Apple TV device. Later, when you launch specific apps, such as Netflix or HBO Now, for example, you need to sign in to each streaming service or network separately using your existing account username and password.

Make sure Bluetooth on your iPhone is turned on. (7)

8 During the setup process, you have the option of turning on Location Services and the Siri feature so they work with Apple TV. Location Services allows Siri to know your location, and the Siri feature itself is used to issue voice commands to the Apple TV device. Turn on both of these features.

9 Apple TV offers a series of precreated animated screensavers. You can choose to download them to your Apple TV device during setup or skip this step by choosing the Not Now option.

10 Two of the final steps in the Apple TV setup process involve allowing your device to send Apple Diagnostic and Usage information to Apple. If you agree to have your device send information to Apple, select the Send to Apple option. Otherwise, select the Don't Send option.

Help Fix Bugs

If you select the Send to Apple option, you can choose to help app developers fix bugs and improve their products by having your Apple TV device send the developers information when a problem occurs as you are using an app. Choose the Share with App Developers option to send problem reports. Otherwise, choose the Don't Share option.

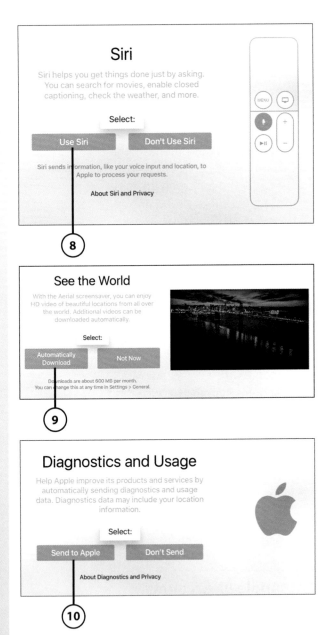

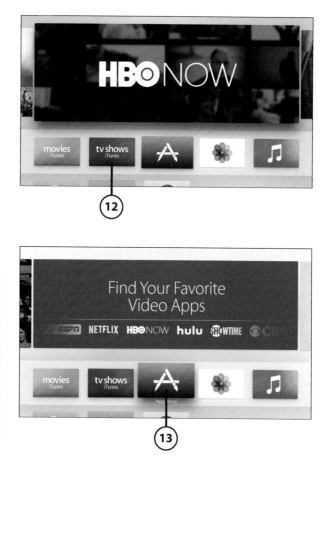

(11) Accept Apple's Terms and Conditions by selecting the Agree option (not shown).

(12) Launch any of the device's pre-installed apps using the Apple TV remote control unit. To watch or rent movies purchased or acquired from the iTunes Store, select the Movies (iTunes) option. To watch television show episodes purchased or acquired from the iTunes Store, select the TV Shows (iTunes) option. To access the Apple TV App Store, select the App Store icon, or to view photos stored within your iCloud Photo Library, select the Photos app icon. Select the Music app icon to listen to music that you've acquired via the iTunes Store or that you want to stream from Apple Music/iTunes Radio.

(13) To launch and use any other app that comes preinstalled on your Apple TV device, or that you've downloaded and installed from the App Store, select that app's icon.

Apple ID Accounts

You need only one Apple ID/iCloud account for all your Apple equipment, including your Apple TV, Mac(s), iPhone, and/or iPad. Using a single Apple ID/iCloud account with all your Apple equipment allows content and information to automatically sync and be shared between your Apple TV, computer(s), and mobile devices. If you don't already have an Apple ID, or can't remember the username (email address) and/or password that's associated with your Apple ID account, visit: https://appleid.apple.com.

How to Stream Content from Your iPhone or iPad to Watch on Your TV

Thanks to the AirPlay function that's built in to your iPhone, iPad, Mac, and Apple TV, when you turn on this feature (as well as turn on Wi-Fi and Bluetooth on your mobile device or computer), anything that's displayed on your smartphone, tablet, or computer screen, or played through its speaker(s), can be sent wirelessly to Apple TV and be played on your HD television set.

To do this from a compatible iPhone, iPad, or Mac app, tap or click the AirPlay icon or button. You can do this from the Videos, Photos, Music, Keynote, or PowerPoint app, for example. AirPlay is also supported by a growing number of other third-party apps.

Google Chromecast

Google Chromecast is a small streaming device that plugs directly into the HDMI port of your television set using the supplied cable. You can purchase it from popular retail stores (like Best Buy, Walmart, Target, or Staples) or order it online (www.google.com/chromecast/buy-tv). An additional (supplied) cable is used to plug the Chromecast device into an electrical outlet.

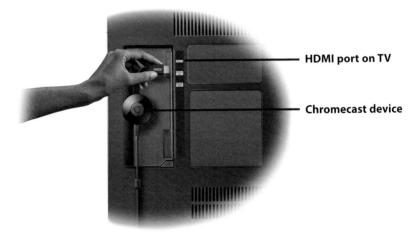

HDMI port on TV

Chromecast device

Photo Credit: ©Google

Then, using the free Chromecast mobile app that's available for the iPhone, iPad, or any Android-based smartphone or tablet, you're able to control the device remotely. Like Apple TV, Chromecast uses a series of built-in apps that allow you to stream video or audio content from the Internet and watch it on your HD television set.

Finding, Downloading, and Installing the Chromecast Mobile App

If you're using an iPhone or iPad, launch the App Store, and in the Search field enter **Chromecast**. Tap the Get button that's displayed in conjunction with the Chromecast's app listing, and at the prompt provide your Apple ID password, or use the Touch ID sensor to accept the free app download.

If you're using an Android device, launch the Google Play app, enter **Chromecast** in the Search field, and follow the onscreen prompts to finish the download and installation process.

After the app is installed on your mobile device, launch it after you've connected your Chromecast streaming device to your television set, and then follow the onscreen prompts to wirelessly link your smartphone or tablet with the Chromecast device and set it up to function with the device's various apps.

When running certain apps via the Chromecast device, you need to enter the username and password associated with that service or app-specific account. This applies to streaming services such as Netflix, Hulu, Pandora, or YouTube, for example.

Some of these apps offer free, on-demand access to television or cable TV networks or streaming music services. Other apps give you access to premium streaming services, such as Netflix, Hulu, or Showtime, for which you pay a monthly fee to stream content.

Apps you download and install onto your Chromecast device get stored within its 2GB of internal storage. Currently, more than 2,000 channel and game apps are available from third parties, so you can choose which apps you want to install on your streaming device.

Google Chromecast is purely a streaming device. You can stream selected content via an app, but you can't store content within the device for later (offline) viewing. Chromecast also requires you to download the free mobile app, and then use your smartphone or tablet as a remote control for the device. It doesn't come with a dedicated remote control unit.

The Cost of Google Chromecast

The price of the Google Chromecast streaming device is $35.00. Don't forget, though, that you might need to pay additional monthly subscription fees to access third-party programming services such as Netflix or Hulu. Some streaming music services that Chromecast is compatible with, such as Pandora, have both a free and a paid option.

Apps to stream content from nonpremium television and cable networks are available for free, but this programming includes commercials, and shows typically are not available until at least 24 hours after their original air date on their respective network.

To discover what apps come preinstalled on Google Chromecast, or what apps you can download and install later, visit www.chromecast.com/apps. In addition to apps from the most popular streaming TV show and movie services (such as Netflix, Hulu, HBO Now, Google Play Movies, and Sling TV), streaming music apps from services like Spotify, Pandora, Google Play Music, iHeart Radio, and NPR One are available.

You also can get Chromecast apps for YouTube and other online-based video and photo sharing services, as well as online-based games. To download and install additional apps, use the Chromecast mobile app on your smartphone or tablet to select apps, and then control them from your mobile device as you're watching or listening to the content via Chromecast on your television set.

Google Chromecast Works with Popular Google Services

The Google Chromecast device works seamlessly with online-based, Google-owned and -operated services, such as Google Play Movies, Google Play Music, and Google Photos. It also works flawlessly with YouTube (a Google-owned video-sharing service), as well as a special version of the Chrome web browser.

Amazon FireTV Stick

Amazon.com offers its Amazon FireTV Stick for $39.99. This device works seamlessly with the Amazon Prime Video streaming service (which offers more than

250,000 movies and TV episodes), as well as Amazon Prime Music (which includes a library of several million songs and albums).

Amazon FireTV is a tiny device that connects directly to the HDMI port of your HD television set. No cable or external power source is required. This device comes with its own handheld wireless remote control. It also includes 8GB of internal storage (for apps), as well as 1GB of internal memory.

Photo Credit: ©Amazon

Along with preinstalled apps for accessing Amazon's streaming video and music services, FireTV offers third-party apps for other popular streaming services, like Netflix and Hulu, as well as television and cable network-specific apps for streaming programming for free.

The Watchlist screen for Amazon Prime Video

As with the other streaming services, you must pay a subscription fee for services such as Amazon Prime Video, Amazon Prime Music, Netflix, or Hulu to access and experience commercial-free television shows, movies, and music. The free television and cable network-related apps include commercials with their programming.

The Third-Party App Selection

The collection of third-party apps available for FireTV is very similar to what's offered by Apple TV and Google Chromecast. The Disney Channel, FOX Sports, NBC News, PBS, Showtime Anytime, and WatchESPN are among the device's channel and game app offerings, which currently exceed 3,000 options.

One nice feature of FireTV is that after it's set up, you can plug the device into the HDMI port of any HD television set to access your favorite shows and content, at home, or even while at a hotel. Keep in mind that this device must have access to a wireless (Wi-Fi) Internet connection.

FireTV Stick Voice Remote

Instead of purchasing the FireTV stick with a standard handheld remote control device, an optional Voice Remote is available for $10.00 more. This voice remote allows you to control the FireTV device, as well as many of its most popular features and functions, using voice commands instead of manual button pushes.

Roku Streaming Stick

Priced at $49.99, the Roku Streaming Stick is very similar to the Amazon FireTV Stick in that it is small and plugs directly into the HDMI port of your HD television set. You control it with the supplied handheld wireless remote control.

Photo Credit: ©Roku

Built in to the device are a handful of apps that allow you to stream video and audio content from a wide range of third-party services, such as Netflix, Hulu, Amazon Prime Video, Google Play, YouTube, and Pandora. You can also choose from more than 2,600 additional apps (from the Roku App Store, which is available from the main menu when using the device) that give you access to specific programming from a variety of providers.

Individual channel and streaming service apps

The Roku Streaming Stick includes 256MB of internal storage (for apps) and 512MB of internal memory, which is less than its competitors. This streaming device, however, does offer a mobile app for the iPhone, iPad, and Android-based devices, with which you can control the playback of video and audio on your television set (via the Roku Streaming Stick device), or wirelessly transfer video or audio content from your mobile device to be experienced on your HD television set.

The Roku Streaming Stick is available from popular retail stores, such as Best Buy, Target, and Walmart, or you can order it online (www.roku.com). More advanced

Roku streaming devices, including several basic models (starting at $49.99) and the 4K Ultra High Definition Player ($129.99), are also available. Roku streaming technology is also built in to a growing lineup of Smart TVs from manufacturers such as Insignia, LG, and Sharp.

Some of the basic Roku streaming models include a voice-controlled, handheld remote control, and the 4K Ultra High Definition Player allows users to stream 4K resolution video content to their 4K-compatible television set. For most users, however, the basic Roku Streaming Stick has sufficient functionality and is easiest to use. It offers a nice selection of available apps, which grants access to plenty of streaming video and audio programing.

>>>Go Further

WHAT YOU SHOULD KNOW ABOUT POPULAR STREAMING SERVICES

Chapter 5, "On-Demand Movies at Your Fingertips," explains more about the various streaming video services that charge a flat monthly fee to access and experience the service's entire library of content (which includes hundreds of thousands of TV show episodes and movies).

It's important to understand that when you purchase a streaming device that includes apps for various streaming services, the price of the device does not include the monthly subscription fee for the various services. To stream content from a service such as Netflix, you need to pay the ongoing monthly fee.

After you subscribe to one of these streaming video services, you can access and stream content from a streaming device that's connected to your HD television set, or you can download the proprietary mobile app for your smartphone or tablet. You can also stream and view programming on your PC or Mac computer by visiting the streaming service's website using your web browser (www.netflix.com, for example) and then signing in to your account.

Remember, although the streaming services offer commercial-free programming, the availability of many TV show episodes and movies is delayed. Each service also has its own deals with television networks, television studios, motion picture studios, independent filmmakers, and other content providers, and offers a unique collection of available programming. In addition, many of these streaming services, such as Amazon Video Prime, Hulu, and Netflix, are now producing their own original TV series and movies that are exclusive to each service.

Binge Watching TV Shows

One thing that has not yet changed when it comes to watching television is that popular TV series are composed of individual 30- or 60-minute episodes (including commercials). A TV series' season typically includes between 8 and 24 episodes, which air on their respective network once per week, at a designated time and day.

So, if you're a fan of *The Walking Dead*, which airs weekly on AMC, you know that during the season when the show airs, a new episode can be seen every Sunday night at 10:00 p.m. Eastern Standard Time.

How TV Show Episodes Are Labeled and Organized

In addition to each episode of a television series having a unique title, episodes of a TV series each have a Season and Episode number associated with them. Thus, if an episode is labeled "503," for example, this means it's the third episode of the show's fifth season. The first digit or digits refer to the series' season number, and the last digits refer to the episode number within that season.

Thanks to on-demand programming, as well as streaming services such as Amazon Prime Video, Hulu, Netflix, and Vudu, many people forgo watching a TV series during its actual season and instead wait for all episodes from a series to become available at once, on an on-demand basis. Then, they watch all episodes from that show's season back-to-back. This is referred to as *binge watching* a TV show.

It's also possible to binge watch all movies in a popular movie franchise. For example, you can watch all the already released *Star Wars* or *Harry Potter* movies on-demand and back-to-back.

Streaming Services Are Ideal for Binge Watching TV

What people love about services such as Netflix, Amazon Prime, and HuluPlus, for example, is that thousands of television series are readily available for binge watching, and more are constantly being added to each service.

One rather new trend is that many of these streaming services are now producing their own original programming. But unlike television networks, the streaming services make all episodes available from a season of original shows available at once.

For example, when Netflix releases a new season of its award-winning series *Orange Is the New Black* or *House of Cards*, all episodes from the new season are made available for streaming on the same day, allowing viewers to watch all new episodes back-to-back, or at their leisure.

There are several benefits, as well as a few drawbacks, to binge watching TV shows. On the plus side, depending on how you access the episodes and stream them, you can watch them on a commercial-free basis. Thus, a half-hour episode without commercials will be between 22 and 24 minutes, and a one-hour episode will be between 44 and 46 minutes.

Also, when you binge watch, you don't have to wait a week to see what happens at the end of each episode that concludes with a cliffhanger. Instead, you can camp out on your couch and watch an entire season's worth of episodes in one or two marathon sessions.

The main drawback is that you need to wait for a TV season to end before you can watch all the episodes from that season back-to-back. There are a variety of options for streaming and watching on-demand shows after a season ends. Some of these options include the following:

- Use the free On-Demand function offered by your cable TV or satellite service provider. This option is typically free (assuming you pay for your cable/satellite TV service), but the availability of episodes and entire seasons of shows varies greatly. When you use this option, commercials are included as you watch each episode. If your cable or satellite service offers a pay-per-view on-demand option for TV episodes (which is typically priced between $0.99 and $1.99 per episode), you can watch these shows.

- Subscribe to a streaming service that offers your favorite show(s). Each streaming service has a flat monthly fee associated with it, as well as a unique collection of television shows and movies that are available. The programming offered by these services is commercial free, but the availability of an entire TV series is sometimes delayed by several months after the program has initially aired on its television network.

- Purchase the entire season of a TV show outright. Some TV shows and movies are still available and sold on DVD and Blu-ray discs. However, these days, it's more common to purchase the digital version of TV shows and movies, which you can download and watch at your leisure. After you purchase the digital edition of a TV show, a show's entire season, or a movie, you own it and can watch it on an unlimited basis. You can stream the content from the Internet or download it to your computer, mobile device, or DVR. When you've downloaded content, an Internet connection is no longer needed to view the content.

Purchase Individual TV Show Episodes or Entire Seasons

Apple's iTunes Store, Amazon.com, and most likely your cable or satellite TV service provider allow you to purchase individual TV show episodes, the entire season of previously aired TV series, as well as movies, in a digital format that you then own.

Instead of acquiring this content on a DVD or Blu-ray disc, the digital file is stored online (on your behalf) or can be stored on the hard disk or within internal storage associated with your computer, mobile device, or DVR.

Purchasing a single episode of a TV series typically costs between $1.99 and $2.99. The cost of an entire TV season of a series, if purchased at once, is usually offered at a discount. Movies can often be purchased in digital form for between $9.99 and $29.99 (although these prices vary a lot).

The biggest benefit to purchasing content, in contrast to streaming it, is that you can download and store the content and then watch it anytime, as often as you'd like, whether or not an Internet connection is available. You can also freely move the content between your own computers and mobile devices.

However, with so many options available for streaming TV show episodes on-demand, as long as you'll have a continuous Internet connection available when you want to watch TV or a particular movie, this is typically a preferred and more cost-effective option.

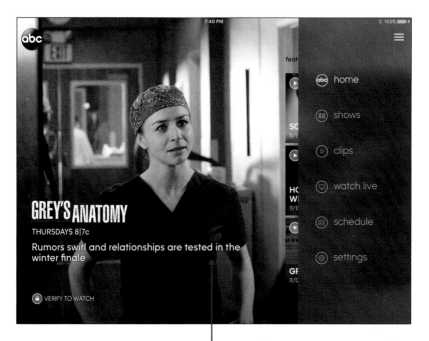

Use mobile apps to stream your favorite shows
from television networks to your mobile devices.

This chapter explains options for watching TV via the Internet using your smartphone, tablet, or computer. What's covered includes

→ Streaming on-demand TV shows to your computer
→ Using mobile apps from TV networks to watch television programs on-demand
→ Using an app offered by your cable or satellite TV service provider to watch programming on your mobile device
→ Experiencing interactive elements of some TV shows using a mobile app

Watching TV on Your Devices

Chapter 3, "Television in the 21st Century," describes how watching television on an HD television set has changed dramatically in recent years, and how programming can now be delivered to your television set in a variety of ways, including by streaming shows and movies from the Internet.

You can also stream or download television programming and movies to your PC or Mac computer, smartphone, and/or tablet. For example, you can purchase and download TV show episodes or movies so that you can watch them at your leisure on your computer or mobile device's screen. You need an Internet connection to download the content, but then you can roam freely as you watch the downloaded video files.

>>>Go Further
THE COST OF PURCHASING TV SHOWS AND MOVIES

When you purchase a single TV show episode, a complete season of a TV series, or a movie in digital form from a service such as Amazon Video, the Google Play Store, or the iTunes Store, you ultimately own that content and can download and store it on your computer's hard drive, in the cloud, or within the internal storage of your smartphone or tablet. You can then watch that programming as often as you'd like, on any computer or mobile device the digital file is compatible with.

The price of an individual TV episode is typically between $1.99 and $2.99. If you purchase an entire season of a TV series at once, it's often cheaper than acquiring the episodes individually.

When you purchase TV shows or movies using the iTunes Store, the iTunes software on a PC or Mac is used to manage and view the content. On an iPhone or iPad, you use the iTunes Store app to acquire the content, and then you view the content with the Videos app.

You acquire TV show episodes from Amazon Video from a PC or Mac by using the Amazon.com website. On an Android-based smartphone or tablet, you purchase content from the Google Play Store and play it using an app that comes preinstalled on your mobile device.

The cost to stream TV shows on your computer and/or mobile device varies. For example, if you visit the website for a particular television or cable network (or use the mobile app from that network), streaming programs is free, although commercials are included.

However, if you already pay for a premium cable network, like HBO or Showtime, you can stream programming from one of these networks on a commercial-free basis, using your computer or mobile device, at no additional cost.

Meanwhile, when you pay a flat monthly subscription fee for a streaming service, such as Amazon Prime, Hulu, or Netflix, which typically costs less than $10.00 per month, you can watch as many TV shows or movies as you'd like from that service, and the programming is commercial free.

Another option is to stream programming from the Internet to your computer or mobile device screen. From a computer, you visit the website for a television network or streaming service. On a smartphone or tablet, you need a specialized app to stream content. Apps for streaming TV shows and movies are available from several types of content providers, including

- Individual TV and cable networks (such as ABC, CBS, FOX, NBC, and PBS)

- Cable/satellite service providers (such as Comcast/Xfinity, DirecTV, DISH, or Time Warner Cable)

- Subscription-based streaming services (such as Amazon Prime, Hulu, and Netflix)

- Other online-based content providers (such as YouTube)

Depending on which of these options you choose, the programming may or may not include commercials, and a monthly subscription fee may be required. When specific programming (such as the most recent episodes of a TV series) becomes available for streaming after its initial broadcast varies. In some cases, you might need to wait 24 hours after an episode airs before it's available to stream or purchase.

As long as your computer or mobile device has Internet access, you can stream current and classic TV show episodes on an on-demand basis. You're also often able to watch live television broadcasts in real-time by streaming shows via the Internet to your computer or mobile device. As a result, you can watch television virtually anytime and anywhere, as long as an Internet connection is available.

It's Not All Good

Streaming Doesn't Always Work Internationally

If you travel abroad, some of the apps and services used to stream television programming that originates within the United States will not work. So, if you want to watch the latest episode of your favorite TV show while traveling, it may be necessary to purchase and download that content, rather than stream it.

Streaming TV Shows on Your Computer's Screen

When it comes to watching on-demand or live television programming on your PC or Mac computer's screen, you have three main options, which are described in the following sections.

Visiting a Network's Website

Programs that air on television networks are often available on-demand 24 hours after they air as part of the network's normal programming schedule. For each series, only a limited number of past episodes are typically offered.

A growing number of networks are also now streaming their programming live (in certain regions), or making shows available on-demand at the same time as they're broadcast. All this programming typically includes commercials, but it is free to access. A continuous Internet connection is required, because the programming is streamed from the Internet to your computer screen.

Look for Full Episode Listings

When looking for on-demand TV series episodes to watch from a network's website, look specifically for Full Episode listings, in contrast to Previews, Clips, or Recaps.

Some of the websites for specific broadcast networks include the following:

- **ABC**—http://abc.go.com—Click Shows to select a program, and then choose which recent episode you want to watch, or click Watch Live to stream programming the same time it airs on the television network. (Watch Live is available in limited markets at the time the book is being written.) After clicking a show title, click the Watch button associated with a particular episode.

Selected show

Watch button

Episode listing

- **CBS**—www.cbs.com—Click the listing for the show you want to stream. A limited number of past episodes are available for each program. If you pay a monthly fee of $5.99 for CBS All Access, live streaming, as well as access to episodes of current CBS series (and classic CBS series no longer airing on TV) become available. Starting with a brand-new *Star Trek* TV series in 2017, CBS All Access will also begin producing and offering exclusive and original programming.

- **FOX**—www.fox.com—Click the FOXNOW Full Episodes option to watch episodes of recently aired series on your computer.

- **NBC**—www.nbc.com—Click the Full Episodes option to see what series and episodes are available to stream on-demand, or click the Live option to stream live programming from the NBC television network to your computer. (The Live option is available in limited markets at the time the book is being written.)

- **PBS**—From the website's main screen, click the Video option, and then click the Programs option to view episodes of popular PBS shows.

Navigate Networks' Websites

Every popular television and cable network has its own website from which you can stream full episodes of shows that air on that network. These websites also showcase the network's programming schedule and offer video previews, clips, and often short recaps of recent episodes.

To find the website for a specific network, follow these steps:

1. Launch your favorite web browser, and visit a popular search engine, such as Bing (www.bing.com), Google.com (www.google.com), or Yahoo! (www.yahoo.com).

2. Within the Search field, type the network's name, followed by the phrase **television network**. For example, to find the website for the Lifetime network, type **Lifetime Television Network**.

3. Click the Search result for the network you're looking for to access the appropriate website.

4. From the network's website, click the option that allows you to watch full episodes of recently aired shows. For example, on Lifetime's website, click the Video option and then click the Full Episodes or Full Movies option.

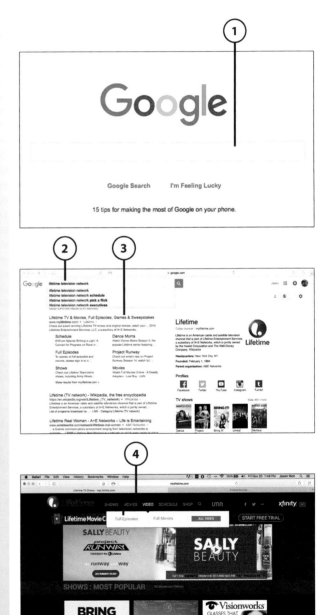

Purchasing TV Shows to Watch on Your Computer

From online-based services such as the Amazon Video Store, Apple's iTunes Store, and the Google Play Store, you can purchase individual TV series episodes or entire seasons of TV series, and then download that content to your computer. In the next section, the iTunes Store is used as an example to show how content is acquired. The process is similar among all of the services.

These video files are provided in a specific file format that's compatible with that service's own viewing and digital file management software. However, after you purchase a TV show in digital form, you own it.

The file can be downloaded and stored on your computer, stored in the cloud, and/or transferred to any of your other computers (or mobile devices) that are linked to the same account you used to purchase the content.

Purchase Content from iTunes

From your Mac or PC, follow these directions to find, purchase, download, and watch a TV show episode using the free iTunes software (www.itunes.com):

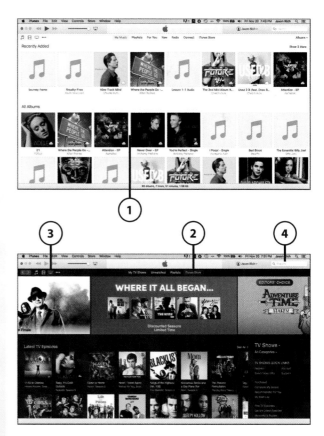

1. Launch the iTunes software on your Mac (shown) or PC.

2. Click the iTunes Store option.

3. Click the TV icon that's displayed in the top-left corner of the screen.

4. If you know the name of the TV series you want to acquire episodes for, enter the series name into the Search field.

5. From the Television screen within the iTunes Store, click the See All option located to the right of the Latest TV Episodes heading to see the latest episodes of popular TV shows that have been added to the service.

6. Click the graphic icon for a specific TV series.

7. Alternatively, click the See All option associated with the New and Noteworthy heading, or click a show listing that's found under the Top TV Episodes heading (not shown).

Choose Between HD or Standard Resolution

Most TV show episodes offered from the iTunes Store and some of the other services are offered in Standard Definition or High Definition resolution. The price per episode of a Standard Definition episode is $1.99, and the price of a High Definition episode is $2.99. The actual program you watch is the same, but the detail, vibrancy of colors, and overall image quality of a high definition episode will be much better when you view it on your computer or mobile device's screen.

The file size associated with HD TV episodes and movies is much larger, which results in longer download times to acquire the files. In addition, if storage space within your computer's hard drive (or your mobile device's internal storage) is limited, you'll be able to store much more content if you acquire smaller size, SD resolution video files.

8 Make sure you're viewing the show description screen for the season you're interested in, click the SD or HD option icon (based on your resolution preference), and then click the Price icon that's associated with the single episode you want to purchase and download.

9 From the series description screen, click the Price button for a single episode or click the Buy Season Pass button to subscribe to purchase an entire season of episodes.

10 Click the Buy button on the purchase confirmation screen. When prompted, enter the password that's associated with your Apple ID account.

11 The purchased episode is downloaded and stored on your computer's hard drive, and simultaneously (and automatically) stored online within your free iCloud account. It's now available to watch on any computer or mobile device that's linked to your Apple ID or that's tied to your iCloud Family Sharing plan (not shown).

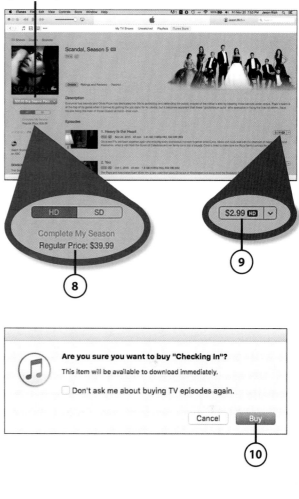

Buy season pass

Unlimited Replays

After you own a TV episode, you can watch it as often as you'd like, delete it from your computer or mobile device, and then redownload it at any time from your iCloud account at no additional charge.

12 Click My TV Shows at the top of the screen to view all TV episodes (and complete seasons of shows) that you own.

13 Click an episode listing to begin viewing that episode. If the episode listing has an iCloud icon associated with it, this means the episode's video file is stored within your online-based iCloud account, but not on the computer (or mobile device) you're currently using. Click the iCloud icon to download the episode. As the episode is downloading, you can begin watching it by clicking its listing.

14 After an episode begins playing, playback controls are displayed at the bottom of the screen. These include a volume slider, a time slider, an AirPlay icon, a Rewind to Beginning icon, a Rewind icon, a Play/Pause icon, a Fast Forward icon, a Fast Forward to End icon, a Closed Captioning icon, and a Full Screen viewing mode icon. Click the X icon to exit the episode and return to the previous iTunes menu (not shown).

Watch TV on Airplane Flights

If you're planning a trip that involves a long flight, instead of relying on the airplane's in-flight entertainment service to offer programming you're interested in, consider purchasing and downloading a collection of TV show episodes and/or movies to watch on your notebook computer, smartphone, or tablet during the flight. Remember, after you purchase and download this content, an Internet connection is no longer needed to view it.

Keep in mind, even if an airplane offers Wi-Fi, the airlines typically disable streaming services and websites, such as Netflix, so you can't use them. This also applies aboard cruise lines, in some hotels, and at some airports.

>>>Go Further

WATCH SHOWS FROM YOUR CABLE OR SATELLITE SERVICE PROVIDER'S WEBSITE

Most cable and satellite television service providers offer a website for their paid subscribers that allows you to stream (and in some cases download) programming from participating networks at no additional charge.

For example, if you subscribe to Comcast/Xfinity for your home's cable television service, visit the My Xfinity website (http://my.xfinity.com) to watch TV shows (and movies) online. Other cable and satellite service providers offer a similar option.

When you're on the website, sign into your account by clicking the Sign In option (and then enter your username and password). Next, click the TV option, and then click the Watch Online option. Listings for current and classic TV series that are available to watch online are displayed.

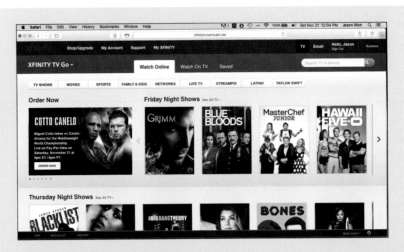

Streaming TV show episodes from your cable or satellite TV service provider's website is a free service for paid subscribers. This is different from Pay-Per-View or Paid On-Demand programming, which is also offered. In some cases, you can also now stream live broadcasts from various TV networks directly to your computer screen (from your cable/satellite TV service provider's website). This is a feature that's becoming more widely available.

To determine what online streaming services your cable or satellite television service provider offers, contact its customer service department, or visit the website that's listed on your monthly bill.

Streaming TV Shows on Your Smartphone or Tablet

Whether you're using an iPhone, iPad, or an Android-based smartphone or tablet, if you want to stream TV shows (or movies) on your mobile device, you need to have a continuous Internet connection. You'll also need to download and install a specific app offered by a television or cable network, your cable or satellite television service provider, or a streaming service. These apps are all available, for free, from the App Store (iPhone/iPad) or the Google Play Store (Android).

Check for Connection Requirements

Some apps require you use a Wi-Fi Internet connection (in contrast to a 3G/4G/LTE cellular data connection) to stream programming. If you plan to sometimes use a cellular data connection, be sure to download an app that functions with that type of connection.

Using Network-Specific Mobile Apps

All the popular television networks offer their own proprietary mobile app that enables you to stream current or recent TV show episodes and watch them, for free, on your mobile device's screen. The number of recent episodes for specific TV series varies, and programming typically includes commercials. Episodes are often made available via the mobile app 24 hours after they air on the network, but this varies.

Some of the network-specific mobile apps also offer the capability to stream live programming directly to your mobile device's screen. Each television network has its own app, and the features, functions, and programming selection offered by each app varies greatly.

To find network-specific apps for your mobile device, visit the app store for your device and enter the name of the network in the Search field. Tap the appropriate search result listing to view the app's description screen. Next, tap the Get button (iPhone/iPad) or Install button (Android) to download and install the free app.

Tap Get to install an iPhone/iPad app.

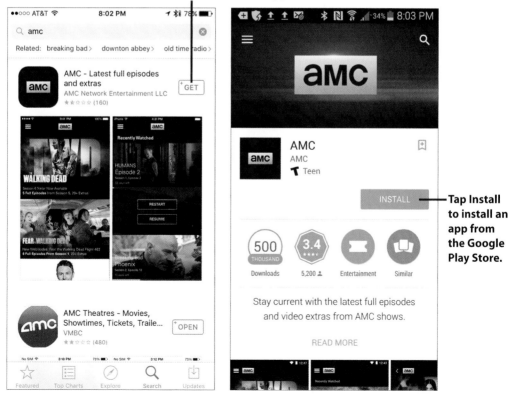

Tap Install to install an app from the Google Play Store.

Table 4.1 lists a small sampling of apps available from the popular television networks.

Table 4.1   Popular Television/Cable Network Apps

Television Network	App Name
A&E	A&E
ABC	Watch ABC (primary app) ABC News (news app) Many local ABC affiliate stations across the U.S. also have their own mobile apps.
AMC	AMC
BBC News	BBC News
Bravo	Bravo Now
CBS	CBS (primary app) CBS Sports (sports app) CBS News (news app) CBS Local (access to local affiliate programming) Many local CBS affiliate stations across the U.S. also have their own mobile apps.
CNN	CNN App
ESPN	WatchESPN
Food Network	Watch Food Network
FOX	FOX Now (primary app) Fox News (news app) Fox Sports Go (sports app) Many local Fox affiliate stations across the U.S. also have their own mobile apps.
HBO	HBO Now (for non-cable TV subscribers) HBO Go (for paid cable TV subscribers)
HGTV	HGTV Watch
Lifetime	Lifetime

Television Network	App Name
NBC	NBC Watch Now (primary app) NBC News (news app) NBC Sports Live Extra (sports app) NBC Sports Talk (sports app) Many local NBC affiliate stations across the U.S. also have their own mobile apps.
PBS	PBS Video (primary app) PBS Kids Video (kids' programming app)
Showtime	Showtime Anytime
SyFy Network	Syfy Now
The CW Network	The CW
TNT	Watch TNT
USA Network	USA Now

Use a Network's Mobile App

When you're ready to begin streaming and watching specific shows using an app from a particular television or cable network, make sure your mobile device is connected to the Internet and then follow these steps, which are demonstrated here using the WatchABC mobile app on an Android smartphone.

Fast Forward Is Not Offered

When streaming TV shows using a network's mobile app (or the mobile app from your cable/satellite TV service provider), you have the option to rewind, but the fast forward option is typically disabled. You can, however, pause the program and restart it at any time in the future from where you left off.

(1) Launch the app from the Home screen.

(2) Tap the app's main menu icon and select Shows (or a similar option) to view a listing of the network's shows (displayed alphabetically).

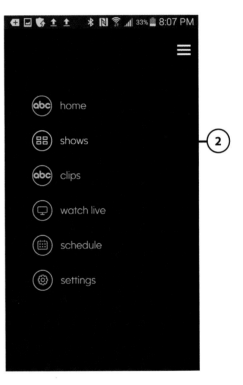

3 Tap the title you want to watch, and then tap the episode you want to stream.

4 Tap the Play icon for the episode.

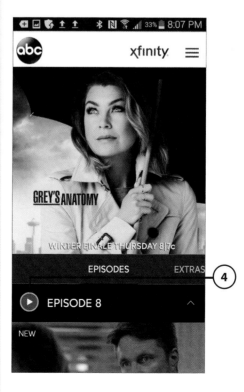

5 Tap the Full Screen icon to view the streaming show in full-screen mode, rather than viewing it within a small window onscreen.

6 To see the largest image possible, rotate your smartphone or tablet to landscape mode. The onscreen icons automatically disappear after a few seconds. To make them reappear, tap anywhere on the screen.

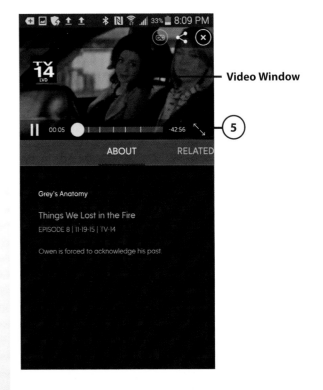

Video Window

Watch Live Programming

If the network's app offers the capability for you to stream live programming, from the app's main menu, choose the Watch Live (or equivalent) option. This feature does not work in all cities or regions across the United States, and in some cases, you need to subscribe to a supported cable or satellite television service to access live programming from the network's app.

Some networks, such as CBS, are experimenting with a paid subscription service that allows you to watch all the network's programming (past or present), on a commercial-free basis, for a flat monthly fee. CBS's paid service is called CBS All Access (www.cbs.com/all-access).

Using a Mobile App from Your Cable or Satellite Service Provider

Instead of loading individual apps onto your mobile device for all the television and cable networks you watch programming from, another option is to install the app offered by your existing cable or satellite service provider.

Many of these service providers, such as Cablevision, Comcast/Xfinity, DirecTV, Dish, and Time Warner Cable, offer their own apps that give you access to the live feed of many popular television and cable networks from your mobile device, as well as stream on-demand episodes of shows starting 24 hours after they originally air on their respective networks.

The programming you're able to stream is the same as what you'd see on your television set as a paid cable or satellite TV subscriber, so if a particular show included commercials, you see those same commercials as you stream the program. However, if you watch programming from premium cable channels, such as HBO or Showtime, via your cable or satellite provider's app, this programming is commercial free.

The Xfinity TV GO app (for Comcast/Xfinity cable TV subscribers), for example, allows you to stream live programming from many popular networks. Simply tap the Live icon that's displayed near the bottom-center of the app screen, and then tap a network's logo to begin streaming that programming.

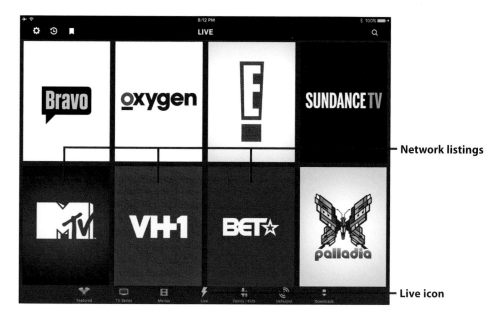

To watch TV shows on an on-demand basis (as opposed to live), tap the TV series icon that's displayed at the bottom of the screen, tap the thumbnail graphic for the TV series you watch to watch (they're listed alphabetically), and then tap the listing for the episode you want to watch. Tap the Play icon to begin streaming that episode.

If you want to stream live programming, tap the Live icon at the bottom of the screen and then tap the logo for the television network you want to watch. (Not all TV networks can be streamed live to your mobile device, however.)

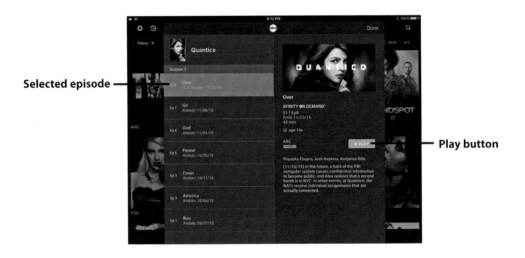

Selected episode

Play button

Use the App's Search Tool to Quickly Find What You Want

All network apps have a Search tool icon (it's shaped like a magnifying glass). Tap this icon, and then enter in the Search field the title of a TV show or movie or any search phrase that will help you quickly find the programming you're looking for. This can be a keyword, actor's name, or episode title, for example. Tap a search result to view that content.

The apps offered by a growing number of cable or satellite TV service providers also offer the capability to download specific TV show episodes, store them within your mobile device, and then watch them at your leisure, even if an Internet connection is not available later. If this function is available, you see a Download button near the Play button for a TV episode listing.

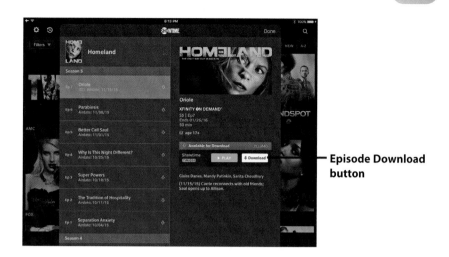

Episode Download button

Using a Streaming Service's Mobile App

To recap, a streaming service such as Amazon Prime, Hulu, or Netflix is a paid, online-based service that offers a vast and ever-growing library of current and past television show episodes, classic television episodes, and current and classic movies from many content providers that you can stream on a commercial-free basis to your computer, smartphone, tablet, video game system, streaming device, or Smart TV.

Many of these streaming services also produce their own original television series and movies, which are available exclusively from that service.

For the iPhone, iPad, and Android-based smartphones and tablets, each of these streaming services has its own mobile app that's available from the App Store (iPhone/iPad) or Google Play App Store (Android). After you begin paying for the streaming service, which typically costs less than $10.00 per month, and set up your own account, you can stream unlimited programming using the app you've downloaded.

For more information about any of these services, and the unique collection of programming each offers, visit the following websites:

- **Amazon Prime Video**—www.amazon.com/gp/video/storefront
- **Hulu**—www.hulu.com
- **Netflix**—www.netflix.com

Use the Netflix App

The layout of the various streaming services' apps vary, but how they function is pretty much the same. To give you an idea of how these apps work, the following are general directions for using the Netflix app on an iPad.

1 Make sure your mobile device is connected to the Internet, and then launch the Netflix app from the Home screen.

2 When prompted, sign in to the service using your username and password (not shown).

3 Scroll through the listings of available TV series and movies, perform a search by typing what you're looking for into the app's Search field, or tap the Categories option/icon to find programming based on a specific genre.

4 Based on your past viewing habits, the app may suggest specific shows or movies you might like. See the listings under the Suggestions for You heading. You can also view listings for newly added programming under the New Releases heading.

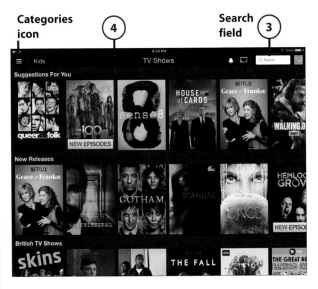

5 Tap the Season pop-up menu and then tap a specific season number (assuming multiple seasons of that series are available). You see individual listings for each episode within that season.

6 Tap the Play option associated with the episode you want to watch.

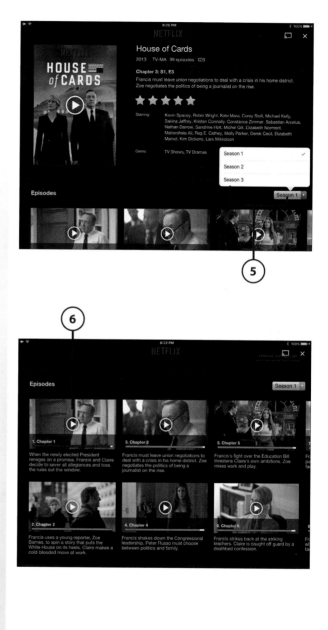

7 Use the onscreen controls to play/pause the programming. In some cases, Fast Forward and Rewind icons and a Time slider are displayed. When a Time slider is shown, drag your finger to the right along the slider to fast forward, or drag your finger to the left to rewind. Additional onscreen controls allow you to turn on/off closed captioning, adjust the volume, and switch to full-screen viewing mode. If the onscreen controls are not visible, simply tap anywhere on the screen.

Mobile Apps That Make Watching TV More Interactive

In an effort to engage television viewers, many networks have begun experimenting with the creation of a mobile app that's designed to be used while watching particular shows on a television set. In this situation, show-specific mobile apps are offered (for free from the App Store or Google Play App Store) that sync up with the live television broadcast and allow viewers to access additional content on a mobile device's screen, interact in real-time with show cast members and/or other fans, plus participate in polls, or provide other types of live feedback.

Each show-specific mobile app offers a vastly different interactive experience. For example, in conjunction with the SyFy cable television series *12 Monkeys* and *Expanse*, the SyFy Sync mobile app is able to take control of the optional Phillips Hue lighting system installed in your room (www.meethue.com) and change the room's lights to match the colors of particular scenes in the show to create a more visually immersive viewing experience.

Special apps for some TV networks' morning shows, nightly news broadcasts, and late-night talk shows are also available. This includes apps for *The Today Show, NBC Nightly News, The Tonight Show, ABC News, 48 Hours, CBS News,* and *ABC News.*

Discover What Show-Specific Apps Are Available

When a specific app is available for a television show, it's promoted during the show's broadcast. You can then enter the television show title within the Search field of the App Store or Google Play Store to find, download, and install the app.

Access thousands of movies on-demand and
watch them on your television, computer,
smartphone, or tablet.

This chapter focuses on streaming movies and on-demand video services that offer movies, and explains:

→ Ways to find and watch movies, when and where you want
→ The difference between on-demand services, streaming services, digital video stores, and renting movies
→ The costs associated with the various movie-related options
→ What you should know about Amazon Prime Video, Hulu, Netflix, YouTube Red, and other video services

5

On-Demand Movies at Your Fingertips

Since the early days of movie making, millions of movies have been produced and released in theaters around the world. Many have since been released on DVD and/or Blu-ray, allowing audiences to purchase or rent them, and then watch these films at their leisure.

As technology has evolved, so has movie distribution. DVDs are quickly becoming outdated, and many video rental stores (like Blockbuster) have already shut down. Although still somewhat popular, Blu-ray discs will likely become outdated within the next few years. Instead, movies are being distributed in digital form, through a wide range of services.

In fact, these services are all vying to offer the broadest range of movie titles and are continuously working closely with movie studios, producers, production companies, and other content providers to acquire the rights to distribute original movies, current Hollywood movies, as well as classic, independently produced, and foreign films.

Thanks to the Internet and these services, you now have plenty of options for finding and watching movies, when and where you want.

This chapter focuses on the different services and technologies used for finding and watching movies, discusses the technology that's required, and estimates the costs associated with each option. You'll also learn which options to use based on whether you want to watch movies on your television set, computer screen, smartphone, or tablet.

Owning, Renting, and Streaming Movies: A Comparison

Thanks to the digital age we're living in, when it comes to finding and watching movies, you can choose between buying and owning a digital movie, renting it, or streaming it. Each option offers advantages and disadvantages.

When you purchase the digital edition of a movie, you own that digital file and can watch it as often as you want, on any of your equipment that supports that file. You can download a movie to your computer or store it online and then stream it to your television set, computer screen, or mobile device anytime you're connected to the Internet.

The purchase price of a movie you acquire in digital form is typically the same as buying a DVD or Blu-ray edition of that movie. Prices vary between $9.99 and $29.99 (but sometimes run higher). However, where you buy the digital movie determines the ways you can watch it.

For example, if you acquire a movie from Apple's iTunes Store, you can watch it anytime on your Mac or PC that's running the iTunes software. You can also watch it on your iPhone or iPad, using the Videos app, or watch it on your television set that has an Apple TV device connected.

If you purchase the digital edition of a movie from your cable or satellite TV service provider, you can watch it on your television set that has the cable or satellite TV receiver box connected to it. In some cases, you can also watch it on your computer or mobile device that wirelessly connects to your cable or satellite TV receiver box or through your cable/satellite TV service provider's special app.

The digital file for a feature-length movie requires between 1GB and 6GB of storage space (so it's a large file). Downloading a collection of movies to your computer's hard drive or your mobile device requires significant storage space. Most movies these days are distributed in high definition, which utilizes even larger digital file sizes that require more storage space.

Standard Definition Versus High Definition

When downloading a movie to watch on your HD television set or computer screen, if you have a choice between watching a Standard or High-Definition version of the movie, go with High-Definition because the picture quality, the detail you see, and the vibrancy of the colors will be much better. If you will be downloading the movie to your smartphone or tablet to watch offline, the Standard Definition edition of the movie will require less storage space, which means the device will be able to hold more movies at once. This is useful if you're loading your mobile device with a bunch of content to watch during a long airplane flight or vacation when you know Internet access will not be available.

Instead of purchasing the digital edition of a movie, many services allow you to rent movies and watch them on-demand. When you rent a movie, you pay a flat fee (typically between $0.99 and $5.99 for a 24-hour period), during which you can watch that movie as often as you want.

With some rental services, the movie file is downloaded to the computer, mobile device, television DVR, or to the cable/satellite TV receiver box. After it's downloaded, you can watch it offline (with no Internet connection required). In other cases, the movie gets streamed from the service to your television, computer, or mobile device's screen, and a continuous Internet connection is required.

Some services, like your cable/satellite TV provider, offer on-demand movies, which is the same as a movie rental service. You pay a flat fee for unlimited access to a movie you select, typically for a 24-hour period.

In addition to buying digital movies or renting them on a per-movie basis, there are streaming services that allow you to watch an unlimited number of movies, as often as you'd like, for a flat monthly fee. Amazon Prime Video, Hulu, Netflix, and YouTube Red are among these services that cost between $7.99 and $11.99 per month. Each streaming service has its own collection of movies available based on distribution deals the companies have worked out with movie studios and content producers.

Whether you're buying, renting, or streaming movies, most of the services you'll be using begin offering Hollywood blockbusters a few months after they've been released into theaters. However, this too is changing. In some cases, one or more of these services obtains the right to distribute certain movies at the same time they're released to theaters, or acquire rights to movies that have never been released in U.S. theaters.

On-Demand Services from Your Cable or Satellite TV Service Provider

When you subscribe to a cable or satellite TV service provider, you connect a receiver box to your HD television set, and you're able to watch hundreds of television channels.

The remote control device that's provided by your cable or satellite service provider might have an On Demand button on it. When you press this button, a menu of available programming is offered. If no On Demand button is offered, press the remote's Menu button, and select the on-screen On Demand menu option.

Instead of watching TV shows and movies when they air on specific channels, you can pick what programming you want to watch and begin watching it whenever you want.

Some on demand services offered by your cable or satellite TV service provider are included with the monthly fee you pay for service. You can usually find and watch popular TV shows and movies on-demand starting 24 hours after they air on a particular channel or network. This programming typically includes commercials.

However, by pressing the same On Demand button on your remote control, you can access a vast collection of movies that you pay to watch on demand. These movies are shown commercial free, and during the rental period (which is typically 24 hours), you can watch them as often as you like for a fee of between $0.99 and $8.99, which automatically gets added to your cable or satellite service bill.

On-Demand Charges Get Added to Your Bill

When you opt to rent an on-demand movie that has a fee associated with it, or purchase the digital edition of a movie from your cable or satellite television service provider, the rental fee or purchase price automatically gets added to your monthly bill. These fees can add up quickly, so pay attention to how many paid on-demand movies you watch, as well as how much they cost, so you don't wind up receiving an extremely high bill at the end of the month.

If you find yourself wanting to watch a lot of on-demand movies, consider a less expensive option, such as paying for a streaming service, such as Netflix (starting at $7.99 per month), which gives you unlimited access to thousands of movies, TV shows, and original programming.

Use the On-Demand Service from Your Cable or Satellite Service Provider

When you opt to watch an on-demand movie that requires payment, the cable/satellite TV service requires you to confirm your decision prior to the movie starting. Most cable or satellite TV service's on demand options work pretty much the same way. Explained here are the directions for using Comcast/Xfinity's On-Demand service.

1. Turn on your television set and cable receiver box.

2. Press the On Demand button on your remote control. The On Demand menu will appear on your television's screen.

I Don't Have an On Demand Button

If your remote control has no On Demand menu, press the Menu button, and then select the on-screen menu option related to On Demand programming. In some cases, you can find specific On Demand channels as part of your channel line-up.

3. Use the arrow keys on your remote control to scroll down to the Movies option. The onscreen button may say New Movies, for example. Highlight this button, and press the OK button on your television's remote control.

4. You see a submenu of an alphabetical listing of movies. These are all movies you will typically pay a rental fee to watch (although some movies are offered for free by some cable and satellite service providers). In some cases, movies are sorted by category, such as New Releases, Romance, Comedy, Thrillers/ Horror, Sci-Fi, and so on.

5. Highlight a movie from the menu and press the OK button on the remote control to view a description and the price for that movie. Often, there is also an option to watch a free trailer or preview for the selected movie.

6. If you want to rent that movie and begin watching it immediately, use the arrow buttons on your remote control to select the onscreen Rent option, and then press the OK button on your remote control. Within a few seconds, the movie will begin playing.

7. Using the remote control, you can pause, fast forward, or rewind as you are watching that movie. After the initial rental period (usually 24 hours), you will need to rent that movie again (for a fee) to continue watching it.

Sometimes It Makes More Sense to Buy a Movie

If you plan to watch a movie two or three times, it's often less expensive to purchase the digital movie and own it outright than to keep paying the rental fee for that same film. If you have kids or grandkids who love watching the same movie over and over, and that movie is not offered on-demand for free, consider purchasing the movie so you have unlimited access to it.

Accessing Movies from the iTunes Store

In addition to selling computers and mobile devices, as well as the Apple TV device that connects to your television set, Apple offers one of the largest digital entertainment collections in the world, which is composed of music, TV shows, movies, music videos, audiobooks, and other content.

When it comes to movies, Apple's online-based iTunes Store offers a vast collection of current, classic, independent, and foreign films that you can rent on an on-demand basis or purchase in digital form.

Anytime you purchase a movie from the iTunes Store, it automatically gets stored online, within your free iCloud account. Apple supplies the online storage space needed (for free) to store this purchased content. You can then download and watch that movie on your Mac or PC using the free iTunes software (www.apple.com/itunes).

Using the iTunes Store app on your iPhone or iPad, you're also able to download the purchased movies to your mobile device, where they will be stored, allowing you to watch them whenever you want later, without requiring a continuous Internet connection (after the download process is complete). In addition, if you have an Apple TV device (see Chapter 3, "Television in the 21st Century," for more information) that same movie is available to watch anytime you want on your HD television set.

New Movies Are Released Weekly

Every week, most services, including iTunes and Amazon Prime Video, expand their movie offerings with newly released films and older movies the companies have acquired the rights to distribute.

New films are typically listed under the heading "New Releases" or "New and Noteworthy," whereas classic movies that are new to the service's line-up are under the heading "Movies Just Added."

Purchase Movies from the iTunes Store Using a Mac or PC

Using any Windows-based PC or Mac computer, access the online-based iTunes Store using Apple's free iTunes software. Among other things, this software allows you to purchase or rent movies. The iTunes software for the PC and Mac are very similar. Within this section, the Mac edition of the iTunes software (version 12.3.1) is shown.

The iTunes Software Gets Updated Periodically

Apple offers free updates to the iTunes software several times per year to introduce new features and fix bugs. Be sure you're using the most current version of the software.

To see if an update is available, launch the software, click the iTunes pull-down menu (displayed near the top-left corner of the screen), and select the Check for Updates option. If a message stating an update is available, follow the onscreen prompts to download and install it.

You need an Internet connection to access the iTunes Store. To find movies to purchase from the iTunes Store, follow these steps:

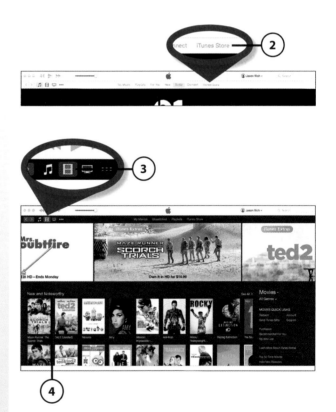

1. Launch the iTunes software on your computer (not shown).

2. From the main iTunes screen, click the iTunes Store option near the top-center of the screen.

3. Click the Movie icon near the top-left corner of the screen.

4. Browse through the movie listings under the various headings, such as New and Noteworthy. Click the title or thumbnail graphic for any movie you're interested in to view its Description screen.

5 If you know the title of the movie you want to watch, type it into the Search field. Within the search field, you can also enter an actor or director's name, the subject matter, a keyword, a search phrase, or anything else that will help you find the movie you're looking for. Click any of the search results to view the Description screen for the desired movie.

6 Alternatively, click the All Genres pull-down menu to view a list of movie genres, and then select a specific genre to see movie listings within that genre.

7 You can also scroll down, and along the right margin of the screen, view a listing of Top Movies (which are currently the most popular within the iTunes Store). Click this option to view more detailed Top Movies listings. After you do this, click the Categories option to sort and view the movies by genre.

8 After you've clicked a movie's listing, you see the Description screen. This screen includes details about the movie and gives you access to its ratings and reviews. Click one of the thumbnail images under the Trailers heading to watch the free preview for that movie.

9 Click the HD or SD tab to select between the Standard Definition or High Definition version. Your choice determines the price, image quality, and file size of the digital video file.

Adjusting Playback Resolution

With iTunes and some other services, when you select HD video resolution, you can then choose between 720p or 1080p resolution. To adjust this setting, access the iTunes pull-down menu, select the Preferences option, click the Playback tab, and then make a default resolution selection from the Preferred Video Version pull-down menu.

10 Click the Buy button to purchase the movie. The purchase price will be displayed within the Buy button.

11 Confirm your purchase decision and, if prompted, enter the password that's associated with your Apple ID account (not shown). The price of the movie will be charged to the credit or debit card that's linked to your Apple ID account.

Alternative Payment Method

Rather than charging the purchase to the card associated with your Apple ID account, you can use a pre-paid iTunes Store gift card to pay for movie purchases or rentals.

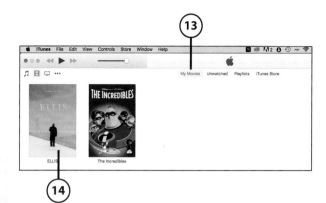

12 The purchased movie will be downloaded to your computer and simultaneously stored within your iCloud account (not shown).

13 Click My Movies in iTunes.

14 Click a movie's listing to view its Description screen, and then click the Play icon to begin watching it.

15 Onscreen controls are displayed to play, pause, fast forward, and rewind, as well as access closed captioning and other features. If these controls are not displayed, click anywhere within the video window (not shown).

16 As a movie is playing, click the Full-Screen icon to begin watching the movie in full-screen mode. Press the ESC key to exit out of full-screen mode at anytime (not shown).

>>>Go Further
RENT MOVIES INSTEAD OF BUYING THEM

You can also rent movies from the iTunes Store rather than buying them outright. When a rental option is available, a Rent button is displayed next to the Buy button when viewing a movie's Description screen. One difference between rented movies and purchased movies is that rented movies can be downloaded to only one computer (Mac or PC), one mobile device, or one Apple TV device, whereas a purchased movie can be accessed from all your computers, mobile devices, and/or Apple TV devices that are linked to the same Apple ID account. The cost to rent a movie from the iTunes Store ranges from $3.99 to $7.99.

The process for finding and downloading a rented movie is the same as purchasing it, except the movie is automatically deleted 24 hours after you first start watching it. It's no longer available for viewing unless you rent it again. As long as you don't start viewing the movie, though, it is stored on your device for up to 30 days before it is automatically deleted.

In many cases, when a new movie is introduced within the iTunes Store, it is made available for purchase first. The rental option is typically not offered until several weeks later.

Click to rent a movie

Purchase Movies from the iTunes Store Using an iPhone or iPad

The iTunes Store app came preinstalled on your iPhone or iPad. When your mobile device has Internet access using a Wi-Fi or cellular connection, you're able to use this app (shown here on the iPad) to access the iTunes Store and purchase or rent movies. To do this, follow these steps:

(1) Launch the iTunes Store app from the Home screen (not shown).

(2) Tap the Movies icon at the bottom of the screen.

(3) If you know the title of the movie you're looking for, enter it into the Search field. Within the Search field, you can also enter an actor or director's name, a subject matter, a keyword, or a search phrase that will help you find what you're looking for. After the search results are displayed, tap a movie's title or thumbnail graphic to view its Description screen.

(4) Browse through the movies listed under the various headings. If you see a movie that's of interest, tap its title or thumbnail graphic to view its Description screen.

⑤ To view movies based on genre, after tapping the Movies icon, tap the Genres option, and then tap a specific genre. Tap the title or graphic thumbnail of a movie to view its Description screen.

⑥ Discover the most popular movies available from the iTunes Store by tapping the Top Charts icon and then tapping the Movies tab. Scroll through the listings, and tap one that's of interest to view its Description screen.

Movies Tab

Top Charts

7 From a movie's Description screen, you're able to view a text-based description of the movie, see its ratings and reviews, and watch a free trailer or preview for the film.

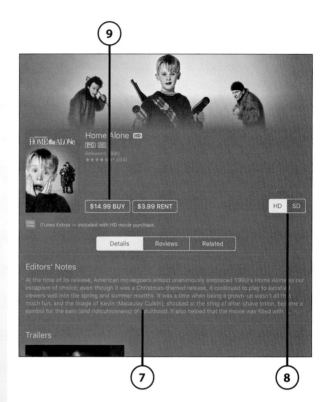

8 Tap the HD or SD icon to choose between the Standard Definition and High Definition edition. Your choice affects the price, image quality, and file size of the digital video file.

9 To purchase the movie, tap the Buy button. Within the Buy button, the price of the movie is displayed. If you want to rent the movie (if applicable), tap the Rent movie. The rental price is displayed within the Rent button.

10 Confirm your purchase or rent decision, and, if asked, enter the password associated with your Apple ID account. Alternatively, place your finger on your iPhone or iPad's Touch ID sensor to scan your fingerprint. The price of the movie is charged to the credit or debit card that's linked to your Apple ID account.

Alternative Payment Method

Rather than charging the purchase to the card associated with your Apple ID account, you can use a prepaid iTunes Store gift card to pay for movie purchases or rentals.

(11) The digital file for the movie will then be downloaded to the mobile device you're using. This can take between 5 and 30 minutes (sometimes longer), depending on the speed of your Internet connection. If you purchased the movie, it will be stored within your iCloud account automatically and made available on your other computers and mobile devices that are linked to the same account.

(12) When the download process is completed, exit out of the iTunes Store app by pressing the Home button, and then launch the Videos app.

(13) Tap the Movies tab to watch a movie that you've purchased. Tap the Rentals tab to watch a movie you've rented. You see a list of the available movies.

(14) Tap the thumbnail image for the movie to view its Description screen.

(15) Tap the Play icon to begin watching the movie.

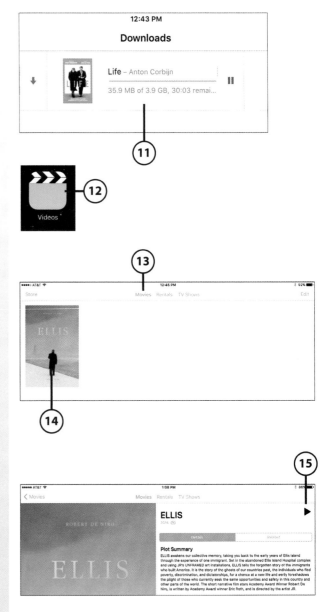

The Video App's Onscreen Controls

While a movie is playing, to make the app's onscreen controls appear, tap anywhere within the video window. After a few seconds, the controls disappear again.

The Video App's On-screen Controls

When playing a video using the Videos app (as opposed to a TV show episodes), you might see Play, Extras, Cast & Crew, and Related options underneath the main control icons. Tapping Play causes the regular video playback control options to be displayed. Tapping Extras allows you to watch what would be DVD or Blu-ray extra features, if applicable, that are distributed with the movie. Tapping Cast & Crew offers an interactive listing of the people who worked on the movie, and tapping the Related option displays movies that are similar to the one you're watching. Not all movies you acquire, however, will include these extra command options.

16 As the movie is playing, the onscreen controls allow you to play or pause the movie, fast forward, rewind, and/or adjust the volume. You can also use the Time slider to manually advance or rewind within the movie. Tap the Closed Captions icon to set up and use this feature.

17 Tap the Widescreen icon to switch between full screen and widescreen as the movie is playing. Most movies look better on the screen when viewed in Widescreen mode.

18 Stop playing the movie by tapping the Play/Pause button or pressing the Home button to exit the Videos app. A virtual bookmark is created, so you can later restart the movie from where you left off.

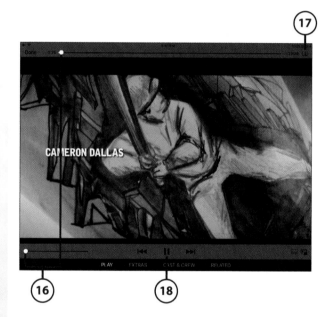

19 If you're using an iPad, tap the Picture-in-Picture icon to shrink down the video window and continue playing the movie while using another app. When the video window shrinks, drag it around the screen with your finger. Press the Home button to access the Home screen, and then launch another app that you want to use. This feature currently only works on the iPad Air, iPad Air 2, iPad mini 2/3/4, and iPad Pro.

20 You can also use the iPad's Split Screen mode to watch a movie on one side of the screen and run a different app on the other. To do this as a movie is playing, or while using the Videos app, place your finger on the extreme right side of the screen and slowly drag to the left. From the App icon menu, tap the app you want to launch. Place your finger on the app divider bar and drag it to the left, toward the center of the screen. The Videos app and the other app will now run independently, side by side.

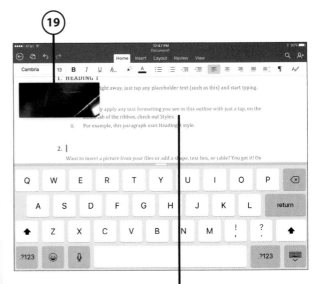

Microsoft Word app

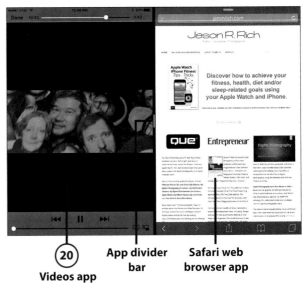

Videos app   **App divider bar**   **Safari web browser app**

Other Digital Movie Stores

In addition to the iTunes Store, Amazon.com, Google Play, and Vudu offer online-based services that allow you to purchase or rent digital editions of movies from your computer, mobile device, or other equipment, such as a console-based video game system.

Amazon.com

In addition to operating the Amazon Prime Video streaming service and selling DVDs and Blu-ray discs, Amazon.com also sells and rents digital movies. To
shop for digital movies to purchase and download, visit www.amazon.com/
Shop-Instant-Video.

When you purchase the digital edition of a movie from Amazon, in addition to
downloading the digital video file to your computer or mobile device, it automatically gets stored within your online-based Amazon account, so you can access it
anytime from any of your other compatible computers or equipment.

From the Rent or Buy screen, you can browse through movie listings displayed in
various categories. The service is shown here on an Android tablet.

Any movie you purchase or rent can be viewed on your computer (via its web browser), on your mobile device (using the Amazon Video app), or using the streaming device that's connected to your television set, such as the Amazon Fire TV Stick, Apple TV, or a Roku device. Some video game consoles also support the Amazon Prime Video service. (Read about streaming devices in Chapter 3.)

Most movies offered by Amazon.com can be purchased (for about the same price as the DVD), rented (for a flat fee per 24-hour period, starting at $2.99), or streamed if you subscribe to Amazon Prime Video.

Download or Stream Movies from Amazon

When you purchase or rent a video, you can download and store it on your computer or mobile device, which means you can view it anytime, even when no Internet connection is available. However, when you use the Amazon Prime Video streaming video service to stream content from the Internet, you have to have a continuous Internet connection.

Google Play Also Sells and Rents Digital Movies

The Google Play Store, which you can access from any computer's web browser (http://play.google.com/store/movies), the Google Chromecast streaming device, or by using the Google Play app on your Android-based smartphone or tablet, also allows you to purchase or rent digital movies.

On an iPhone or iPad, you can use the free Google Play Movies & TV app to watch movies and TV show episodes you acquire from the Google Play Store, but you must purchase the content directly from the website, not from the iOS mobile app.

From the main Google Play menu, tap or click the Movies & TV option (shown here on an Android tablet). Then tap or click the Shop option. Listings for movies can be found under a series of headings, such as New Movie Releases, Most Popular Movies, or New to Rent. You also have the option of typing the title of a movie (or any keyword or search phrase) into the service's Search field to find exactly what you're looking for.

Yet another option is to tap or click the Genres option to see the available genre categories. Tap or click a selection and then browse through the relevant listings.

When you find a movie listing that you're interested in, tap or click its title or thumbnail graphic to reveal its Description screen. This screen includes a text-based description of the movie, a free trailer you can watch, and options for purchasing or renting the movie.

If you purchase a movie, the digital movie file downloads to the mobile device or computer you're using, but it's also automatically stored online within your Google Play account, which means you can access it from any other computer, mobile device, or streaming device that's compatible with Google Play.

From the Google Play menu screen, after you tap or click the Movies & TV option, tap the My Movies & TV option to see a listing of the movies and TV shows you own, and that are stored within your Google Play online account. Tap or click any of these listings to watch that content.

Vudu

Vudu is a service operated by Walmart that allows you to buy or rent digital movies from your computer, mobile device, and some streaming devices that connect to a television set (including Google Chromecast and Roku devices). The Vudu selection includes more than 100,000 titles and expands weekly.

To use the service from a PC or Mac computer, launch your computer's web browser and visit the service's website at www.vudu.com. You can then sign up for a free account and pay for your movie purchases or rentals using a major credit card, debit card, or PayPal. You're can then download or stream movies you purchase or rent.

To use the Vudu service from an iPhone, iPad, or Android-based smartphone or tablet, download the free Vudu app from the App Store (iPhone/iPad) or Google Play Store (Android).

Streaming Movie Services

Instead of purchasing the digital editions of individual movies, or renting movies for one 24-hour period at a time, another option for accessing movies on-demand is to subscribe to a streaming service, such as Amazon Prime Video (www.amazon.com), Hulu (www.hulu.com), Netflix (www.netflix.com), or YouTube Red (www.youtube.com/red).

Each of these services offers a vast and ever-growing selection of movies that you can stream, on an unlimited basis, to your HD television set (using an optional streaming device), your computer (via its web browser), your smartphone (using a mobile app), or your tablet (using a mobile app). Some of these services are also compatible with your cable or satellite TV receiver box, TiVo DVR, and/or Internet-connected console-based video game system.

The Amazon Prime Video streaming service is shown here using the Amazon Video app on an iPad.

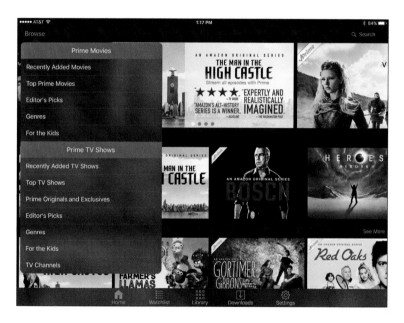

Visit the iPhone/iPad App Store or the Google Play Store to download and install the free Amazon Prime Video, Hulu, or Netflix app. You can access the YouTube Red service using the regular YouTube mobile app.

A Continuous Internet Connection Is Required

To use any streaming video service, you have to have a continuous Internet connection. The content you watch is streamed to your computer or device but not stored within it.

YouTube Red

Since its launch in October 2015, the premium YouTube Red (www.youtube.com/red) streaming service from Google began offering a growing selection of premium content, which will eventually include original television and movie programming, in addition to ad-free access to all existing YouTube videos and the Google Play Music streaming music service. YouTube Red is priced at $9.99 per month and is quickly evolving into a video-streaming service like Amazon Prime Video, Hulu, and Netflix. You'll learn more about YouTube in Chapter 6, "Streaming Video with YouTube and Other Services."

Subscribing to a streaming video service offers a handful of benefits, including the following:

- You pay a flat fee (less than $9.99 per month) for unlimited access to the service's entire collection of movies, TV shows, and original programming.

- You're able to access your account and stream content to any or all of your compatible mobile devices, computers, and streaming devices.

- Most streaming video services offer a selection of more than 100,000 movie and TV show titles, including Hollywood blockbusters, independent films, classic films, original films (produced exclusively for that service), and foreign films that aren't readily available for viewing elsewhere.

- Although there is a huge overlap in terms of the movie titles offered by the streaming video services, each also has exclusive deals with certain movie studios, producers, and content providers, and offers content that's exclusive to that service.

- All programming (movies, TV shows, and original content) can be viewed without commercials on most services.

- You need only one account with a particular streaming video service to be able to access content from your computer, mobile device(s), and/or streaming devices that are connected to your television set. You can also start watching a movie on one computer or device, pause it, and then pick up where you left off on a different computer, mobile device, or streaming device.

The services all work pretty much the same way. Within this chapter, Netflix is used for demonstration purposes because it's currently the most popular video streaming service.

Get More Information About Each Streaming Video Service

To learn more about Netflix, visit www.netflix.com using the web browser on your computer or mobile device. Netflix is priced between $7.99 and $11.99 per month, depending on the service plan you choose. The least expensive plan, for example, does not offer HD or Ultra HD resolution programming and allows you to stream Netflix programming to only one screen at a time.

Visit www.hulu.com for more information about Hulu. The Hulu service has two service options, priced at $7.99 and $11.99. The difference is that one offers limited commercials within some programming, and the more expensive plan is 100% commercial free.

To learn about Amazon Prime Video, visit www.amazon.com, click the Shop By Department option (located near the top-left corner of the webpage), and select Amazon Video, followed by the Included with Prime submenu option.

One perk of subscribing to Amazon Prime Video for the annual fee of $99.00 is that you're also given unlimited access to Amazon Prime Music (a streaming music service), and you receive free two-day shipping on all orders you place, for any product(s), on Amazon.com.

After you learn how to navigate your way around a service like Netflix on your computer, the process of accessing the same service from your mobile device, a streaming device that's connected to your TV, your TiVo DVR, or your console-based video game system is very similar.

Use Netflix from Your Computer

From your PC or Mac computer that's connected to the Internet, launch your favorite web browser, and then visit www.netflix.com. Follow these steps to navigate your way around the service, and begin enjoying the content it offers:

1. From the www.netflix.com home page, click the Sign In button.

2. When prompted, enter the email address that's associated with your Netflix account, as well as your account password. Click the Sign In button to continue. (If you don't yet have an account, click the Sign Up Now option and follow the onscreen prompts.)

3. Netflix allows each person in a family to set up a profile within one master Netflix account, which saves each person's preferences, viewing history, and other information. To add personal profiles to the account, click the Manage Profiles button. Otherwise, click the profile you've created for yourself, if applicable (not shown).

4 Based on movies and TV shows you've watched via Netflix in the past, the service offers recommendations to you. In addition, listings for various movies and TV shows are displayed under various headings, like Recently Added, New Releases, and Trending Now. If you find something you like, click its listing. The selected content begins playing.

Hover your mouse and click the arrow for more details.

Learn More Information About a Movie Before Watching

If you hover your mouse over a Netflix movie or TV show listing, a Description window gives you details and a description of the content. Click the downward-pointing arrow to reveal the full Description screen for that listing.

Search result

5 Another way to find a movie to watch is to type a movie title, actor's name, director's name, keyword, or search phrase into the Netflix Search field. Click one of the search results to begin watching that content.

6 To search for content based on genre, from the Browse screen click the Browse option, and then click one of the genre listings. You can then scroll through the listings and choose what you want to watch.

(7) If you come across a movie or TV show that you want to watch at some point in the future, but you don't want to immediately access its Description screen, click the + My List option. This adds the content to your personal Watch list, which you can access anytime by scrolling down to the My List heading on the Netflix Browse screen.

(8) Tap the Play icon on an image to begin playing a movie.

(9) As a movie is playing, onscreen controls are displayed that allow you to play/pause, fast forward, or rewind (using a Time slider), switch between a normal and widescreen view, turn on/off closed captions, and adjust the volume. If the onscreen controls are not visible, click anywhere within the video window (not shown).

(10) During a movie, or when it's finished playing, click the Back to Browse icon to return to browsing for additional content to watch. If you leave a movie (or TV show) partway through, a virtual bookmark will automatically be saved, so you can pick up where you left off when you return to that content (not shown).

Use Netflix from Your Tablet or Smartphone

All the functionality that Netflix offers from the web browser of your computer can also be utilized from your smartphone or tablet. However, when using a mobile device, such as the iPad (which is shown throughout this section), be sure to download the free Netflix app.

First, Install the Netflix App

For the iPhone or iPad, the Netflix app is available from the App Store. If you're using an Android-based device, you'll find it within the Google Play Store.

Within the Search field of the app store, enter the keyword **Netflix**, and then tap the listing for the Netflix app. From the iPhone/iPad's App Store, tap the Get button to download and install the app. From the Google Play Store, tap the Install button when viewing the listing for the app.

It's Not All Good

Wi-Fi Works Best

When using the Netflix app, or the app for any streaming video service, consider connecting to the Internet via a Wi-Fi connection unless you have an unlimited 3G/4G/LTE wireless data plan. Streaming HD video content from the Internet to your mobile device requires a lot of data usage, so if you have a cellular data allocation of 5GB, for example, this will quickly get used up.

Even if you have an unlimited cellular data plan, most cellular data service providers throttle back the speed of the Internet connection after you utilize a certain amount of data in any given month.

When you use a Wi-Fi Internet connection, data usage is not typically a concern, and the Internet connection speed is typically faster, which allows Netflix (or the streaming video service you're using) to display a higher quality video image on your mobile device's screen. If the Internet service you're using, however, does not offer unlimited bandwidth, streaming video and music content will quickly use up your monthly allocation.

Keep in mind that some public Wi-Fi hotspots, especially those aboard airplanes and on cruise ships, block the use of streaming video services. So, if you want to be able to watch a movie or TV shows, you'll need to purchase or rent the content and download it to your mobile device or computer in advance.

After you've installed the Netflix app on your mobile device, follow these steps for using the app to stream movies, TV shows, and original content whenever your mobile device has a continuous Internet connection available:

1. Launch the Netflix app from the Home screen of your smartphone or tablet.

2. When prompted, sign in to your account using the appropriate email address and password (not shown).

3. From the Profile selection menu, tap your personal profile, if applicable. To create or manage the Profiles, tap the pencil-shaped Edit icon and then tap a profile icon (not shown).

4. From Netflix's Browse screen, begin searching for a movie, TV show, or original programming to watch. Scroll down to view content listings displayed under headings, such as Trending Now, Popular on Netflix, Recently Added, or New Releases. Tap any listing to view that content's Description screen.

5 Search for content based on genre by tapping the Menu icon and then tapping a genre option. From the displayed listings, you can select a movie and tap its listing to view its Description screen.

6 Within the Search field, you also have the option of entering a movie title, actor's name, director's name, a keyword, or any search phrase that will help you find what you're looking for. Within the search results that are displayed will be relevant movie listings. Tap a listing to display its Description screen.

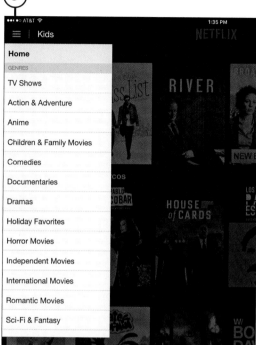

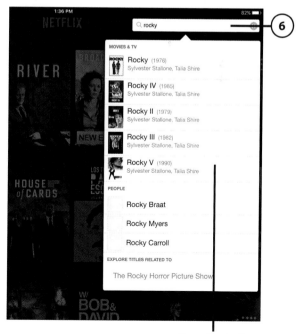

Search results

7 From a movie's Description screen, you're able to view a text-based description of the movie and see its average star-based rating. Tap the Play icon to begin playing the movie.

Save a Movie for Later

If you want to watch the movie at a later time, tap the Add to My List button, and keep browsing for content.

7   **Add to My List button**

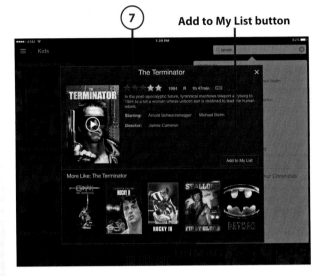

8 Tap anywhere on the screen to display onscreen control icons, which include a Play/Pause button, Time slider (to fast forward or rewind), a Rewind 10 Seconds icon, volume controls, a Closed Captions icon, and an icon for switching between standard and widescreen mode. Tap the control you want to use. After a few seconds, the onscreen controls disappear, allowing you to watch the movie.

9 Exit the movie by accessing the onscreen controls and then tapping the Back to Browse icon to return to the Netflix Browse screen. If you're partway through a movie, a virtual bookmark is automatically saved, so you can pick up watching that movie from where you left off the next time you access it.

9   **8**   **Closed Captioning icon**   **Volume control**

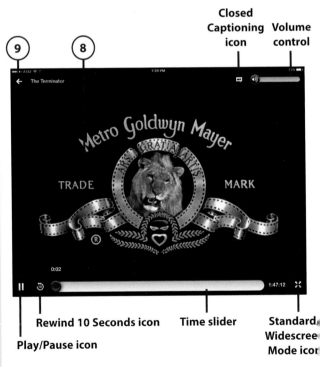

Rewind 10 Seconds icon   **Time slider**   **Standard/Widescreen Mode icon**

Play/Pause icon

Take Advantage of Recommendations

As you watch more and more content on Netflix, or whichever streaming video service you opt to use, that service will analyze your viewing habits and recommend additional movies, TV shows, and original programming for you to watch, based on your interests. These recommendations will often introduce you to movies that you might not otherwise stumble upon yourself.

Use Netflix from Your Streaming Device

There are several ways to watch Netflix streaming video or programming from other popular streaming services on your HD television set. The easiest way is to connect a compatible streaming device to your TV set. These devices include the Amazon Fire TV Stick, Apple TV, Google Chromecast, or the Roku Streaming Stick, which are described in Chapter 3.

These streaming devices connect directly to your HD television set and your home's wireless Internet connection. Using apps that either come preinstalled on the streaming device or that you download for free to the streaming device, you can access Amazon Prime Video, Hulu, Netflix, or most of the other streaming video services that you've subscribed to.

It's Not All Good

There Are Compatibility Issues

Due to licensing and distribution agreements, not all streaming video services work with all streaming devices (sold separately) that connect to your television set. Before investing in a streaming device, make sure it supports the streaming video service(s) you want to be able to access. You'll find this information on the product's packaging and/or by visiting the streaming device's website.

When you turn on your television and select the Input for the streaming device, the main menu for that device will offer options for the various streaming services it's compatible with. After you launch that app via your streaming device, you'll discover that using a streaming service on the device is just like using it on your computer or mobile device.

Streaming Services with TiVo DVRs and Console Video Games Systems

If you have a TiVo DVR, an Xbox 360, Xbox One, PlayStation 3, PlayStation 4, or another popular DVR or console-based video game system connected to your television set, it too has apps for the popular video streaming services built in to or accessible from it.

From the main TiVo menu, or the main menu of your video game system, select the streaming service option and enter your account information (which needs to be done only once). You then have full access to that service's library of content that's available to stream from the Internet to your television set (via the DVR or video game console).

YouTube offers free, on-demand videos covering just about every topic imaginable.

In this chapter, you learn all about the YouTube online video sharing service, including

→ What YouTube is and how it works
→ Accessing YouTube from a PC or Mac web browser
→ Accessing YouTube from your smartphone or tablet
→ Accessing YouTube from your streaming device

6

Streaming Video with YouTube and Other Services

Is there something you want to learn how to do? Would you like to be entertained? Well, from any Internet-enabled computer, mobile device, streaming device, or smart TV, you can access YouTube.

Operated by Google, YouTube is an online-based video sharing and streaming service that gives you free, unlimited, and instant access to the largest video content–producing community in the world. The service has more than one billion users and an ever-growing, on-demand library of video content for people to watch, learn from, and enjoy.

As an online community, YouTube allows anyone to produce and publish video content and then share productions with the world in a public forum. Each content provider—whether it's a 16-year-old kid, a company marketing its product, a television or movie studio, an independent film maker, an amateur or professional musician, a poet, a performer, or a public figure—can create a unique YouTube channel and build an online following of loyal viewers.

Using your computer, mobile device, or Internet-connected computer, you're able to subscribe to specific YouTube channels to watch videos and receive notifications when new videos on that channel are published, and you can use YouTube to find and watch videos about just about any topic imaginable.

Some YouTubers Are More Popular Than Hollywood Celebrities

People who create a YouTube Channel and then produce videos on an ongoing basis are called *YouTubers, vloggers,* or *online personalities.* These are people of all ages, from all over the world, and from all walks of life, who produce videos about topics they're passionate about.

Some YouTubers have attracted more than 10 million subscribers to their YouTube channels and have become more influential and popular than many Hollywood celebrities.

In fact, videos produced by some YouTubers have larger audiences on a regular basis than prime time network television shows. Although some YouTubers create their videos in a professional studio, most are shot using consumer-level equipment, edited on a computer, and produced on a shoestring budget. It's the content within the videos and the personalities of the YouTubers that attract audiences.

YouTube is a free service that's advertiser supported. This means that as you're watching videos, you see display ads on the screen, as well as actual commercials in conjunction with most of the programming. If you want to experience YouTube without ads, you can subscribe to the optional YouTube Red service for $9.95 per month (www.youtube.com/red).

Beyond serving as a free, online-base entertainment tool that allows you to watch music videos, concert performances, short films, YouTuber-produced videos, and all sorts of other entertaining programming, YouTube offers educational and informative content as well. For example, if you want to learn a new skill, if your kitchen faucet is leaking and you want to do the repair yourself, if you'd like to perfect your golf swing, or you want to prepare a meal from scratch and need cooking instruction, you can find videos on these topics and millions of other easy-to-understand tutorial videos covering virtually any topic imaginable on YouTube. Some tutorials feature experts in their field, whereas others star every-day people who simply want to share their knowledge, skills, and/or options with the public.

People have the ability to create their own YouTube Channels, and then share their own videos, including you! As the channel creator, you can choose who has access to your videos. So, you can publish videos from your last vacation on YouTube and invite only your friends and family to watch them, or you can pub-lish the videos and make them public, so anyone will be able to find and poten-tially view them.

YouTube Videos Tend to Be Short

Unlike a typical television program that is 30 or 60 minutes long (including com-mercials), most YouTube videos are less than 10 minutes, although longer videos can be uploaded and shared on the service.

The majority of video content published on YouTube is offered for free. However, the service has recently begun offering premium channels that you can pay to subscribe to in order to watch premium content. Out of the millions of channels on YouTube, as of early 2016, less than 300 of them were paid channels. If you try to watch content on a premium, paid channel, the channel's Subscribe button displays a dollar sign ($), and you need to provide payment information to access that content. Your credit or debit card will be charged a monthly subscription fee until you cancel your subscription to that premium YouTube channel.

At some point, YouTube will most likely begin offering feature films produced exclusively for the service, as well as extended-length programming produced by television and motion picture studios. The service may also stream Hollywood movies (in addition to trailers, movie clips, and behind-the-scenes footage from movies) as well as independent films and short films. Some of this content may require a paid subscription in the future or utilize a pay-per-view business model.

Creating a Free Google Account

Although it's not a requirement that you have a Google account to use YouTube and watch videos, having one allows you to create video playlists, store lists of your favorite videos, subscribe to YouTube channels, keep track of videos you've watched, and ultimately create your own YouTube channel (so that you can upload and share your own videos).

If you already use one of Google's other online services (such as the Google Search Engine, Gmail, Google Maps, Google Docs, Google Drive, Google Play, Google+, or Blogger) or use an Android-based mobile device, you might already have a Google account. You can use this same account username and password with YouTube. Simply click or tap YouTube's Sign In button and enter your existing Google account username and password.

Otherwise, to create a free Google account, or retrieve a forgotten username or password, visit https://accounts.google.com and select the appropriate on-screen option for creating an account or retrieving/editing information pertaining to an existing account. Alternatively, while accessing the YouTube service, click or tap the Sign In button, and from the Sign In screen, tap or click the New Account button. The site walks you through the steps to create an account.

Accessing YouTube

To access YouTube, you need a continuous Internet connection because all videos are streamed from the online-based YouTube service to the computer, mobile device, or television set you'll be watching videos on. You can use pretty much any device that has a screen and access to the Internet to access YouTube and watch videos.

YouTube Red Allows You to Store Videos

If you subscribe to the YouTube Red service, one added feature is the capability to download and store videos on your computer or mobile device, and then be able to watch them anytime later, with or without an Internet connection.

Without a YouTube Red subscription, you have only the capability to stream video content. As a result, the content is not stored within the computer, mobile device, or streaming device that you're using to access the YouTube service.

Access YouTube from Your PC or Mac Computer

From your desktop or notebook computer, launch your favorite web browser, and then visit www.YouTube.com. The figures for the following steps show the Chrome web browser on a Mac.

1 From the YouTube Home page (www.YouTube.com), click the Sign In button.

2 When prompted, enter your Google account username and password. Your account user-name will then continuously be displayed in the top-right corner of the YouTube browser window.

3 Enter a keyword or search phrase for whatever you're looking for in the Search field, and then view the list of search results.

Relevant search results

4 Scroll down the YouTube home page to see videos listed under the various headings, such as Recommended.

5 Click the Browse Channels option to view listings of free and premium (paid) YouTube channels you can subscribe to. They're sorted by category, such as Best of YouTube, Paid Channels, Music, Comedy, Film & Entertainment, Gaming, Beauty & Fashion, Automotive, Animation, Top YouTube Collections, Sports, Tech, Science & Education, Cooking & Health, and News & Politics.

6 Click a category to see more specific subcategories. Below each category and subcategory, you see relevant YouTube Channels that contain the type of programming or content you're looking for (not shown).

7 When you come across a YouTube Channel you want to subscribe to, click or tap the Subscribe button for that channel. You can then click the Manage Subscriptions option to quickly find and view content from each channel you've subscribed to.

4

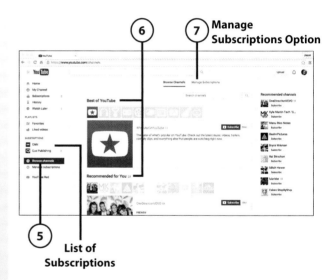

6 **7** Manage Subscriptions Option

5 List of Subscriptions

8 By clicking any video's title or thumbnail, you're able to begin watching that video. As the video is playing, it's possible to pause it anytime, or exit out of the video and begin watching a different video. You also have the option to Like or Dislike a video, leave a comment (which is public), share the video with your online friends, add the video to a Playlist, add the video to your account's Favorites list, or add the video to your account's Watch Later list.

Access YouTube from Your Smartphone or Tablet

From your iPhone, iPad, or Android-based smartphone or tablet, you have two options for watching YouTube videos. First, you can launch a web browser and then visit www.YouTube.com. On an iPhone or iPad, the Safari web browser comes preinstalled. On an Android-based mobile device, the Internet and/or Chrome web browser comes preinstalled.

Alternatively, you can download and install the free (official) YouTube mobile app, which makes it much easier to access and navigate your way around the YouTube service utilizing the smaller size touchscreen that's built in to your smartphone or tablet. In the App Store for the iPhone/iPad and the Google Play Store for Android mobile devices you can find third-party apps that allow you to view and stream YouTube videos and manage your YouTube subscriptions. For example, there's the Video Tube app ($2.99) and the YouPlayer app (free). Some of these apps offer a different user interface, as well as functionality that's not offered by the official YouTube mobile app from Google, Inc.

>>>Go Further

THE YOUTUBE MOBILE APP

If you're an iPhone or iPad user, to find and install the free YouTube app, from the Home screen of your device, launch the App Store app. Within the Search field, enter the keyword **YouTube**.

Select the listing for the official YouTube app from Google, Inc. Tap the Get button, followed by the Install button. When prompted, enter your Apple ID account password or scan your fingerprint using the device's Touch ID sensor.

After the YouTube app is installed, launch it from the Home screen.

To find and download the free YouTube app onto your Android-based mobile device, access the Google Play Store, and within the Search field enter the keyword **YouTube**. Tap the listing for the official YouTube app from Google, Inc., and tap the Install button. After the app is installed, launch it from the Home screen.

Use the YouTube Mobile App

(1) Make sure your mobile device is connected to the Internet using a Wi-Fi or cellular (3G/4G/LTE) connection (not shown).

(2) From the Home screen, launch the YouTube app (not shown).

(3) Tap the Sign In button and enter your Google account username and password. (You can set up the app to remember this information so you need to do only this once.)

4 Tap the Home icon to view a list of Recommended videos, or tap the Subscriptions icon to view a listing of your YouTube channel subscriptions, and see listings for new videos added to those channels.

5 Tap the Account icon to manage your YouTube account. From here, you can access your History, view videos that you've uploaded to your own YouTube channel (My Videos), manage app-specific notifications (Notifications), and access your Watch Later list of videos, as well as view your list of Playlists.

6 Tap the Search icon to find a video based on a keyword or search phrase.

7 Tap the Menu icon to adjust app-specific settings.

8 Tap a video's title or thumbnail image to view that video.

9 As a video is playing, tap the Pause button (which appears in the center of the video window when you tap on the window) to pause the video's playback. Tap the Play icon to resume playback of the video.

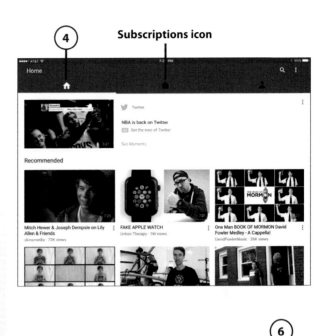

Subscriptions icon

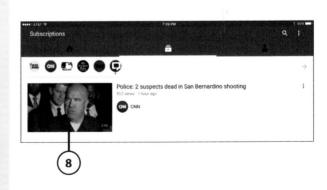

10 Use the slider that's displayed below the video window to fast forward or rewind.

11 Tap the Full-Screen icon, located to the right of the slider, to switch to Full-Screen mode, and view the video on the entire screen of your mobile device (instead of within the video window).

12 Before, during, or after watching a video, scroll down to see the video's title, text-based description, the number of views it has received, and other information about the video.

13 Rate a video by tapping the Like or Dislike button.

14 Scroll down within the right column of the screen to read text-based comments other people have posted about the video, publish your own (public) comment, and see thumbnails for other related videos.

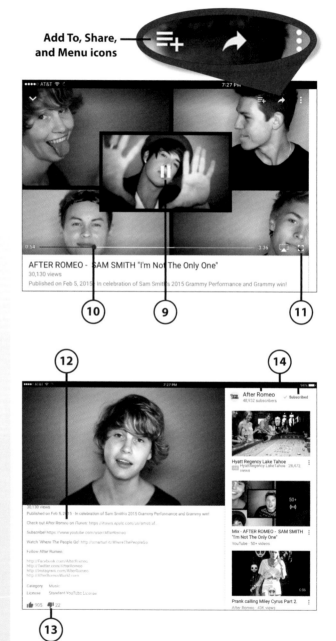

Add To, Share, and Menu icons

(15) If you're using an iPad, while a video is playing within the video window, place your finger near the center of the video window and swipe in a downward-diagonal direction (toward the bottom-right corner of the screen). The video continues playing as a video thumbnail, and the previous YouTube app screen is displayed. As you're viewing this thumbnail video, place your finger on it and swipe to the left to make the video window disappear altogether, or tap on the smaller window to enlarge it.

(16) Also while a video is playing, tap within the video window to make the Add To, Share, and More icons appear. Tap the Add To icon to access a submenu that contains the Add to Watch Later and Add to Playlist commands.

(17) Tap the Share icon to share details about the video with other people via instant message, email, or using social media (Google+, Instagram or Twitter). You can also use the Copy Link command to acquire the specific website address for the video you're watching, and then copy that link into another app.

>>>*Go Further*

THE OPTIONAL YOUTUBE CAPTURE APP

If you want to record, edit, publish, and share videos on YouTube from your mobile device, you can download and use the free Google Capture mobile app that's available from the app store.

From this single app, you can record video (instead of using the mobile device's Camera app), and then edit the video using the app's built in editing tools. This includes the capability to add titles to your videos.

When you're ready, from the Google Capture app, you can upload your videos to your own YouTube channel and then share them with the general public or invite only specific people to access the videos.

Using the Google Capture mobile app to film, edit, publish, and share videos is the easiest and most convenient way to create your own YouTube content.

Access YouTube from a Streaming Device, Smart TV, or Video Game System

If you have a streaming device hooked up to your HD television set (such as an Amazon Fire TV Stick, Apple TV, or Google Chromecast), these devices either come with a YouTube app installed or allow you to download a free Google app, which utilizes the device's Internet access to grant you full access to the YouTube service to watch YouTube videos on your television set.

A YouTube app is also built in to (or available for) all the various console video game systems that connect to the Internet and your television set (such as the Nintendo Wii U, PlayStation 4, or Xbox One), plus you can access YouTube from a TiVo DVR and even some cable TV receiver boxes.

Smart TVs that have Internet access and that allow you to utilize apps also either come with or have a YouTube app available. To access the YouTube service, select the Menu option from any of these devices, and then launch the YouTube app.

Although the YouTube app on each device is slightly different, all work in much the same way as the YouTube website.

Finding Videos to Watch

All videos published on the YouTube service include a title, description, and have keywords associated with them. Each is also categorized based on its topic. When you want to find specific videos to watch, there are several quick and easy ways to do this.

The first method for finding videos that are of interest to you is to use the YouTube Search field. Regardless of how you're accessing YouTube, displayed prominently on the screen is a Search field. Within this field, type what you're looking for. So, if you want to learn how to knit a baby blanket for your grandchild, within YouTube's Search field you would enter **How to knit a baby blanket**, and literally thousands of search results will be presented. As you can see here, each search result represents a free instructional video you can watch at your leisure.

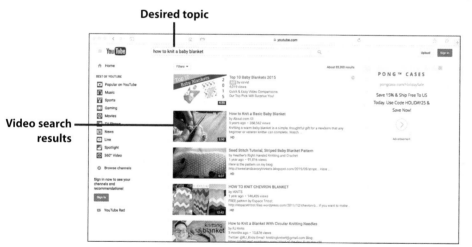

The following list includes some suggestions for ways to search for a topic:

- How to [*insert topic*]
- Tips for [*insert topic*]
- How to assemble [*insert product name*]
- How to use a [*insert product name*]
- Introduction to [*insert topic*]
- How do I [*insert topic*]?

Within the YouTube search field, you can also enter the name of a person, company, product, service, musician, song title, type of music, news event, or anything else that will help you find what you're looking for.

YouTube Offers Only Streaming Video Content

Unlike a regular search engine (such as Google.com or Yahoo.com), which will direct you to relevant websites, YouTube's search results lead only to listings for videos you can watch.

Another way to quickly find YouTube videos to watch that are of interest to you is to click one of the category options listed below the Best of YouTube heading. These categories include Popular On YouTube, Music, Sports, Gaming, Movies, TV Shows, News, Live, Spotlight, and 360-degree Video.

You'll also discover headings and video listings for Trending Videos, which are currently the most watched. And, after you've created your free account, YouTube begins to recommend videos based on your preferences and previous viewing habits. Simply click the title or thumbnail image for a video to begin watching it.

Subscribe to YouTube Channels

If you have a YouTube (Google) account, you can subscribe to YouTube channels. Subscribing to a channel is free, and it enables you to be notified when your favorite content producers (YouTubers) publish new videos. Every video on YouTube is associated with a channel. When you discover a channel you want to subscribe to, or you find a video you like and want to see other videos from that content creator, simply tap or click the Subscribe button that's associated with that channel. If you later want to unsubscribe from a channel, simply click or tap the channel's Subscribed button.

Provide Feedback to YouTube Videos

YouTube is very much an online community that invites participants like you to be active on the service. After watching a video, you can "Like" or "Dislike" the video (by clicking on the thumbs-up or thumbs-down icon), share a video, or leave a comment about the video. While looking at a video's listings, you can also see how many views it has received to determine its popularity.

Share button ———————————————— **Like/Dislike Icons**

————————— **Comment Field**

Deciding Which Videos to Watch

One way to decide which videos to watch is to pay attention to how many views and Likes it has received. The more views and Likes a video has, the more popular it is.

Although a video's title should give you a good idea about what the video is about, some titles can be misleading. Prior to watching a video, read its text-based description, which will give you an idea about what the video contains. You can also read comments posted by people who have watched the video. Other viewers' comments can help you determine whether watching the video is a good use of your time.

When someone produces a video that's funny, quirky, unusual, or extremely entertaining, for example, it can go *viral*. This means that people watch the video and share it with their online friends; those people watch the video and then share it with their online friends, and so on. This trend continues until millions of people have watched that video. As videos become very popular, they wind up on YouTube's Trending list or can be showcased on the main YouTube page, making them even easier to find.

In some cases, these viral videos have made ordinary people into household names, or even online celebrities, in a matter of days. There is no formula for creating what will become a viral video, although most people who produce content for YouTube strive to have their videos go viral.

By repeatedly watching the same video(s), clicking or tapping the Like icon, and sharing videos you enjoy with your online friends, you can help videos become popular.

Playing Videos and Creating Playlists

Watching a YouTube video is much like watching any other type of video on your computer or mobile device. In addition, you can create playlists of videos, which are groups of videos you want to be able to quickly find and watch anytime later.

Watch Videos

To watch YouTube videos, follow these steps:

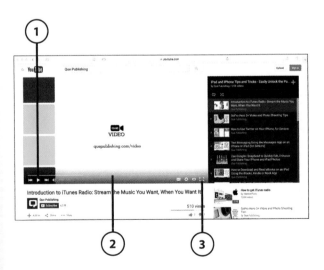

(1) Pause the video at any time by clicking or tapping the Pause icon. When a video is paused, the icon changes to a Play icon. Tap the Play icon to restart the video.

(2) Use the Time slider to move forward or back in the video. Drag the slider to the right to fast forward through the video, or move it to the left to rewind the video.

(3) Switch from watching the video within the video window to watching it in full-screen mode on your computer or mobile device by clicking or tapping the Full Screen icon.

4 Tap the Share icon to share details about the video with your online friends.

5 If you're signed into your YouTube (Google) account, you can add the video to your account's Watch Later list, Favorites list, or to a Playlist.

6 Read the details about the video, including its title, description, and the name of the channel or person that uploaded the video.

7 Click or tap the Subscribe button to subscribe to the channel operated by the YouTube content producer that created and/or published the video you're watching.

8 See how many views the video has received.

9 Click or tap the Like and Dislike button associated with the video. When you rate the video this way, YouTube is better able to make recommendations for other videos you might like.

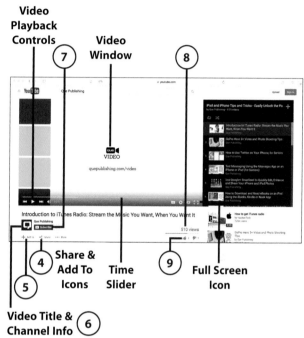

Video Playback Controls

Video Window

7

8

Share & Add To Icons

4

Time Slider

9

Full Screen Icon

5

Video Title & Channel Info **6**

YouTube's Recommendations

As you're watching a video, you see thumbnails and information about related videos, as well as other videos from that same YouTube Channel operator. YouTube is trying to help steer you to other content that you might find interesting.

Where's the Exit?

As you're watching a video, you can exit out of it and select a different video to watch. You are not obligated to watch a video from beginning to end.

>>>Go Further

PLAYLISTS VERSUS YOUR WATCH LATER OR FAVORITES LIST

A *playlist* is a list or group of videos that you like, and that you want to playback in the future, in a specific order. For example, you can create a Playlist containing a dozen of your favorite music videos.

You give each playlist its own title, and each playlist can have as many videos within it as you choose. You can also create an unlimited number of separate playlists within your account. When you access YouTube's Playlists option, you select the Playlist you want to watch and view those videos (one after the other), without having to tinker with the video playback controls.

Alternatively, if there's a single video that you want to quickly be able to find and watch later, add it to your Watch Later or Favorites list. To do this, tap or click the Add to Watch Later or Add to Favorites option while watching a video. Information about these videos is stored separately, so when you access your Watch Later or Favorites list, you see listings for each separate video. Tap a listing to begin (re-)watching that video.

Anytime you subscribe to a YouTube channel, create or edit a Playlist, or update your Favorites or Watch Later list, this information is stored automatically within your account. So, when you access YouTube from any computer, mobile device, or streaming device, all your account information and content will be accessible and up to date.

Thus, if while using the iPhone edition of the YouTube app, you store details about a video in your Watch Later list, you can then access YouTube from your Windows PC, sign into your account, and access your Watch Later List.

Create a Playlist

To create a Playlist, you need to sign into the YouTube service using your YouTube (Google) account information. Keep in mind, the location of command icons and menus varies based on which web browser or YouTube mobile app you're using.

1. Sign into your YouTube account, and then find and start watching any YouTube video.

2. Tap or click the Add To menu icon to reveal the Add to Playlist option.

3. Click or tap Add to Playlist.

4. Give the playlist a title, such as Music Videos, as shown in the figure.

5. Choose whether you want the playlist to be public or private. The selected video will then be added to that playlist.

6) After you've created at least
one playlist, you can add other
videos. Click or tap the Add to
Playlist option and then select
the Playlist title where you want
to add the video.

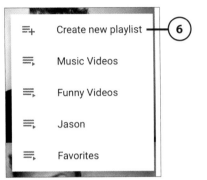

≡₊   Create new playlist —————(6)

≡₊   Music Videos

≡₊   Funny Videos

≡₊   Jason

≡₊   Favorites

>>>Go Further
THE FAVORITES AND WATCH LATER LISTS

When you create an account and begin using it with YouTube, two lists are automatically created for you: Favorites and Watch Later. As you're watching videos, if you tap or click Add to Favorites (or Add to Playlist and then select the Favorites option), the video you're watching will be added to the Favorites list.

Alternatively, as you're watching a video or looking at a listing for a video, you can add it to your account's Watch Later list by clicking or tapping Add to Watch Later.

You can later click or tap your account's Favorites or Watch Later option, and then view the listing of videos you've added. It's possible to play these videos one at a time, or in some cases, play them back-to-back as a playlist.

It's Not All Good

Remember, Videos Are Not Downloaded

Unless you have a paid YouTube Red account, when you create a Playlist or add a video to your Favorites or Watch Later list, only information and a link to each video is saved within your account. You will still need Internet access when you click a video's listing in order to stream (watch) it to your computer, mobile device, or the television set.

Listen to your favorite radio stations
and programs, such as *Morning Edition*
from NPR, from your computer.

This chapter explains how radio has evolved and how it's now possible to listen to your favorite radio stations, music, and programs from your computer, smartphone, tablet, or Internet-connected television set. This can be done in several ways, including

→ Using a web browser to access a radio station's website
→ Using a radio network or radio station's mobile app on your smartphone or tablet
→ Using a music streaming service, such as Amazon Prime Music, Apple Music, Pandora, or Spotify

The Evolution of Radio: Beyond AM and FM

For decades, using an AM/FM radio receiver was the only way to enjoy listening to radio stations. However, each radio station's signal reaches only so far, and when you leave that signal's radius, the signal drops. Thus, using an AM/FM radio receiver has its limitations, but it continues to be a viable way of enjoying localized programming.

Terrestrial Radio Is Quickly Becoming Outdated

Local AM and FM radio stations, which are listened to using an AM/FM radio receiver, are now referred to as *terrestrial radio stations*. This differentiates them from satellite and Internet-based radio stations, which utilize different technologies to broadcast their signals.

Sirius/XM satellite radio uses different technology and a different type of receiver to deliver programming that's heard coast to coast. A special satellite radio receiver is required to listen to Sirius/XM radio in your car or home. However, you can also listen to the broadcasts via the Internet on your computer, smartphone, or tablet.

Subscribing to Satellite Radio Costs Money

In addition to requiring the special receiver, it's also necessary to pay for an ongoing monthly subscription to the Sirius/XM radio service, which includes unlimited access to more than 150 channels that feature extremely diverse programming.

Yet another form of radio programming is Internet-based. Instead of broadcasting over radio airwaves (using land-based transmitters), or using a satellite, Internet radio distributes programming over the Internet and can be heard using a computer, smartphone, tablet, or television set that's connected to the Internet.

It's Also Possible to Store Your Digital Music Library

Instead of streaming music and programming from the Internet within your computer or mobile device, it's possible to store hundreds or thousands of songs (as well as complete albums) that you purchase or acquire. You can then manage your digital music library and listen to it anytime, with or without an Internet connection. How to do this is covered in Chapter 8, "Digital Music: No More Records, Tapes, or CDs."

Understanding Streaming Radio Options

Terrestrial, satellite, and Internet-based radio use different technologies and offer many stations or channels you can experience 24 hours per day. However, thanks to the Internet, all these broadcasting methods have gone digital.

As a result, terrestrial radio stations, satellite radio programming, and Internet radio stations can all be streamed from the Internet to an Internet-connected computer or mobile device. When you're using a computer, you use your web browser to access a specific radio network or station's website, which has a feature that enables you to stream the station's broadcast. When you're using a mobile device or Internet-connected television, you use a specialized app to stream the station's signal. In other words, you no longer need an AM/FM receiver or satellite radio receiver to listen to radio programming.

Mobile Apps Allow Access to Virtually All Radio Stations

Almost every terrestrial radio station that broadcasts over the AM or FM airwaves also now streams its programming over the Internet, allowing listeners to use a specialized app for that radio station or radio network to listen to its programming using an Internet-enabled device instead of a traditional AM/FM radio receiver.

For paid subscribers to the Sirius/XM satellite radio service, the Sirius/XM mobile app allows listeners to enjoy satellite radio programming via their Internet-connected computer or mobile device as well (without requiring a satellite radio receiver). In addition to listening to the satellite radio broadcasts, the Sirius/XM app offers on-demand programming for some of its more popular shows and channels.

Internet radio stations broadcast exclusively via the Internet. There are three online-based delivery methods available for these online-based radio stations:

- **Internet radio networks/stations**—These are online-based services that offer one or more specialized channels or stations that produce and offer programming. This programming might include music, news, talk, sports, or religious shows. Most Internet-based radio stations and networks are free to access. You need to visit the service's website from your computer's web browser or use the network's proprietary mobile app with your Internet-enabled mobile device.

A Continuous Internet Connection Is Required

When streaming music or radio programming via the Internet to your computer or mobile device, you have to have a continuous Internet connection. The programming you listen to is played on your computer or mobile device, but it's not stored within the device's internal storage.

- **Podcasts**—These are audio or video programs that are recorded and distributed, for free, on an on-demand basis. Instead of listening to a podcast live, you use a specialized app on your computer or mobile device to download and store the digital file for the program, which you enjoy at your leisure. Every day, thousands of podcasts are published online.

- **Streaming music services**—A handful of popular streaming music services are now available via the Internet for you to access from a web browser, music playing software, or a specialized mobile app. Some streaming music services are free, but the programming includes commercials. Others have a monthly subscription fee associated with them but are offered on a commercial-free basis.

  Streaming services offer thousands of preprogrammed stations or channels. In many cases, you can customize your own station to play only music or programming that you personally enjoy. Amazon Prime Music, Apple Music/iTunes Radio, Pandora, and Spotify are examples of streaming music services that are covered in this chapter.

Choose Just One Service and App

This chapter discusses a handful of music streaming options that are available using a PC or Mac, as well as any smartphone, tablet, or most Internet-connected television sets. Because the features, functions, and music/programming selections overlap a lot among these services, chances are you'll need to use only one or two of these options to listen to the music and radio programming that's of greatest interest to you.

Based on the equipment you'll be using, choose a service that offers a website and/or app that provides the functionality and versatility you want, along with the most programming or content that you'll enjoy.

Introduction to Sirius/XM Satellite Radio

Like any terrestrial radio station, the programming that you hear on Sirius/XM satellite radio originates from studios located in various locations around the country. However, that programming is beamed to satellites in space and then is transmitted to special receivers located within the homes and cars of paid Sirius/XM subscribers.

At the same time, all the different Sirius/XM channels are streamed over the Internet, and you can access them via the Sirius/XM website (www.siriusxm.com) or using the proprietary Sirius/XM mobile app that's available from the App Store (for iPhones and iPads), or the Google Play Store (for Android-based smartphones and tablets). In some cases, in addition to streaming live programming, it's possible to listen to specific shows on-demand, which means you can hear them exactly when you want, from your computer or mobile device.

In addition to more than 70 commercial-free music stations that focus on specific music genres, Sirius/XM simulcasts several popular terrestrial radio music stations; offers channels with unique sports play-by-play, talk and entertainment; has multiple comedy, news, traffic, and weather-related channels; plus offers other exclusive programming.

>>>Go Further

THE FEES ASSOCIATED WITH SIRIUS/XM RADIO

For a flat monthly fee, you're able to listen to some or all of Sirius/XM's more than 150 channels, each of which offers specialized programming, 24 hours per day, seven days per week.

Subscription plans range from $10.99 to $14.99 per month. Some programming is offered commercial-free, whereas other channels include commercials just like terrestrial radio stations do.

Any subscription plan that includes the "All Access" programming tier includes free streaming via the Internet from the Sirius/XM website and mobile app (which is available for the iPhone/iPad, Android-based smartphones and tablets, as well as for the Kindle Fire eBook readers).

If you're already a Sirius/XM subscriber, but Internet streaming is not included within your older subscription plan, you can either switch to one of the newer plans that includes streaming or add streaming to your existing plan for an extra $4.00 per month.

However, if you're new to Sirius/XM, and do not have a satellite receiver in your home or car, it's possible to sign up for a streaming-only subscription to the service for $14.99 per month. With this subscription you can listen to Sirius/XM programming from your computer (via the Sirius/XM website) or a smartphone or tablet (with the Sirius/XM mobile app).

For more information about Sirius/XM subscription plans, visit www.sirius.com/ourmostpopularpackages.

Stream Sirius/XM Programming

Depending on whether you want to listen to Sirius/XM from your computer or mobile device, follow the steps offered in the following two sections. Keep in mind that you need a continuous Internet connection to use Sirius/XM's streaming feature.

Listen to Sirius/XM from Your PC or Mac Computer

After you subscribe to a Sirius/XM plan that includes streaming, follow these steps to listen to the programming from your Internet-connected computer:

(1) Launch your computer's web browser (not shown).

(2) Visit www.siriusxm.com.

(3) Click the Listen Online option near the top-right corner of the screen.

(4) Enter your account username and password at the prompt.

(5) From the Featured Channel Lineup, click the channel you want to listen to. Make sure your computer's speaker volume is turned up, and start listening to the selected programming.

Listen to Sirius/XM from Your Smartphone or Tablet

After you subscribe to a Sirius/XM plan that includes streaming, follow these steps to listen to the programming from your Internet-connected smartphone, tablet, or compatible eBook reader:

1. Download the free Sirius/XM mobile app to your smartphone, tablet, or eBook reader. You need to do this only once. If you're using an iPhone or iPad, visit the App Store (shown here). Then to find the app, within the Search field, enter **Sirius/XM Radio**. If you're using an Android-based smartphone or tablet, visit the Google Play Store.

2. Launch the Sirius/XM mobile app by tapping its app icon.

(3) Make sure your mobile device is connected to the Internet. Using a Wi-Fi connection is ideal, although a cellular connection also works (not shown).

(4) Tap the Log In button and then enter your Sirius/XM username and password. The Welcome screen opens.

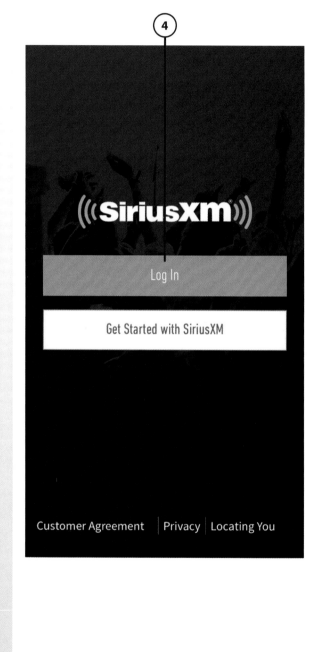

5 Either tap a featured channel to start listening or tap the Channels option (located at the bottom of the iPhone screen or on the left side of the iPad's screen) to view a directory of channels.

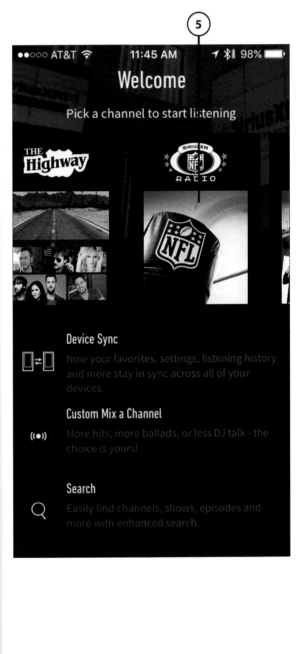

(6) Tap the type of programming you're looking for, such as Music, Sports, or Talk & Entertainment. A submenu for the chosen genre opens.

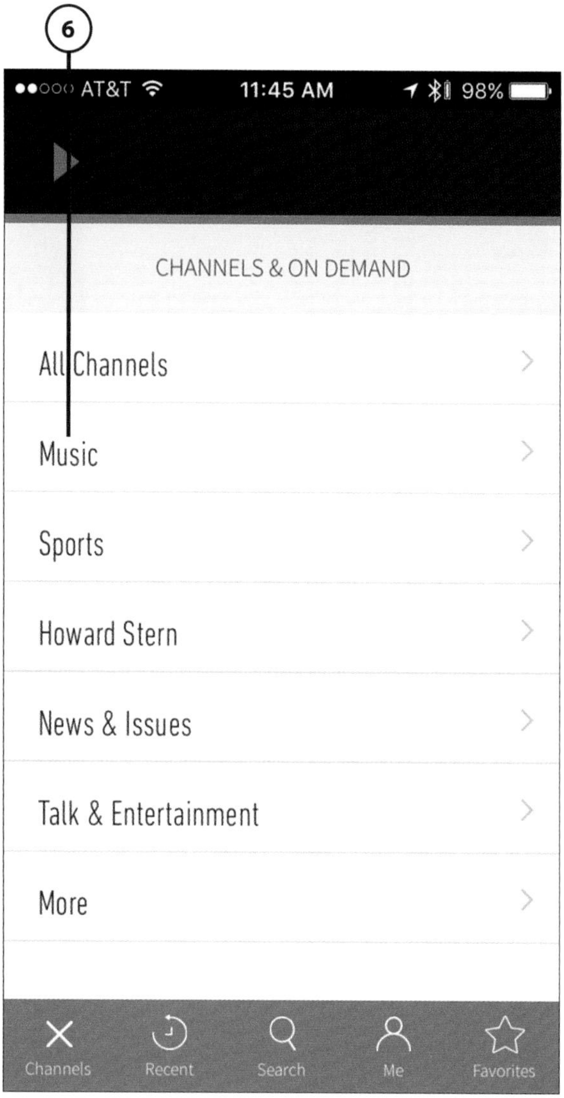

(6)

••○○○ AT&T 📶   11:45 AM   ✈ *⚡ 98% 🔋

▶

CHANNELS & ON DEMAND

All Channels   >

Music   >

Sports   >

Howard Stern   >

News & Issues   >

Talk & Entertainment   >

More   >

✕   🕘   🔍   👤   ☆
Channels   Recent   Search   Me   Favorites

(7) Select a specific genre.

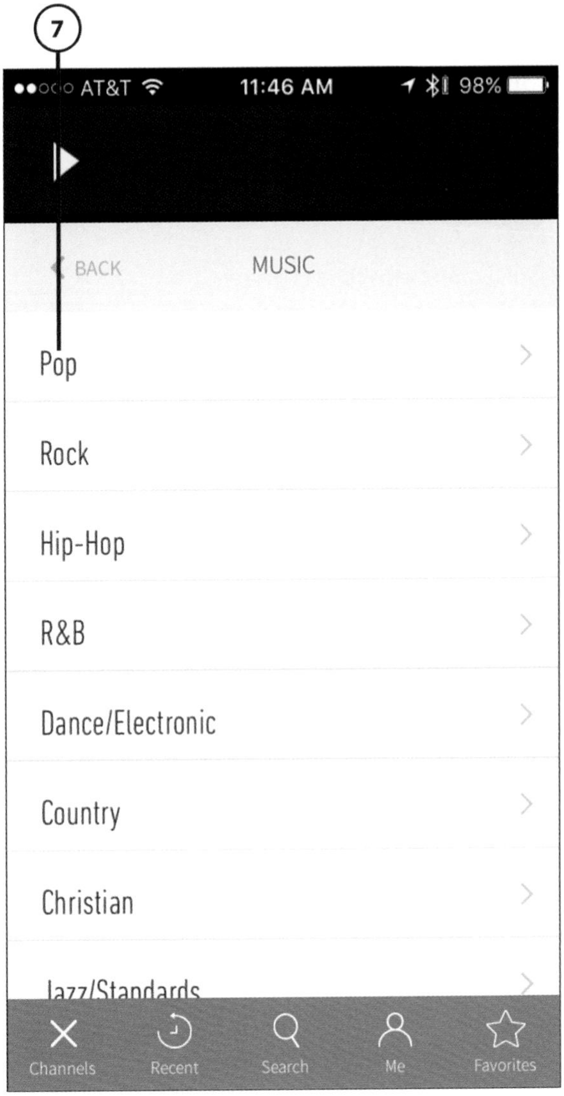

(7)

●●○○○ AT&T 📶   11:46 AM   ✈ ⚹❘ 98% ▬▬

▷

‹ BACK   MUSIC

Pop   ›

Rock   ›

Hip-Hop   ›

R&B   ›

Dance/Electronic   ›

Country   ›

Christian   ›

Jazz/Standards   ›

✕   ↻   🔍   👤   ☆
Channels   Recent   Search   Me   Favorites

8 Tap a specific channel to start streaming the programming from that channel.

Listen to On-Demand Programming

In some cases, you see Now Playing and OnDemand tabs for a channel you have selected. You access prerecorded shows that the channel offers by tapping the OnDemand tab and selecting from the available show options. (The Now Playing tab allows you to hear whatever is currently airing on that channel.)

From the OnDemand menu, choose the specific show you want to listen to. Most shows are listed by title, date, and the time of the original airing (when applicable).

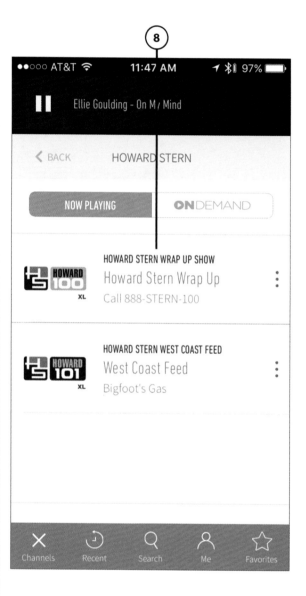

(9) Tap the Favorites icon (the star) for a station to make it easier to find the channel later. To see a list of your favorite channels, tap the Favorites icon to access the Favorites menu.

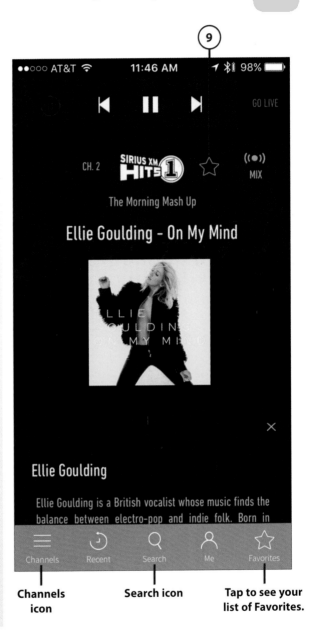

Channels icon

Search icon

Tap to see your list of Favorites.

Find the Channel You Want

The Sirius/XM service includes more than 150 channels. To choose a specific channel, tap the channel's icon or tap the Search icon, and then enter the name of the channel, show, or on-air personality you want to listen to. Tap one of the search results to start streaming that programming.

Accessing Streaming Radio Stations

From your smartphone or tablet, it's possible to install and use a handful of specialty apps for streaming radio networks and stations. Some of the free apps that allow you to access a variety of stations are listed in this section. To find additional mobile apps that can be used to stream radio programming, visit the app store for your mobile device, and within the Search field, use a search term such as *Radio* or *Talk Radio* and then browse through the search results to find related apps.

Alternatively, from your Internet-connected computer, launch the web browser, access your favorite search engine, and within the Search field, enter a related search term, which can include the call letters for your favorite radio station, a specific music genre, or a radio programming format (such as talk radio, sports talk radio, or news/talk radio).

Internet Required

Remember, to use any of these streaming radio options, a continuous Internet connection is required.

iHeart Radio

With the iHeart Radio mobile app (or website), you can quickly locate any of several thousand participating radio stations from across the United States and begin streaming and listening to any of these stations, for free, regardless of where they are located or broadcasting from.

One great thing about this app is that you can find stations by state or region. Thus, it's easy to locate radio stations in your home state, or choose a radio station to listen to from any other state. For example, you can be in New York City and listen to a radio station broadcasting from Los Angeles or Topeka, Kansas. The programming offered by iHeart Radio includes commercials.

Using External Speakers

If you're streaming to your tablet or smartphone, you can use AirPlay (iOS products) or Bluetooth to listen to the audio using external speakers or headphones that are wirelessly connected to your mobile device. Otherwise, your device's built-in speakers are used.

Controlling the Volume

When playing any audio from your smartphone or tablet, use the volume up or volume down buttons located on the side of your device to adjust the volume, or use the app's onscreen volume slider.

>>>*Go Further*

CONTROLLING THE AUDIO FROM THE IPHONE/IPAD'S CONTROL CENTER

When using the iPhone or iPad to play any audio using a specialized app that's compatible with Control Center, you can exit out of the app after the music/audio begins playing so that you can use other apps at your leisure. To quickly control the audio that's playing in the background, access the Control Center—which includes music controls—by placing your finger near the bottom of the screen and swiping up.

From the Control Center menu, you'll have access to a Pause/Play button, Fast Forward and Rewind buttons, as well as a Volume slider.

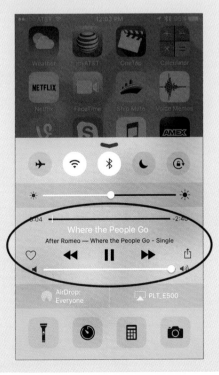

Use the iHeart Radio Mobile App

Follow these directions to begin using the mobile app on your iPhone, iPad, or Android-based mobile device.

(1) After launching the iHeart Radio app, tap the Get Started button to create a free username and password.

Logging In to iHeart Radio

You use the Get Started button only on your first time using the app. After you've created an account, you tap Log In when you first launch the app, and you can skip to step 3.

(2) Enter your email address, create a password, and then enter your ZIP Code, your birth year (as a four digit number), and gender. Tap the I Agree check box to add a check mark to it, and then tap the Create Account button.

(3) Tap the images that represent the type(s) of music or radio programming you enjoy listing to. A check mark appears in the top-right corner of each selected listing.

(4) Tap the Done button.

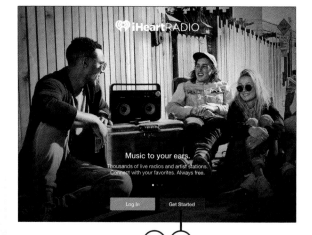

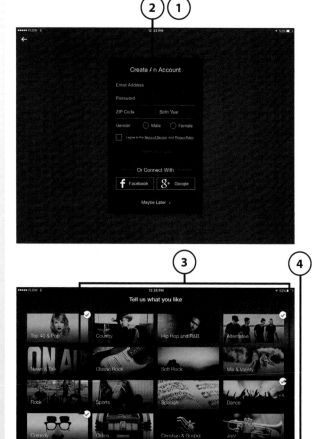

(5) The app makes recommendations of radio stations from around the country that you might be interested in. Tap any station listing to begin streaming its programming.

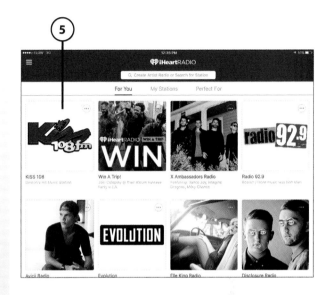

(6) From this Now Playing screen, you can see what station you're listening to, Like or Dislike the station and current song (by tapping the thumbs-up or thumbs-down icon), press the Play/Stop button to stop the program from playing (streaming), tap the Favorites icon to save the station as one of your favorites, share information about the station with others by tapping the Share menu, or return to the previous menu by tapping the Back icon. Some of these options become visible and accessible after you tap the More (…) icon.

Back icon   **Dislike a song**   **Like a song**

(7) Tap the iHeart Radio menu icon to access a list of your favorite stations, find and listen to the live broadcast of a participating station (by tapping the Live Radio option), or create a custom station by tapping the Add Station (+) icon or the Artist Radio option. After you do this, type the name of a recording artist or band, and the app will create a custom radio station featuring music and programming from that artist/band. This custom station will also feature music from similar artists/bands.

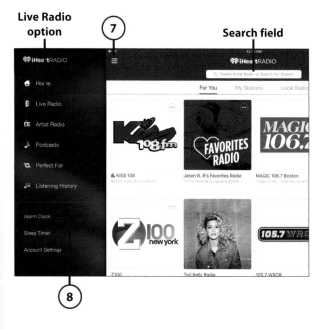

Live Radio option

Search field

Add Songs to Your Favorites List

As you begin using the iHeart Radio app (or any streaming app), be sure to tap the Like (thumbs-up) icon when you hear songs you enjoy. The more you do this, the faster the app learns your music preferences to suggest and play music that you're most apt to enjoy, rather than music or programming that just fits within a particular genre or category.

(8) Tap Alarm to remind you to listen to specific programs that you enjoy (when they're about to air live), or use the Sleep option to set a timer so the app will shut down and stop streaming/playing the programming after a certain amount of time, such as 15 minutes, 30 minutes, or one hour.

Find the Music You Want

Tap the Search field displayed within the iHeart Radio app, or any similar app, and type the name of a song, album, artist, or band that you want to hear, or enter your favorite radio station's call letters. The app then helps you create a custom station or recommends existing stations that play your desired music.

Radio.com

Like many of the other radio station mobile apps that allow you to stream programming from participating terrestrial radio stations, when you launch the Radio.com app, you'll immediately see listings for Popular Stations, as well as options to help you quickly locate other stations that offer specific types of programming, such as Local, Music, Sports, or News & Talk.

Tap the Local option, for example, so that the app utilizes the GPS capabilities of your mobile device to figure out where you are. It then lists all participating radio stations in that region. Tap a listing to begin streaming that station's programming.

Alternatively, to locate stations based on the type of programming offered, regardless of the point of origin, tap the Music, Sports, or News & Talk option, and then tap one of the listed stations.

Notice that if you tap the Music tab, along the top of the station listing screen are tabs that describe specific music genres, such as Top, Pop, Rock, Country, Classic, and Urban. Tap one of these tabs to narrow your search, or tap the More tab to see other options. Then tap a station listing to begin hearing the streaming live broadcast from that station.

Tap the Menu icon to reveal the app's main menu. From here, you can quickly find stations and access app-related Settings, such as Alarm and Sleep Timer.

Menu icon

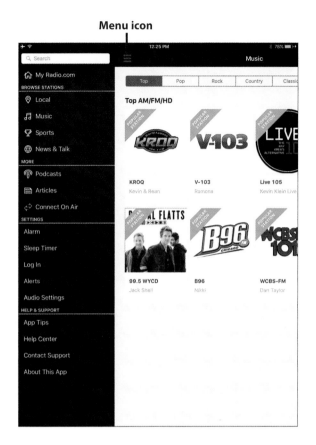

As you're listening to the streaming broadcast of a particular station, you see information about the station, the program, and the song that's being played.

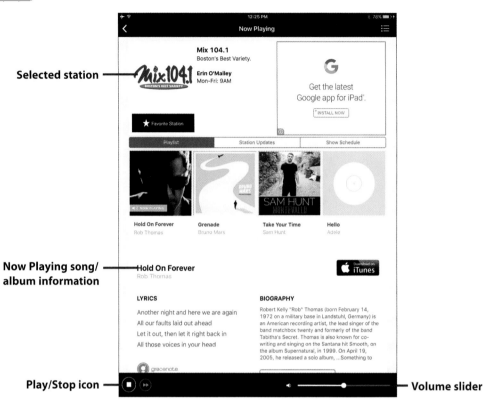

Selected station → *(points to Mix 104.1 station info)*

Now Playing song/album information → *(points to Hold On Forever)*

Play/Stop icon → *(points to controls)*

Volume slider → *(points to volume control)*

NPR News and NPR One

The NPR One and NPR News apps are offered for free from National Public Radio. You can find each app in the Apple App Store or the Google Play Store. You use these apps to find and then listen to the broadcast from any participating NPR radio station within the United States. You can also choose from an ever-growing selection of prerecorded, on-demand NPR shows.

The NPR News app has more of a focus on news and talk programming, in contrast to music and entertainment.

Stream NPR Stations from Your Computer

To stream your favorite NPR radio station from your PC or Mac, launch your web browser and visit www.npr.org. Next to the NPR logo that's displayed in the top-left corner of the screen, click the Station name, and then click the Find Stations option. Select the NPR station you want to listen to, and then click the Play icon that's displayed near the top-center of the browser window.

When you launch the NPR News app, your smartphone or tablet determines your location so you can quickly begin streaming the programming from one of the local NPR affiliate stations. Alternatively, you can quickly find and listen to any NPR station, from anywhere.

Use the NPR News App

After installing the NPR News mobile app onto your smartphone or tablet, launch the app, and then follow these directions to use the app:

1. Tap any of the news headlines on the main screen to read and/ or listen to the associated news story (on-demand). Alternatively, tap the Topics tab to find specific types of programming to listen to.

2. Tap the Newscast tab to quickly get caught up on the latest news.

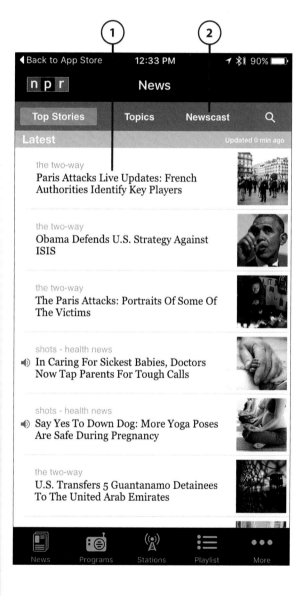

(3) Find a specific NPR program, such as *All Things Considered* or *Morning Edition*, and listen to the most recent broadcast (on-demand) by tapping the Programs button and then tapping the name of the program you want to hear.

More Options for On-Demand NPR Programs

After you select an NPR radio program that you want to listen to on-demand, you see a menu that lists the dates/times of recently aired shows. Choose a specific broadcast.

(4) Tap the By Title or By Topic tab to re-sort the available program listings, which include the date the broadcast originally aired (not shown).

List of programs

◀ Back to App Store   12:36 PM   ⭐ ❋ 90% 🔋

n p r   Programs

All Programs   Topics   🔍

All Things Considered   >

Morning Edition   >

Weekend Edition Saturday   >

Weekend Edition Sunday   >

Weekends on All Things Considered   >

Car Talk   >

Fresh Air from WHYY   >

TED Radio Hour   >

All Songs Considered   >

Here & Now from NPR and WBUR   >

Wait Wait...Don't Tell Me!   >

News   Programs   Stations   Playlist   More

(3)

5 Find a specific NPR affiliate station by tapping the Stations option. Then tap the Find Nearest button to locate the local NPR stations in your geographic area. Alternatively, within the Search field, enter any city, state, ZIP Code, or a station's call letters to quickly find a specific station. Tap a search result, and the desired station begins streaming its programming.

◀ Back to App Store   12:36 PM   ⌁ ⚡ 89% 🔋

n p r   **Stations**

Favorites   All   **Locate**

Nearby Stations

WGBH
Boston, MA   89.7 >

WBUR
Boston, MA   90.9 >

WELH
Providence, RI   88.1 >

WCAI
Woods Hole, MA   90.1 >

WNYC
New York, NY   820 >

WCRB
Lowell, MA   99.5 >

WICN
Worcester, MA   90.5 >

WPKT
Norwich, CT   89.1 >

WNNZ
Amherst, MA   640 >

Find by ZIP   **Find Nearest**

News   Programs   Stations   Playlist   More

5

(6) After audio begins playing, use the audio controls displayed on the screen to play/pause the broadcast. If you're listening to an on-demand program, additional controls are available.

Understanding the Controls

On the iPhone (shown here), you see a time slider that you should use to fast forward or rewind through a broadcast. On an iPad, tap the Back 30 icon to rewind the program by 30 seconds and then continue playing it. (Remember, not all these options are available when listening to a live broadcast.) If you're using an Android mobile device with the NPR app, while audio is streaming you will see a Play/Pause icon near the bottom of the screen. Place your finger near the bottom of the screen and swipe up to reveal the Play/Pause, Fast Forward, Rewind, and Rewind 30 Seconds icons, as well as a time slider.

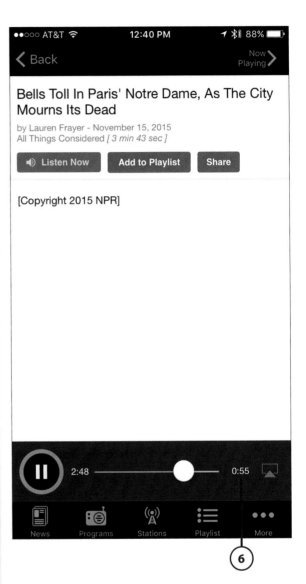

(7) Tap the Topics button to quickly find NPR programming based on a topic you're interested in. Tap on a category, and then choose a specific topic. For example, if you tap News, the following topics are listed within a submenu: News, U.S., World, Politics, Business, Science, Health or Technology. Tap your desired selection.

●●○○○ AT&T 🛜   12:41 PM   ✦ ✳︎ 88% 🔋

n p r   **Programs**   Now
                                        Playing ›

All Programs   Topics   Q

News   ›

U.S.   ›

World   ›

Politics   ›

Business   ›

Science   ›

Health   ›

Opinion   ›

Technology   ›

Sports   ›

Arts & Life   ›

News   Programs   Stations   Playlist   More

Find Your Favorite Local Radio Stations Online

Using any Internet search engine, within the Search field enter the name or call letters for your favorite radio stations to quickly locate their respective websites and streaming broadcasts. From the station's website, click the Listen Now icon (or an equivalent icon) to stream that station's broadcast to your computer.

Alternatively, from your mobile device enter the name or call letters for the radio station into the Search field of the app store for your device to find, download, and then install the free app that allows you to stream that station's programming to your smartphone or tablet.

To discover radio stations from around the world that you can stream to your smartphone or tablet, within the Search field of the app store, enter the word **Radio**, and then browse through the various app options.

Discovering Streaming Music Services

A handful of streaming music services offer vast libraries of digital music. Some of these services allow you to create customized, online-based radio stations that feature only the music you like (mixed with similar music recommended by the service you're using), whereas others allow you to choose specific artists, bands, albums, or songs to create virtual playlists that then stream from the Internet to your computer or mobile device.

A few of these streaming music services are offered for free, but they include advertising within the programming. Other services require you to have a paid subscription, in which case the programming is typically presented ad free.

This section offers an introduction to several popular streaming music services and explains how to get started using them. Keep in mind, however, this is only a sampling of services that are available to you via the Internet web browser on your computer or using a specialized mobile app on your smartphone, tablet, or Internet-connected television set.

Amazon Prime Music

For a flat fee of $99.00 per year, it's possible to subscribe to Amazon Prime, which gives you access to Amazon Prime Music. To enroll in Amazon Prime, point your web browser to www.amazon.com and then click or tap the Try Prime option.

What the Amazon Music with Prime Music Service Offers

The Amazon Music with Prime Music service (and app) gives you instant access to more than a million songs, on-demand, which you can stream from the Internet to your computer or mobile device and enjoy listening to at your leisure. This service allows you to create your own virtual playlists, access an ever-growing assortment of curated playlists created by the service's music experts, or quickly find and play a specific song or album.

When streaming music is not an option, if you're a paid Amazon Prime member, you can pre-load songs and playlists to your computer or mobile device and later listen to that content offline.

Keep in mind, a free version of Amazon Music is offered, but ads are included with the programming, and you can use the free service only when a continuous Internet connection is available.

Use the Amazon Music with Prime Music Mobile App

After downloading and installing the free Amazon Music with Prime Music mobile app onto your smartphone or tablet, launch the app, and follow these steps for using the app to begin enjoying your favorite music (shown here on an Android smartphone):

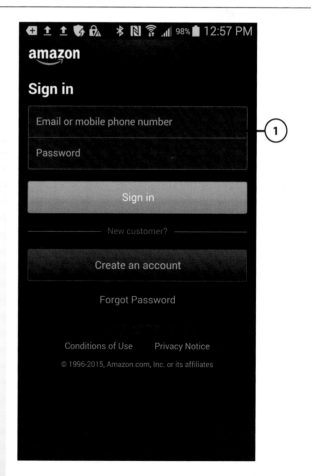

1. Sign in to the online-based service using the email address and password that are associated with your Amazon Prime account.

(2) Tap a tab along the top of the main screen to quickly find and listen to music you're interested in. These tabs are labeled Recommended, Stations, Playlists, Spotlight, New to Prime, and Popular.

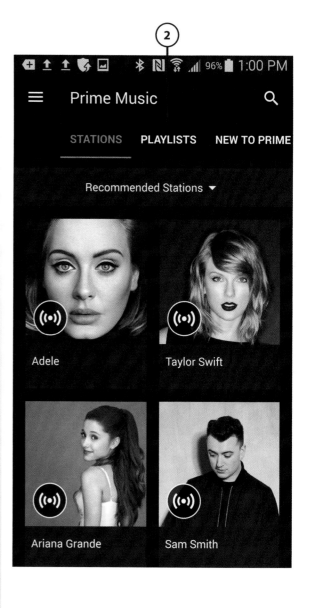

(3) Tap the Menu icon to find and
stream music from the Prime
Music service. You can also tap
the Your Library option to listen
to music you've purchased from
Amazon and that's stored on the
computer or mobile device you're
using. If you tap Recent Activity,
you see a listing of music you've
previously enjoyed using the app
or Amazon Prime Music website.

Some Music Can Be Downloaded

When viewing a song or album listing,
if a Download icon appears as part of
the listing, you can use your Amazon
Prime account to download and store
that music within your computer,
smartphone, or tablet and then listen
to it offline. Tap the Download icon to
download and store the music without
having to purchase it (in contrast to
streaming it from the Internet).

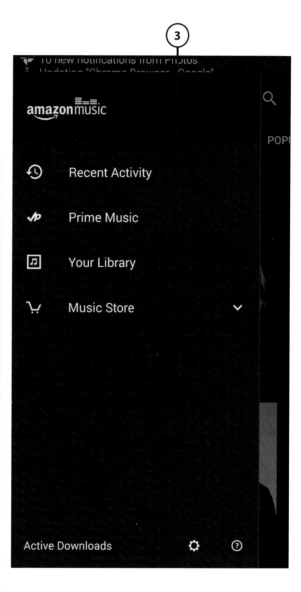

(4) When you tap an album and begin playing it, each song is listed separately. Tap the first song listing to hear the album in order, or tap a subsequent song listing to begin playing the album from the desired song. Use the Shuffle icon to play songs from the selected album in a random order. Tap the Add to Queue icon to add the selected album to a queue, and then listen to several albums, back-to-back, without having to reaccess the app.

Shuffle icon   **Add to Queue icon**

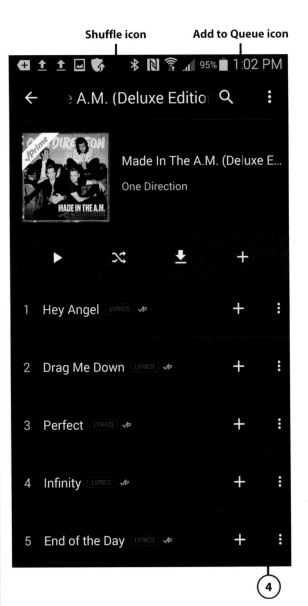

5 As a song is playing, use the music controls to customize your experience. There's a Play/Pause button, Rewind button, and Fast Forward button available to you. In some cases, as music is playing, song lyrics are displayed (karaoke style).

6 Use the Repeat icon (the end-to-end arrows) to keep playing the same song over and over until you pause it, or tap on the Shuffle icon (the interwoven arrows) to play songs from the currently selected album, queue, or playlist in a random order.

7 Tap the More icon while a song is playing to see other options.

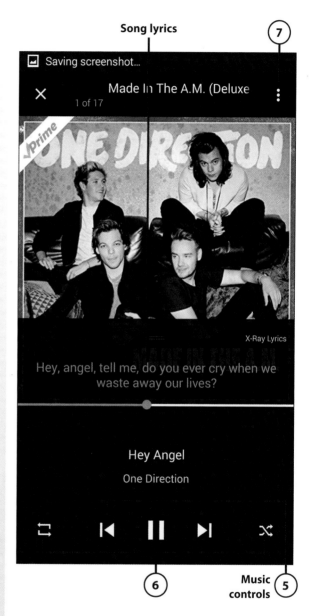

Song lyrics

7

6

Music controls **5**

(8) From the More menu, you can add a song to your Library, download the song to later listen to it offline, add the song to a playlist, view details about the album the song comes from (when applicable), or shop for additional music from the artist/group that's playing. Some of these More menu options have submenus associated with them that offer additional music management tools and options.

Add to Library

Download

Add to playlist —(8)

Go to album

Shop for One Direction

(9) Tap the Search icon to quickly find a song, album, artist, or band that you want to listen to using this streaming music service. Tap a search result to begin listening to that music (not shown).

>>>Go Further

QUICKLY DISCOVER THE MUSIC YOU WANT TO HEAR

Here's a brief description of each of the main menu options that are displayed as tabs across the top of the Amazon Music with Prime Music app.

- **Recommended**—Based on your listening habits and music you've acquired from Amazon, this feature recommends music to you. Recommended music may come from artists and bands that are similar to your favorites, for example. Tap a listing to hear music that's recommended to you.

- **Stations**—Create and listen to a custom radio station. When you do this, enter the name of an artist, band, song, or album, and the service creates a personalized station that plays music that includes and is similar to the artist or band you selected.

- **Playlists**—Create custom playlists of songs that you want to hear, in the order you want to hear them. The music from the virtual playlists is then streamed to your computer or mobile device. Read more about creating and managing custom playlists in Chapter 8. In addition to playlists you create for yourself, it's also possible to acquire curated playlists that have been created by Amazon's music experts or share playlists with your online friends.

- **Spotlight**—Learn about new music from artists and bands you love, as well as music from up-and-coming artists that Amazon Prime chooses to feature and showcase. The music this feature introduces to you is based on your previous listening habits and taste.

- **New to Prime**—Amazon Prime's digital music library is always expanding. Tap this option to discover music (current songs and albums, as well as classics and oldies from all music genres) that have recently been added to the service's library.

- **Popular**—Discover what music, from all genres, is currently popular among Amazon Prime's other subscribers. Access top albums and songs from all music genres, or access the pull-down menu to select a specific genre. There are more than 25 music genres to choose from.

Rating and Reviewing Music

Amazon Prime Music, in addition to most of the other streaming music services, allows its members to rate and review music. These ratings and reviews are then displayed publicly.

Ratings on Amazon Prime Music are star based, and range from one (worst) to five (best) stars. In addition to a song or album's average star-based rating, how many people have rated it is also displayed in parentheses next to the rating.

Thus, a song or album with thousands of five-star ratings is probably awesome, but if a song/album has an abundance of one-, two-, or three-star ratings, this probably means that people haven't enjoyed it.

Apple Music

If you're a Mac, iPhone, iPad, or Apple TV user, Apple has made it very easy to access its subscription-based Apple Music streaming music services.

How to Access Apple Music

From a Mac or PC, use the iTunes software to access Apple Music. On an iPhone and iPad, you use the Music app, which comes preinstalled with iOS 9, to access the service. If you're using an Android device, visit the Google Play Store (or the App Store for your mobile device) to download and install the free Apple Music app.

Apple Music

Apple Music is a subscription-based, commercial-free, streaming music service that allows you unlimited listening for almost any song in the iTunes Store's massive digital music library. This gives you almost instant access to more than 30 million songs (including complete albums) on demand.

After you subscribe to Apple Music, you can create custom playlists, access curated playlists created by music experts, listen to individual songs, enjoy entire albums, receive personalized music recommendations, and discover new music from established or up-and-coming artists.

Apple Music Subscription Fees

The monthly subscription fee for Apple Music is $9.99 per month for one user. However, a family plan (which up to six family members can share) is priced at $14.99 per month.

A free, three-month subscription to Apple Music is offered. To learn more about this service and activate a trial subscription, visit www.apple.com/music.

Upon subscribing to Apple Music, you're able to enjoy it from all your computers and mobile devices that are linked to the same Apple ID/iCloud account. All your custom playlists, for example, automatically sync between your computers and mobile devices. So as long as a continuous Internet connection is present, you have unlimited access to all your favorite music.

Music Downloads Are Permitted

In some cases, if a continuous Internet connection will be unavailable where you want to listen to music via Apple Music, you can download music and playlists, store that content within your computer or mobile device, and then listen to it anywhere (offline), and anytime, at your leisure. When this is possible, a you see a download icon next to the song.

Take Advantage of Siri to Select Music

If there's a song you want to hear, and you're an Apple Music subscriber, activate Siri on your iPhone or iPad by pressing and holding down the Home button for two seconds. When prompted say, "Play [insert song title]." Within seconds, that song will begin playing.

More recently released iPhone and iPad models have the "Hey Siri" feature built in to the operating system. When this feature is active, simply say, "Hey Siri, play [insert song title]." There is no need to first manually activate Siri.

iTunes Radio

Up until late-January 2016, iTunes Radio was a free music streaming service offered by Apple. However, this services was discontinued as a free music streaming service, and its functionality has since been incorporated into Apple Music. Thus, it's only accessible to paid Apple Music subscribers, with the exception of Beats One, which is a single streaming radio station operated by Apple.

The Beats One programming is streamed live around the world, and can be heard for free from the Music app on your iPhone or iPad, the Apple Music app that's running on an Android mobile device, or via the iTunes software on your computer. This free, Internet-based radio station features disc jockeys playing popular and new music, as well as original music-related programming.

A continuous Internet connection is required to access iTunes Radio via Apple Music, and it's programming is now 100 percent commercial free. When you select a specific iTunes Radio station to listen to, you can often skip to the next song on a playlist, but you do not have the capability to customize the playlist.

Many preprogramming stations feature specific music genres, artists, or groups to choose from.

Use the Like Button

As you're listening to Apple Music and iTunes Radio, while music is playing use the heart-shaped Like button when you like a particular song, album, or artist. This will help the service make more personalized music recommendations, as well as create playlists and programming that you're more apt to enjoy because they'll be more closely based on your listening habits and preferences.

Use Apple Music and iTunes Radio via the Music App

The Apple Music and iTunes Radio services are completely integrated into the Music app that comes preinstalled with iOS 9 on all iPhones and iPads. To begin using either or both of these services, launch the Music app from your mobile device, and follow these steps.

The Music App Has Multiple Uses

The Music app on the iPhone and iPad, as well as the iTunes software on a Mac or PC, is also used to manage your personal digital music library, which you'll learn more about in Chapter 8.

1. Tap the For You icon to discover personalized music recommendations based on your past listening habits, personal preferences, and music that's already part of your digital music collection.

2. Tap the New icon to learn about new music from established and up-and-coming recording artists and bands. Apple often features unsigned artists and bands here. It's a great way to discover new music that falls into the genre(s) of music you enjoy listening to.

3. Tap the Radio icon to begin streaming the Beats One station. See the "Stream Your Favorite Music Using iTunes Radio" sidebar later in this chapter for more information.

4. While music is playing, music controls are displayed near the bottom of the screen, including Play/Pause, Rewind, and Fast Forward.

5. Tap the center of the music controls to view a Now Playing screen for the song being played.

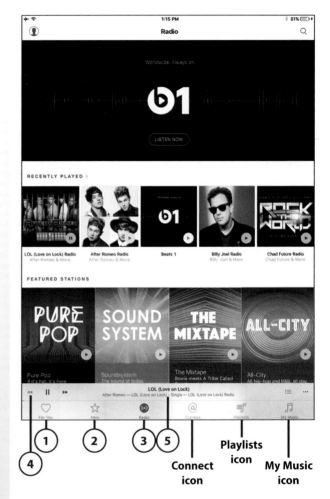

>>>Go Further

ADDITIONAL FEATURES IN THE MUSIC APP

Use the Connect icon to access exclusive content created and published by your favorite recording artists and bands. This content might include song demos, photos, video clips, blog entries, tour information, or behind-the-scenes content. You can choose specifically which artists and bands you want to follow, and then view all their updates as they're published.

Use the Playlists and My Music command icons to manage your personal music library. You can also use the Playlists icon to create a personalized playlist using music from the Apple Music service (if you're a subscriber) or to access curated playlists created by Apple music experts.

Tap the My Music icon to access and manage the digital music you own and that's stored within the mobile device you're currently using. Read more about how to use the Playlists and My Music features in Chapter 8.

(6) Tap the What's Next icon to see what song(s) are coming up on the selected station's playlist.

Exiting the Now Playing Screen

The down-arrow icon in the top-left corner of the screen closes the Now Playing screen and returns you to the Radio screen within the Music app.

(7) Tap the More icon (the ellipsis) to learn more about the artist or group whose music is being played. For example, from this menu you can Like the song, create an iTunes Radio station based on the song/artist, share information about the music with others, or add the currently playing song to a playlist.

Tap to exit the Now Playing screen.

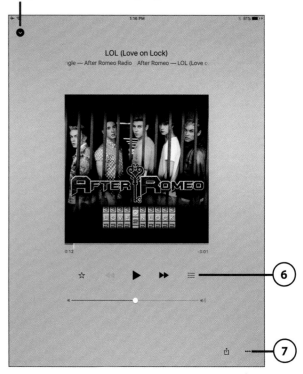

Playing Apple Music in the Background

While you're listening to Apple Music, you're able to exit out of the Music app, but the music will continue playing in the background. Meanwhile, you can use other apps. Return to the Music app by pressing the Home button twice to access the app switcher, and then reopen the Music app. You can also access Music app controls from the Control Center.

If you're using a compatible iPad, use the Slide Over or Split Screen features to run the Music app simultaneously with another app on the same screen.

>>>Go Further

STREAM YOUR FAVORITE MUSIC USING ITUNES RADIO

If youre an Apple Music subscriber, when you tap the Radio icon in the Music app, you'll see a banner for the Beats One station. Tap the Listen Now button to begin playing this broadcast (as long as a continuous Internet connection is available).

Under the Recently Played heading are a selection of iTunes Radio stations you've listened to in the past, and under the Featured Stations heading are a collection of stations that Apple has created based on popular music genres. Scroll through these station listings and tap the one you want to begin listening to (streaming).

In addition to music programming, iTunes Radio offers a growing selection of sports programming (thanks to ESPN Radio), as well as news and talk programming (offered by NPR, for example).

Scroll down to discover hundreds of preprogrammed stations that feature specific music genres. For example, under the Pop heading are station options that feature Pure Pop, Soft Pop, or Oldies.

Tap the Search field and type the name of a song, album, artist, band, or music genre. iTunes Radio creates a custom station for you that plays music you requested, along with similar or related music. Radio stations differ from playlists because you don't select the specific songs that play, have control of the song order, or have the ability to repeat a song. If you don't like a song, tap the Skip (Fast Forward) icon to jump to the next song in the playlist. Now that iTunes Radio is part of Apple Music, the programming is commercial free, but you need to be a paid subscriber to the Apple Music service to listen to it.

Use Apple Music and iTunes Radio via the iTunes Software

You can access all the Apple Music and iTunes Radio features from any Mac or PC that's running the iTunes software and that has Internet access. To use these features, follow these steps:

(1) Launch the iTunes software on your Mac or PC. If you don't have this free software already installed, visit www.itunes.com and click the Download button.

(2) Click the Music icon.

(3) Click the Radio tab that's displayed in the top-center of the screen, and then click the station listing you want to listen to. The My Music, Playlists, For You, New, Connect, and iTunes Store command tabs are also in the top navigation of the screen.

(4) Click the Search field and then click the All Apple Music tab. Next, enter the title of any song or album, or any artist, band, or music genre, to find what you're looking for, or create a custom iTunes Radio station. Available iTunes Radio stations are near the bottom of the search results, under the Stations heading. Click a search result to begin streaming that station or programming.

Search results

Pandora

Pandora is a streaming music service that you can access easily from any computer via its web browser. Simply visit www.pandora.com.

If you're using a smartphone or tablet, a free Pandora app is available for all iOS and Android mobile devices. There's also a Pandora app available for streaming devices that connect to television sets (including the Amazon Fire TV Stick, Google Chromecast, and Roku Streaming Stick). In some cases, a Pandora app is available via your cable/satellite TV receiver box, or from your DVR that's connected to your television set.

Streaming Sticks and Devices Connect to Your TV

Refer to Chapter 3, "Television in the 21st Century," to learn more about the Amazon Fire TV Stick, Apple TV, Google Chromecast, and the Roku Streaming Stick. Any of these devices connect to your HD television set and are used to stream compatible video or audio programming (including Pandora) from the Internet through your TV's speakers or sound system.

Pandora offers a free service that includes ads within its programming. For a flat monthly fee of $4.99, though, you can access commercial-free programming. The premium (paid) Pandora service is called Pandora One.

Upon launching the Pandora mobile app (shown in this section on the iPad) or by visiting the website, you're prompted to set up a free account. Tap or click the Register for Free button and create a username and password. As with all streaming music services, a continuous Internet connection is required to use Pandora.

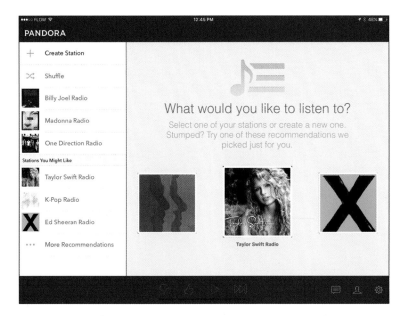

After you've set up the free account, Pandora asks you what types of music you enjoy listening to. Select specific music genres (such as pop, rock, or country), or select specific bands or recording artists.

You can select from many precreated streaming stations that offer specialized programming. However, by tapping the Create Station button, you can create your own custom station by entering the name of a recording artist, band, song title, album title, or music genre.

As songs begin playing, music controls are displayed along the bottom of the screen. You can Like or Dislike a song by tapping the thumbs-up or thumbs-down icon, respectively. Rating songs this way helps Pandora create more personalized stations and playlists for you.

The screen displays information about the station you're listing to, as well as the currently playing song. In some cases, song lyrics are also displayed.

Tap the Share icon to share details about the music you're listening to with other people. Tap the Buy icon to purchase the song or album from the iTunes Store or Amazon.com, and add it to your digital music library. Tap the More (the ellipsis) icon to create a new Pandora station based on the artist/band or the track/song you're listening to.

Share icon — Buy icon — Settings icon

Skipping to the Next Song

If you're not in the mood to listen to the currently playing song, tap or click the Fast Forward/Skip icon to jump to the next song within the playlist. If you're using a free Pandora account, you're limited to how many times per day this feature can be used.

Access Pandora's Settings Menu

Tap the Settings menu icon to access a menu that includes multiple options for managing your Pandora account and the operation of the service. For example, tap the Sleep Timer to set a timer for when the music should stop playing, or turn on the Alarm Clock so Pandora starts playing music at a specific time.

>>>Go Further

SPOTIFY

Spotify is a service that's very similar to Pandora. Upon setting up a free Spotify account, you're able to stream music to your Internet-connected computer or mobile device on an unlimited basis.

Spotify is free, but includes commercials. With Spotify, you can create your own station or and listen to precreated stations, manage your digital music library, discover new music, and listen to music from dozens of different music genres.

As you're listening to a station, it's possible to pause the music at any time, skip to the next song within the playlist, and learn more about the currently playing song, album, and/or artist. You're also able to Like or Dislike songs and create new stations based on songs you discover and enjoy.

Although it's possible to create a custom station, you cannot create custom playlists, select what specific songs will be played, or designate the order in which the songs play. The advantage is that after you create a custom station, the Spotify service tries to cater to your personal music taste and selects only songs you'll enjoy (based on past listening habits, songs you've Liked, and feedback you've previously provided).

For more information about Spotify, visit www.spotify.com from your web browser, or download the free Spotify mobile app that's available for the iPhone, iPad, and all Android-based mobile devices.

Discovering Podcasts

Think of a podcast as a prerecorded radio program or video-based show. If a particular podcast is produced daily or weekly, for example, you're able to subscribe to it for free, and your podcast player (which you'll learn more about shortly) will automatically download the audio or video file to your computer or mobile device. You can then listen to or view it, on-demand, at your leisure.

Anyone is able to produce and distribute a podcast about any topic whatsoever. Thus, there are many to choose from. The podcast player you opt to use will help you find and download podcasts that you're interested in.

>>>Go Further
THE DIFFERENCE BETWEEN YOUTUBE AND PODCASTS

Chapter 6, "Streaming Video with YouTube and Other Services," covers the online-based YouTube service, which allows you to find and watch a vast selection of free video content by streaming videos from YouTube (via the Internet) and viewing them through your web browser or the YouTube app on your smartphone or tablet.

You can subscribe to YouTube channels, and then watch videos published by specific YouTube content providers and YouTubers. This content is not stored on the computer or mobile device you're viewing it on.

Podcasts can be either audio based or video based, and they're different from YouTube videos in that they can be downloaded and stored on your computer or mobile device to be enjoyed anytime. After the content has been downloaded, a continuous Internet connection is no longer needed to listen to or watch podcasts.

How to Easily Find Podcasts

In addition to the tools offered by the podcast player app you opt to use, online-based podcast directories list and review podcasts. To find these directories, within any Internet search engine, enter the search phrase, **podcast directory**.

Some of the directories you may find useful include Podcast Directory (www.podcastdirectory.com), Learn Out Loud (www.learnoutloud.com), iPodder (www.ipodder.com), PodCast 411 (www.podcast411.com), and Digital Podcast (www.digitalpodcast.com).

Podcasts cover a wide range of specialized topics that typically fall into the entertainment, comedy, or news/talk genre. Unlike a streaming broadcast, you download a podcast to your computer, smartphone, tablet, or digital music player and listen to it using a podcast player app.

The Podcasts app, for example, comes preinstalled with iOS 9 on all iPhones and iPads. However, similar apps, such as Overcast: Podcast Player, Pocket Casts, Downcast, and Stitcher Radio for Podcasts, are available for iOS and Android mobile devices. You'll find these apps available for free from the App Store (iOS) or Google Play Store (Android).

When you use a podcast player app to find and then listen to a podcast, that content gets downloaded as a digital file to your computer or mobile device. You can listen to it at any time later, with or without an Internet connection being present.

Use the Podcasts App on an iOS Device

Most podcast players for computers and mobile devices work pretty much the same way. They help you find and subscribe to podcasts that you want to listen to, as well as download the appropriate content files, and then listen to or view selected podcasts.

(1) Launch the app and tap the Featured icon to see a listing of recommended podcasts. You can view the general listing or tap the Categories option, and then view podcasts sorted by topic.

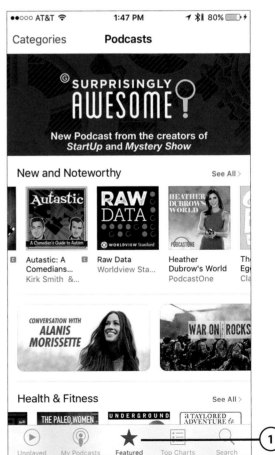

(2) Tap a podcast listing to read its description. If you want to subscribe to that podcast, tap the Subscribe button.

(3) Tap an iCloud icon to download a specific episode of the podcast. It's possible to download individual podcast episodes without becoming a subscriber.

Podcast description

●●○○○ AT&T 🔹 1:49 PM 🔹 ✳📶 80% ▭◆

‹ Top Charts 📤

S SERIAL	**Serial** This American Life › News & Politics ★★★★☆ (4,793)

SUBSCRIBE — **(2)**

Details	Reviews	Related

Description

Serial is a new podcast from the creators of This American Life, hosted by Sarah Koenig. Serial unfolds one story - a true story - over the course of a whole season. The s …more

1 **Episode 01: The Alibi**
It's Baltimore, 1999. Hae Min Lee, a popular high-school senior, disappea...   54:00 ☁

2 **Episode 02: The Breakup**
Their relationship began like a storybook high-school romance: a pr...   37:00 ☁ — **(3)**

3 **Episode 03: Leakin Park**
It's February 9, 1999. Hae has been missing for three weeks. A man on hi...   28:00 ☁

4 **Episode 04: Inconsistencies**
A few days after Hae's body is found, the detectives get a lead that opens t...   34:00 ☁

▶ Unplayed | 🎙 My Podcasts | ☆ Featured | ☰ Top Charts | 🔍 Search

(4) Tap the Top Charts icon to see a listing of the most popular podcasts. Separate lists for Audio Podcasts and Video Podcasts are displayed in their order of popularity.

(5) If you want to search for a podcast based on its title, host's name, subject, or a keyword/phrase, tap the Search command icon, type what you're looking for, and then tap any of the search results.

(6) Tap the Unplayed icon to play any podcast episode that the app has previously downloaded (or that you've downloaded manually) but that you have not yet listened to. Tap the My Podcasts command icon to see a listing of all podcasts you're currently subscribed to.

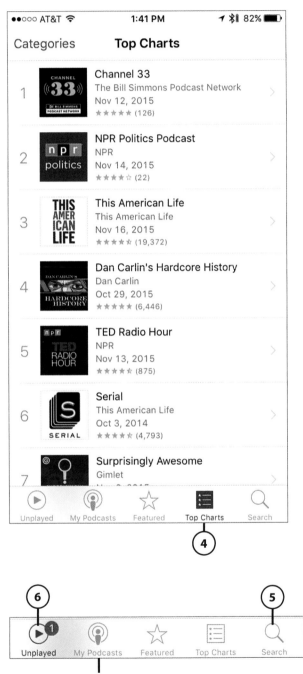

My Podcasts icon

(7) From the Unplayed or My Podcasts screen, tap the listing for the podcast you want to listen to.

(8) Player controls, along with details about the podcast, display on the screen. Use the player control icons to play/pause the audio or video. Tap the Back 15 icon to rewind by 15 seconds, or the Forward 15 icon to fast forward by 15 seconds. Tap the Up Next icon to see the next podcasts in your current playlist.

(9) Tap the More icon to see additional options.

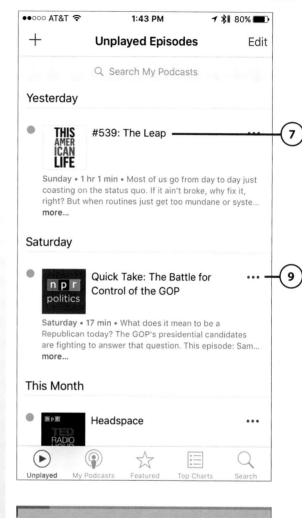

(10) Tap the More icon to access this menu, which allows you to manage the podcast episode you're currently listening to. This menu offers options for saving and deleting podcasts that are stored within your mobile device, as well as creating custom playlists, and discovering more information about the currently playing podcast.

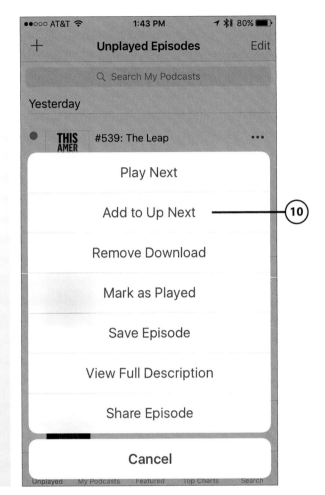

iTunes Software and Podcasts

If you're a Mac or PC user, among the many things that you can use the free iTunes software for is to find, download, subscribe to, listen to, watch, and manage podcasts.

After you launch the iTunes software, click the Podcasts icon. You can then use the software's built-in tools by tapping the My Podcasts, My Stations, Playlists, and iTunes Store tabs that are displayed near the top center of the screen.

The Overcast App Helps You Quickly Find and Enjoy Podcasts

The Overcast app for iPhone, iPad, and Apple Watch offers all the tools needed to find, subscribe to, download, and listen to (or watch) podcasts. To learn more about the Overcast app, visit https://overcast.fm.

>>>Go Further

ACCESSING PODCASTS FROM AN ANDROID DEVICE

For Android mobile devices, some of the best podcast-related apps include Stitcher Radio for Podcasts, Pocket Casts, BeyondPod, Podkicker Pro, and Podcast Addict. These and other apps are available from the Google Play Store.

From the Google Play Store, find, download and install a free app, such as Stitcher Radio for Podcasts. When you launch the app, create a free account or sign in using your existing Facebook or Google account. From the Topics screen, begin browsing for podcasts to enjoy.

Browse the podcast categories and subcategories to find a podcast that interests you. After you select a specific podcast, you see a list of available episodes for that podcast.

Tap any podcast listing to access its description screen and on-screen controls. Tap the Info ("i") icon to view additional information about the selected podcast. To stream the podcast and play it immediately, tap the Play icon. To download the podcast so you can play it later (potentially offline), tap the Listen Later option.

Access downloaded podcasts by tapping the Menu icon and selecting the Listen Later option to see a listing of previously downloaded and saved podcasts that are available to you.

You can stream music from the Internet or download digital music files from your computer or mobile device.

This chapter explains how you find, download, store, manage, and enjoy listening to digital music files on your computer, smartphone, or tablet. It covers

→ Using online music stores to find, purchase, and acquire music
→ Using the iTunes software on a PC, Mac, iPhone, or iPad
→ Using Groove Music player on a PC
→ Using the Music app on the iPhone or iPad to manage and enjoy your digital music collection
→ Managing and enjoying your digital music collection on an Android-based smartphone or tablet

Digital Music: No More Records, Tapes, or CDs

Thanks to the digital era we're living in, music (including individual songs or entire albums) is now distributed in digital form and can be transferred over the Internet to be stored, copied, synced, or managed just like any other digital file. With the proper app or software, you can play these digital music files on any computer, smartphone, tablet, smart watch, or digital music player. Digital music files can be stored within your computer, smartphone, tablet, digital music player, and/or on the Internet (in the cloud). In other words, there are no more vinyl records, cassette tapes, or CDs.

As a result, you can carry your entire digital music collection with you so that it's available virtually anytime and anywhere. Plus, the digital music player app or software allows you to truly customize your music listening experience. For example, you can easily create *playlists,* which allow you to organize your music into lists and then determine the order in which songs from each playlist are heard.

A Digital Music Player App Is Required

Just like you need a word processing application to work with a document file, or a photo editing/viewing application to view or edit a digital photo, you have to have a digital music player app on your computer or mobile device so that you can play a digital music file.

For the Mac and PC, many digital music player apps are available. One of the most popular is Apple's iTunes software, which comes preinstalled on all Macs and is available as a free download on all PCs (www.itunes.com). The Groove Music player software comes preinstalled in all Windows 10-based PCs.

Another option for both Macs and PCs is Amazon Music Player, which is also available for free and can be used to manage and listen to music, including music acquired from Amazon's online-based Digital Music Store (www.amazon.com).

Your mobile device also comes with a digital music player preinstalled. It's called Music (iPhone/iPad) or Play Music (Android). You can also download other music apps from the App Store (iPhone/iPad) or Google Play Store (Android).

This chapter focuses on creating, managing, and enjoying your digital music collection, composed of music that you have purchased or acquired.

Streaming Versus Storing Music

Although you can listen to streaming music and downloaded music using the same music player app, managing your digital music collection is different from using a streaming music service. A streaming service (covered in Chapter 7, "The Evolution of Radio: Beyond AM and FM") allows you to play music from the Internet, but the music is not stored within the equipment you're using.

Acquiring Digital Music

Digital music can also be purchased from many online-based sources, including Amazon.com, Google Play, the iTunes Store, and the Windows Store. Each of these online stores offers its own software and mobile apps for managing and listening to your digital music collection. iTunes is one of the most popular apps and services and is covered in detail later in this chapter.

To access the Amazon Music Store, visit the Amazon.com website, click the Shop by Department pull-down menu option, select the Music, Movies, and Games option, and then click Digital Music. To download the free software or mobile app needed to manage and enjoy your Amazon music purchases, click the Music Apps option that's displayed at the top of the screen within the Digital Music store.

Next, scroll down and select the type of computer or mobile device you'll be using (shown here), and follow the onscreen prompts to download and install the appropriate (free) software or mobile app.

To access the Google Play Music Store, launch the Google Play Store app, and then tap the Entertainment option. Next, tap the Music option. You can then browse and shop for music. After you've downloaded a music file, you can listen to it using the Play Music app that comes preinstalled on your Android-based device.

If you're using a Windows PC, from the Desktop access the Windows Store, and then click the Music option. You can manage and enjoy the music you acquire from the Windows Store using the Groove Music software that comes preinstalled with Windows 10. Groove is covered in more detail later in this chapter.

In almost all cases, the music you acquire from any online-based music store will be distributed in an industry-standard MP3 file format, which means you can import it into almost any music player software (or mobile app). In some cases, however, you will need to convert the music files you purchase from a proprietary file format to the MP3 file format using your music player software or mobile app, which will most likely be able to handle the conversion. There are also free software packages for PCs and Macs that you can download to handle music file conversion, such as Switch (www.nch.com.au/switch/index.html) or Converter Lite (www.converterlite.com).

Although it's possible to shop for music using a variety of music stores, you'll find it much easier to manage, organize, and sync your personal music library if you stick with one online music store and one music player application and/or mobile app.

>>>*Go Further*

THE COST TO PURCHASE DIGITAL MUSIC

The price of music sold by online music stores is set by the record labels or independent recording artists/bands that release the music. For a single song, the price is usually between $0.69 and $1.29. The price of albums also varies, from less than $10.00 to $20.00 (or more).

Every week, the online music stores offer select music for free. When you acquire free music, this becomes part of your digital music collection. You own it, and you can manage those songs just like any others that you've paid for.

Save Money Using the Complete My Album Feature

When shopping for music online, if you purchase one or two individual songs from an album, but later decide you want to purchase the entire album from that artist or band, return to the album's Description screen and click the Complete My Album (or equivalent) option. The Buy button associated with the album offers a discounted (prorated) price based on the number of songs from that album you've already purchased. In other words, you do not have to repurchase music you already own.

Using iTunes on the Mac or PC

The iTunes Store is an online-based business operated by Apple that allows you to purchase music (as well as other digital entertainment files) using the iTunes software either on a Mac or a PC. Thanks to its collection of more than 43 million songs, the iTunes Store offers one of the largest collections of digital music in the world.

From the iTunes Store, you can purchase individual songs or complete albums. As you acquire each song or album from the iTunes Store, it becomes part of your personal digital music collection. These digital music files immediately get downloaded to the computer or mobile device you're using, and automatically and simultaneously get stored online, within your personal (free) iCloud account. At this point, the digital music file becomes accessible on all of your computers and/or mobile devices that are linked to that iCloud account.

You need to use the iTunes software on your PC or Mac to manage and listen to the music you acquire from the iTunes Store.

Purchase Music from the iTunes Store with a Mac or PC

To find and purchase an individual song or an entire album from the iTunes Store, using the iTunes software on your Mac (shown) or PC, follow these steps:

(1) Make sure your computer is connected to the Internet, and then launch the iTunes software on your Mac or PC. If you need to first download the software (or update the software), visit www.iTunes.com and click the Download button.

(2) Sign in to the iTunes software using your Apple ID username and password. In most cases, this is the same as your iCloud username and password (not shown).

Your Apple ID Account

You need only one Apple ID account for all your computers and mobile devices. To create a new Apple ID account (or retrieve a lost or forgotten password), visit https://appleid.apple.com.

(**3**) Click iTunes Store near the top center of the screen.

(**4**) Click the Music icon.

Accessing iTunes Purchases from Android Devices

There are free, third-party apps available for Android mobile devices—such as Sync iTunes, iSyncer for iTunes, and Get My iTunes—that allow you to manage and listen to music acquired from the iTunes Store. You can get these types of apps from the Google Play Store.

(**5**) Scroll through the Featured music listings. If you find a listing that's of interest, click it to reveal that music's description.

The See All Option

To view all music listings under a particular heading, be sure to click the See All option. Many more music listings will be displayed that relate to the type of music the heading describes.

(**6**) Enter a song title, album title, artist or group name, or any keyword or search phrase into the Search field. As you're viewing the search results, tap any listing to reveal that music's description.

(**7**) Click the All Genres pull-down menu and then click a specific genre. Browse through the music listings within that genre and click any listing to reveal that music's description.

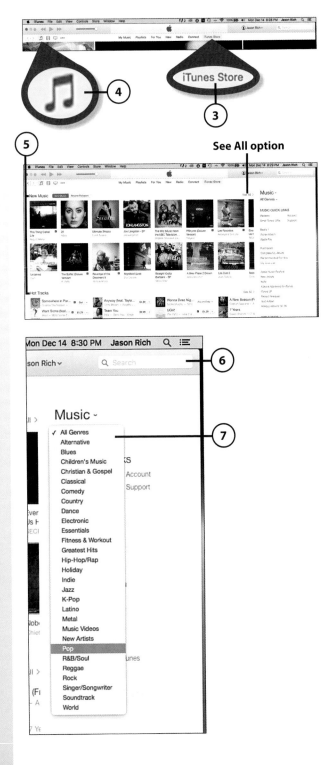

8 Click the Top Songs or Top Albums heading to view the complete chart of songs in that category.

9 Click the listing for a single song or an album to see the music's description.

Previewing Music Before Purchasing It

When viewing the Description screen for a song or album, click a song's title or graphic thumbnail (album artwork) to hear a free preview of that song before you purchase it.

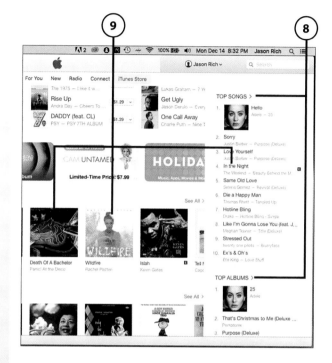

Ratings and Reviews

Individual songs and albums are rated and reviewed by customers. The average star-based rating (between one and five stars) is displayed on the main description screen for a song or album. To see the star-based ratings chart associated with that music, and read the text-based reviews it's received, click the Ratings and Reviews tab.

10 Click the Buy button under the album art to purchase the full album, or scroll down to the specific song (track) you want to purchase and click the Price icon associated with that individual song.

11 Enter the password that's associated with your Apple ID account to confirm your purchase decision and then click the Buy button. The music you purchased will be downloaded to the computer you're using and also placed within your iCloud account.

12 Click My Music at the top of the screen to manage and listen to your music.

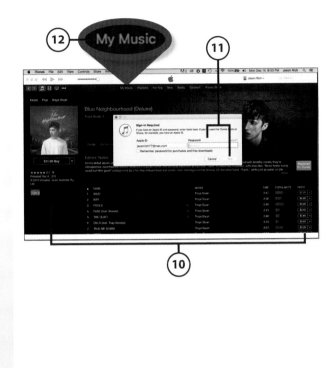

Paying for iTunes Store Purchases

Music purchases made using the iTunes Store are automatically charged to the credit card or debit card that's linked to your Apple ID account. You also have the option to pay for iTunes Store purchases using prepaid iTunes Store Gift Cards, which can be purchased in many denominations from retail stores, gas stations, convenience stores, and pharmacies, as well as online (www.apple.com/itunes/gifts).

The iTunes Store often offers selected music for free. In this case, the Buy button (associated with an album) or the Price button (associated with a song) will display the word "Free," instead of a price. Click this Free button and confirm your acquisition by entering the password that's associated with your Apple ID account.

The free music you acquire becomes part of your personal digital music collection, which you own. These music files can be downloaded and treated the same way as purchased music.

Select and Play Music

The following steps help you access and use the more popular features of the iTunes software to manage and play your music:

1. Make sure your computer is connected to the Internet. Then, after launching the iTunes software on your Mac (shown) or PC, click the My Music option. By default, a list of all songs that you own is displayed in alphabetical order by song title.

2. An iCloud icon indicates that you own the song, but you have not downloaded it to the computer you're currently using. The digital music file is stored online, within your iCloud account. Click the iCloud icon to download the song.

3. Click the Songs pull-down menu to display a list of Albums you own (instead of songs) or to sort your music by Artist, Composer, or Genre. Click a sort option.

4. Double-click a song's listing or album artwork to play the song or album.

5. Use the music controls displayed at the top of the screen to pause the music, fast forward, rewind, or adjust the volume.

6. Read details about the currently playing song in the Now Playing window.

7 Add a song to your Favorites list by clicking the heart icon.

8 Click the More menu icon to access a pop-up menu that allows you to add the song to a playlist, share the song, or handle other management tasks related to the song.

Learn More About the iTunes Software

The Mac and PC version of the iTunes software is extremely powerful and can be used to manage and enjoy various forms of digital entertainment. When it comes to working with your digital music collection, only some of the software's key features are explained here.

To learn how to use all aspects of the iTunes software, visit www.apple.com/support/itunes.

Create and Manage Playlists

Use these steps to create and manage playlists:

1 Click Playlists. A listing of your currently available playlists, including those precreated on your behalf by the iTunes software, are displayed in the left column below the Playlists heading.

2 Click a listed playlist to view, play, or edit it.

3 Click the + icon and select New Playlist to create a new playlist from scratch.

4 Create and enter a title for your playlist, such as "Favorite Pop Songs," "Workout Music," or "Driving Music."

5 Click Edit Playlist to add songs to the playlist.

6 Click the More (…) icon associated with a song listing and select Add to Playlist.

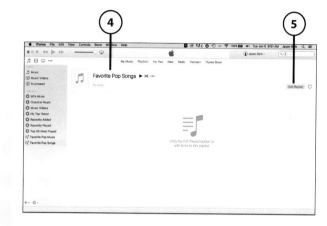

Another Way to Add Songs

As a song is playing, click the More menu icon within the Now Playing window and then click Add to Playlist to either add that song to an existing playlist or begin creating a playlist from scratch that includes the currently playing song.

7 When prompted, select the title of the newly created playlist.

8 Repeat steps 6 and 7 until you've added all the desired songs to your playlist. You can add as many songs to each playlist as you desire, and songs can come from multiple albums or music genres.

9 Enter a description for the playlist in the Add Description field.

10 Click the musical note graphic to add a custom thumbnail image to the playlist.

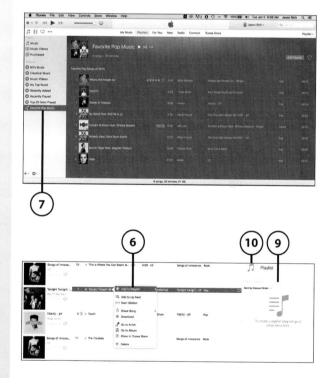

11. Click Done to save your playlist.

12. Click the Play icon on the Playlist screen to begin playing the playlist from the beginning. Alternatively, click the Shuffle icon to play songs from the playlist in a random order.

13. Click Edit Playlist to edit your playlist.

14. Click the More (…) icon and select Delete to delete the playlist.

15. View the playlist at any time by clicking the playlist title under the Playlists heading in the left column of the screen.

iTunes Playlists Automatically Sync

As soon as you create or edit a playlist, that information automatically syncs with your iCloud account and then becomes accessible from all other computers and mobile devices that are linked to your Apple ID/iCloud account. Thus, you can access, edit, manage, and play the playlist immediately on any device connected to the account.

Thumbnail image

Shuffle icon

>>>*Go Further*

CONSIDER ITUNES MATCH SO YOU CAN SYNC YOUR ENTIRE MUSIC COLLECION

In addition to buying music from the iTunes Store via the iTunes software on your PC or Mac, the same iTunes software can be used to convert and import your own audio CDs into digital format. This process is called *ripping* CDs. It's also possible to import digital music files acquired from other services into the iTunes software.

However, if you want your entire digital music library (up to 100,000 songs) to sync with all your computers and mobile devices, and be stored within your iCloud account (rather than just your iTunes Store purchased music), you'll need to subscribe to the iTunes Match service for $24.99 per year. More information about this service is available at www.apple.com/support/itunes/itunes-match.

Purchase Music from the iTunes Store with a Mobile Device

When using an iPhone (shown here), iPad, or iPod touch, you can acquire music from the iTunes Store using the iTunes Store app that comes prein-stalled with iOS 9. Use the following steps to use the app:

1. Make sure your mobile device is connected to the Internet, and then from the Home screen of your iPhone, iPad, or iPod touch, launch the iTunes Store app.

2 Sign in to the app using your Apple ID username and password (not shown). The app remembers your login information after the first time you sign in.

3 Tap the Music icon.

4 Tap the Featured tab and scroll through the music listings or tap the Search icon to find listings for specific music. Tap the Charts tab to view the list of Top Songs and Top Albums. Tap Genres to look through music listings for a specific genre.

5 Tap a specific listing to reveal its description screen.

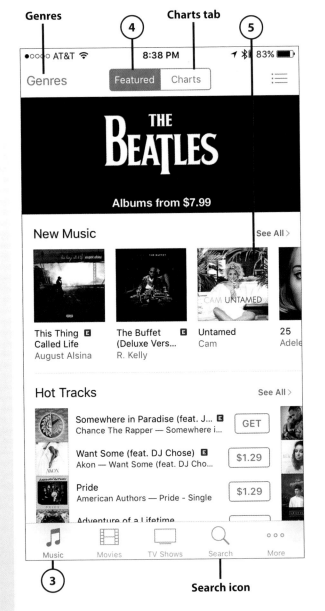

Genres

4

Charts tab

5

●○○○○ AT&T 🔒   8:38 PM   ✈ ∗ 83% ▮

Genres   Featured   Charts

THE BEATLES

Albums from $7.99

New Music   See All ›

This Thing 🅴   The Buffet 🅴   Untamed   25
Called Life   (Deluxe Vers...   Cam   Adele
August Alsina   R. Kelly

Hot Tracks   See All ›

Somewhere in Paradise (feat. J... 🅴   GET
Chance The Rapper — Somewhere i...

Want Some (feat. DJ Chose) 🅴 $1.29
Akon — Want Some (feat. DJ Cho...

Pride $1.29
American Authors — Pride - Single

Adventure of a Lifetime

Music   Movies   TV Shows   Search   More

3

Search icon

6 Tap the Buy button to purchase the entire album, or scroll down to see a listing of songs within the album, and tap a song's Price button to acquire just that one song.

7 Tap the Reviews tab to see the ratings chart and read reviews for the music.

8 Tap a song title to preview that song.

9 Tap the Buy Album or Buy Song button and then confirm your purchase decision by entering the password that's associated with your Apple ID (iCloud) account. The music is downloaded to the mobile device you're using and is also stored within your iCloud account.

Use Your Device's Touch ID Sensor

If you have a more recent iPhone or iPad model, place your finger on the device's Home button to scan your fingerprint (using the Touch ID sensor) and confirm your purchase decision, rather than manually typing the password that's associated with your Apple ID account.

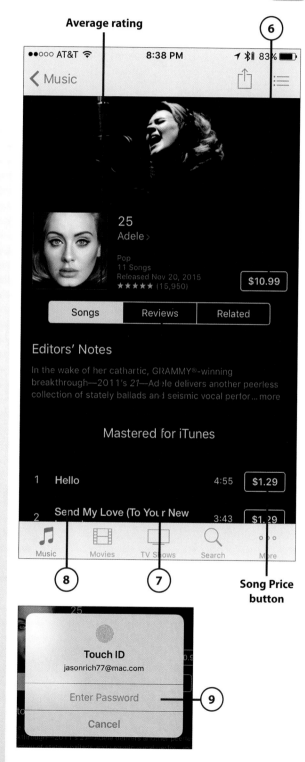

Average rating

6

8   7

Song Price button

9

Use the Music App

You use the Music app to manage and listen to music on your iPhone, iPad, or iPod touch. To begin playing your music and/or to create and manage playlists, follow these steps (shown here on an iPhone):

(1) After acquiring music from the iTunes Store, launch the Music app from the Home screen (not shown).

(2) Tap My Music to find, select, manage, and listen to digital music files you own (and that are stored within your mobile device or within your online-based iCloud account).

Do More with the Music App

For complete information on how to use all the Music app's features to listen to music, stream music (via iTunes Radio and Apple Music), create and manage playlists, and manage your personal music collection, visit https://support.apple.com/en-us/HT204951.

(3) Tap the Library tab to view the music you own.

(4) Tap the pull-down menu to see a list of choices for sorting your music.

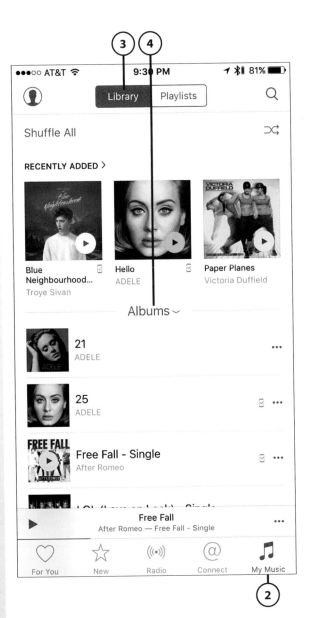

5 Select a sort option. Your music will be listed alphabetically within the category. In this example music is sorted by Albums. Some of your other sorting options include Artists, Songs, Genres, Composers, and Compilations.

6 Tap a listing to see a detail screen for that listing.

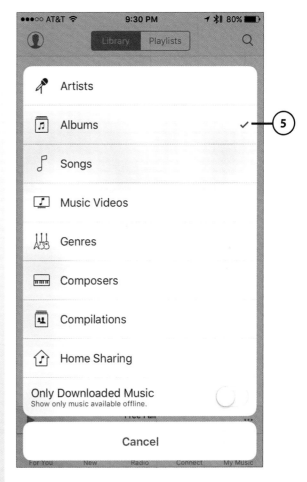

7 Tap any individual song listing to begin playing that song.

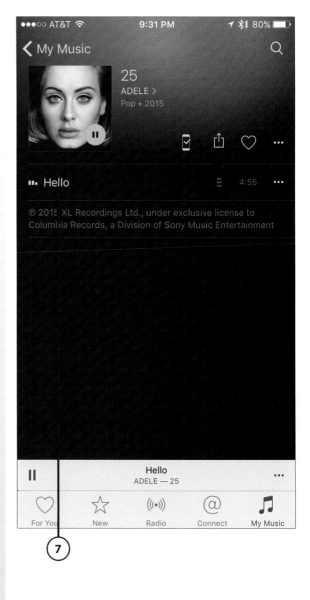

8 Onscreen controls for the music that's playing are displayed near the bottom of the screen. Place your finger on these controls and swipe up to view the Now Playing screen, which displays more controls and more information about the music that's playing.

9 Tap a song's More (…) icon to access a menu for managing that song.

(10) Tap Play Next to have this song be the next song you hear.

(11) Tap Add to Up Next to see a listing of songs in the current playlist or album that come after the song you're currently listening to.

(12) Tap Add to a Playlist to add this song to a playlist or create a new playlist with this song in it.

(13) Tap Create Genius Playlist so the Music app creates a playlist for you based on this song.

(14) Tap Delete to delete this song from your device.

(15) Tap the back arrow to return to the main Music screen.

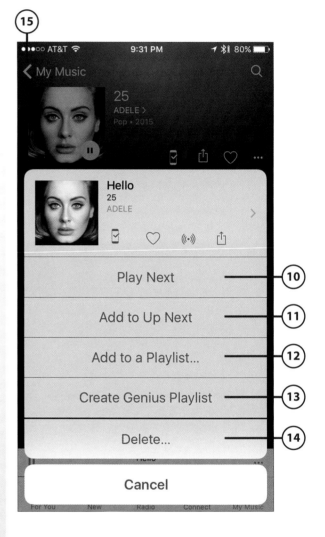

16 Tap the Playlists tab to create, manage, and play playlists.

17 Tap New Playlist or tap a playlist name to begin playing that playlist. Tap the More (…) icon that's associated with a playlist to delete or manage it.

18 Tap the Search icon and type a song title, artist or group name, album title, or keyword to find what you're looking for.

16

●●●○○ AT&T 🔇   9:31 PM   🠕 ✻▮ 80% 🔋

Library   **Playlists**   🔍 — **18**

RECENTLY ADDED ❯

Purchased   Driving Music   90's Music

All Playlists ⌄

➕   New Playlist   — **17**

⚙   Music Videos   ⋯

⚙   My Top Rated   ⋯

⚙   Recently Added   ⋯

‖   Hello   ⋯
       ADELE — 25

♡   ☆   ((•))   @   🎵
For You   New   Radio   Connect   My Music

More icon

Each Music App Screen Gives You Access to Features and Functions

Each separate screen within the Music app enables you to access a variety of features and functions to access, manage, organize, and listen to music that's stored within your mobile device, music you own that's stored within your iCloud account, or music that you stream from the Apple Music service (via the Internet).

Anytime you purchase new music from the iTunes Store, it becomes accessible from the Music app. Anytime you create or edit a playlist, that information syncs with your iCloud account and becomes accessible from all your other computers and mobile devices that are linked with your iCloud account, assuming you turn on this syncing feature.

Using the Groove Music Player on a PC

For Windows PC users, the Groove Music player software is the default go-to app if you want to play digital music on your computer. You can acquire the Groove Music Player from the Windows Store, however, it comes preinstalled with Windows 10, and it's one of your options for managing and listening to your personal digital music collection.

Discover More About the Groove Music App

To discover how to use all the features and functions built in to the Groove Music app, sync your digital music collection with your Microsoft OneDrive account, and access streaming music using the optional (paid) Groove Music Pass service, visit www.microsoft.com/en-us/groove.

Play Your Music with the Groove Music Player

To use the Groove Music app, follow these steps:

 Launch the Groove Music app from the Start screen by clicking its tile.

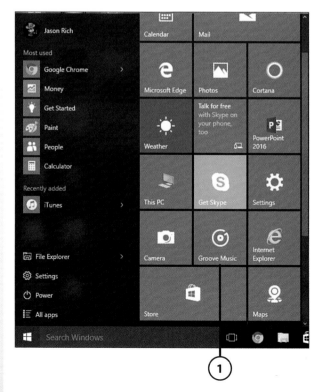

2 Click the Menu icon to search for specific music or sort the digital music you have stored within your PC (and/or online-based OneDrive account) by album, artist, or song title.

3 Click the gear-shaped Settings icon to adjust the app's settings and customize its functionality.

4 From the Settings menu, one option is to turn on the ability to automatically download songs you add to the Groove Music Player on the computer you're currently using.

5 Tap the back arrow to return to the main Groove screen.

6 When viewing a listing of your music that's stored on your computer by song title, album title, or artist, double-click a listing to begin playing that music, or click the Play icon that's associated with the listing.

7 Use the onscreen music controls to play, pause, fast forward, rewind, and control the volume. You can also use the time slider and the Shuffle or Repeat icon.

8. Click the + icon to create a new playlist from songs within your music collection. You can then access and manage those playlists from the Groove Music Player app on the computer you're using, or have them sync (via your OneDrive account) with all your other computers and compatible mobile devices.

9. Click Get Music in Store to shop the Windows Store for new music.

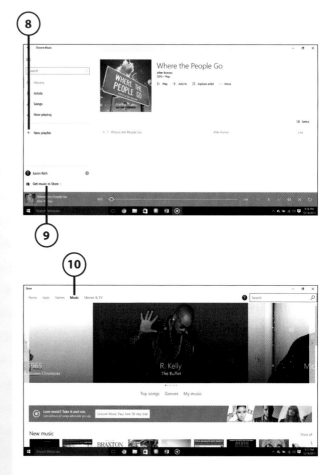

Internet Connection Required

Your PC must be connected to the Internet to access the Windows Store.

10. Click the Music tab to shop for music in the Windows Store. Shopping for music on all of the different online-based music stores, whether it's the Windows Store or iTunes Store is very similar.

Try Out the Groove Music Pass Streaming Service

Microsoft offers an option for streaming music. Groove Music Pass is a paid subscription service that works seamlessly with the Groove Music app. It gives you unlimited streaming access to more than 40 million songs from your computer(s), mobile devices, and/or Xbox video game console. To learn more about this service, visit www.microsoft.com/en-us/store/music/groove-music-pass. A free 30-day trail of this service is available from within the app.

Using the Music App on an Android Device

On an Android-based smartphone or tablet, you can use the Play Music app that comes preinstalled on your Android-based device to manage and listen to the music you acquire from the Google Play Music Store.

1 Launch the Google Play Store app when your mobile device is connected to the Internet (not shown).

2 Tap the Entertainment tab.

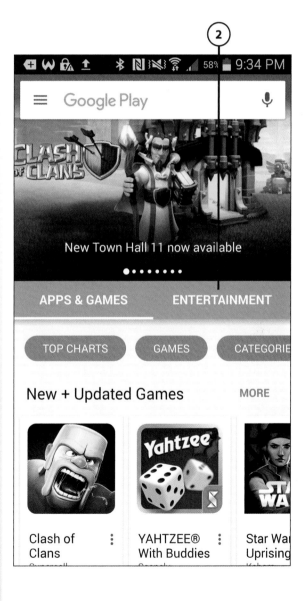

3 Tap the Music button.

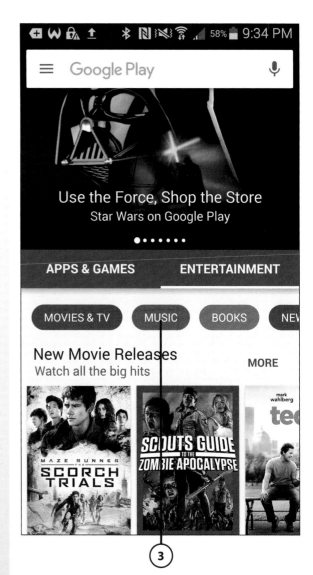

4 Find the music you want by browsing through the listings.

5 Tap Top Songs, Top Albums, New Releases, Genres, or Pre-Order to find music in one of those categories.

6 Enter what you're looking for by tapping the Search icon and then entering a song title, album title, artist name, or any keyword or search phrase into the Search field.

Completing the Purchase

Purchasing songs from the Google Play Store is much like purchasing a movie or book. Refer to Chapter 5, "On-Demand Movies at Your Fingertips," or Chapter 11, "Reading eBooks," for more information on the purchase process.

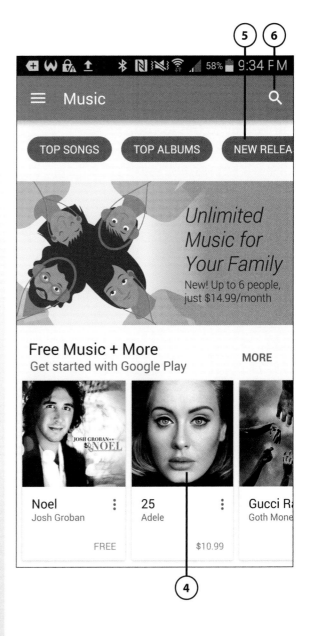

(7) Tap the Listen button to begin playing the newly purchased music immediately. The Play Music app launches.

Another Way to Get to Your Music

Another way to access the newly purchased music is to tap the Menu icon within the Google Play Store, tap Music, and then tap My Music. You see a listing of the music you own. Tap any listing to play that music using the Play Music app.

Google's Streaming Music Service

The Play Music app and Google Play Music Store are tied to Google's streaming music service. One way to access this content is to tap the Menu icon and then select the Browse Stations option or the Listen Now option.

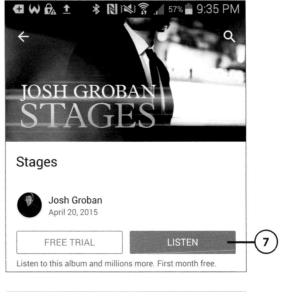

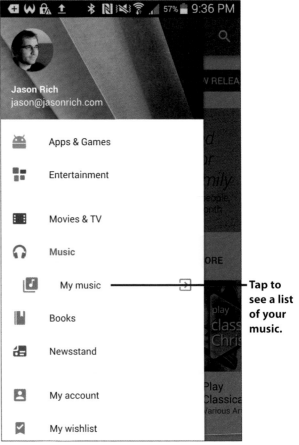

Tap to see a list of your music.

8 To create and manage customized playlists composed of music you own and that's stored within your mobile device (or online), tap the Menu icon, select the My Library option, and then tap the Playlists tab.

9 Tap the thumbnails displayed below the Auto Playlists option. You see the song listing for that playlist.

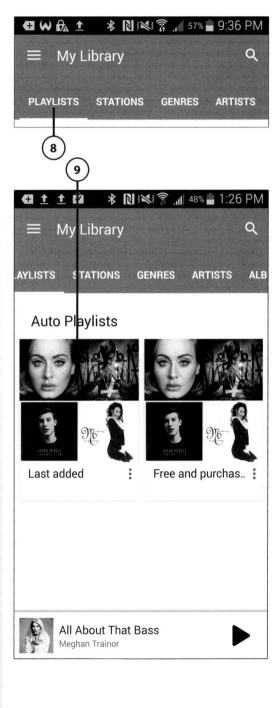

(10) Tap the More icon (three vertical dots) for any song you want to add to a new playlist, and select Add to Playlist.

(11) Within the Add to Playlist window, tap New Playlist.

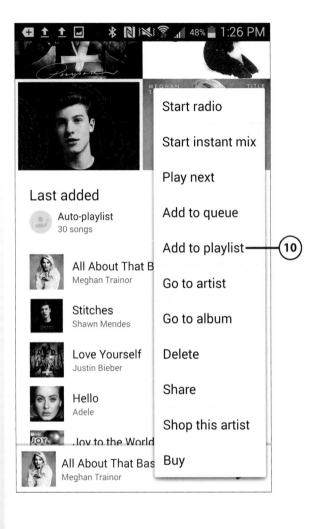

(12) Type a Name and Description for the new playlist, and then tap the Create Playlist button.

(13) Add another song to the playlist by tapping the More icon associated with another song in the song listing and selecting Add to Playlist. This time, tap the name of the already-created playlist you want to add the song to (not shown). Repeat this step until you've added all of the desired songs to the new playlist.

New playlist

Favorite Songs

Best Pop Songs of Jan 2016 ————(12)

Public
Anyone can see and listen   OFF

Cancel   Create playlist

(14) Tap the Back icon (the left-pointing arrow located in the top-left corner of the screen) to return to the main Playlists menu. A listing for your newly created playlist will be displayed.

(15) Tap your playlist listing, followed by the Play icon, to begin listening to the newly created playlist.

Alternative Music Apps for Android Devices

If you prefer, you can use the optional apps that are compatible with iTunes, Microsoft Groove Music, Amazon Music, or another service to acquire and manage your digital music collection on your Android device. Search the Google Play Store for the service name to find the appropriate app.

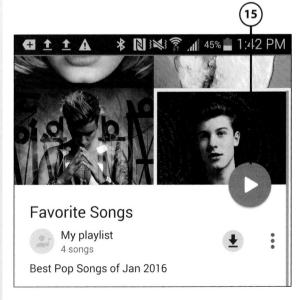

Favorite Songs

My playlist
4 songs

Best Pop Songs of Jan 2016

Computer, online, and video games offer count-less hours of interactive entertainment that can test your reflexes, make you think, and allow you to challenge opponents.

In this chapter, you'll learn all about computer, online, and console-based video games—all of which offer fun, challenging, and interactive entertainment experiences. You'll discover

→ The different types of gaming experiences available to you

→ The differences between computer, online, mobile device, and console-based video games

→ How to find games that you will find enjoyable to play yourself, when challenging your friends, or when competing against your kids or grandkids

Having Fun with Games and Interactive Entertainment

Watching TV shows and movies, listening to music, and reading eBooks or digital publications are all examples of passive forms of digital entertainment. Computer games, online games, mobile device games, and console-based video games, however, offer a different form of highly interactive digital entertainment. When playing interactive games, the actions you take and the decisions you make directly impact the outcome of the experience.

Video games require you to challenge your mind and/or reflexes, and often compete against the clock, other human players, or computer-controlled opponents as you strive to achieve specific goals within a computer-generated world or environment.

There are several ways to experience interactive games, and these experiences vary greatly, based on the types of games you choose to play.

A wide range of different types of gaming experiences are available that use a combination of computer animation, video, audio, graphic effects, and other multimedia elements. Based on their content and required skill level, for example, some games cater to specific audiences, whereas others are suitable for people of all ages.

Whether you enjoy card games, puzzle challenges, high action shoot'em ups, challenges that test your reflexes, or games that make you think, you'll soon discover how to find games that you personally enjoy playing, using the equipment you have available.

Understanding Gaming Options

Whereas some interactive games cater to an audience of people of all ages, most are designed for people with specific interests. However, all games fall into a genre, and many game genres are available, so you can choose games based on your interests, skill level, and the type of interactive experience you're looking for.

For example, you can now play just about every popular board game and card game as an interactive game on your computer, smartphone, tablet, or console-based video game system. An app called 3D Chess Game is shown here on the iPad.

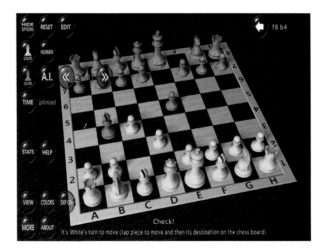

Crossword puzzle challenges, Sudoku, trivia games, bingo, casino simulation games, and many types of puzzle games are all extremely popular among adults. Sudoku 2 is shown here on the iPad.

Kids and teens, however, tend to like more action-oriented games, such as first-person shooting games (which are violent), driving simulations, role-playing adventure games, and other types of games that require fast reflexes but less thinking and strategizing. There are, however, also educational (or edutainment) games available for younger kids.

Understanding Game Ratings

Just like movies, games have a rating system to help you choose games that are appropriate to the age of the people playing them. For example, when it comes to computer games, console-based video games, and games for mobile devices, the Entertainment Software Rating Board (www.esrb.org/ratings/ratings_guide.aspx) provides ratings for every individual game (and game app).

The various game ratings include the following:

- **EC (Early Childhood)**—These are games suitable for young children, including preschoolers. Most of these have some type of educational component.

- **E (Everyone)**—These games are suitable for people of all ages. They contain no violent or objectionable content. An E rating does not necessarily mean, however, that the game is exclusively for kids. For example, a Sudoku game or crossword puzzle game that appeals mainly to adults will typically have an E rating.

- **E 10+ (Everyone 10+)**—Games with this rating are suitable for kids over the age of 10, as well as teens and adults. They may be too difficult, however, for people under the age of 10 to figure out.

- **T (Teen)**—These are games designed for people over the age of 13. They may contain mild violence, high-intensity action, simulated gambling, or other content that is not suitable for young children.

- **M (Mature)**—This rating is given to games that have a lot of graphic violence or that contain sexual content and/or strong language. They are not suitable for players under the age of 18.

- **AO (Adults Only)**—These are games that should not be played by anyone under the age of 18 because they involve gambling (with real money), strong and explicit sexual content, or graphically depicted (and realistic) violence.

- **RP (Rating Pending)**—In some cases, when a brand new game is being advertised, but has not yet been released or evaluated by the Entertainment Software Rating Board, the game is labeled with an RP rating. However, before the game is released, it will be given an appropriate rating based on its content.

It's Not All Good

Kids and Teens Are Probably More Tech Savvy Than You

Most kids and teens are very savvy when it comes to technology, and they enjoy playing the more action-oriented and often violent video games (especially if they have an older brother or sister who plays them).

For example, extremely popular video game series, such as *Grand Theft Auto* and *Call of Duty*, are available on all computers, console-based gaming systems, and mobile devices. However, they are rated M (Mature). These games are fun for older teens and adults to play, but due to their violent content, strong language, and, in some cases, sexual innuendo, they are not suitable for kids or younger teens.

Yet, kids and teens will try very hard to get access to these and other games like them. So, if you choose to buy interactive games for your kids or grandkids, pay careful attention to each game's rating, read each game's description carefully, and avoid exposing your kids or grandkids to game content that is not appropriate for them.

The game ratings provide guidelines, but ultimately, it's your job as a parent or grandparent to choose content that's suitable. Don't believe it when your child or grandchild says, "All of my friends at school have this game," especially if that game has an M rating.

Using the Parental Controls that are built into most gaming consoles and devices, you're able to restrict kids and teens from accessing games and content that are inappropriate based on a game's ratings, plus you can prevent young people from making in-app (in-game) purchases. How to set up these controls varies, based on the equipment you're using.

Benefits of Interactive Games Versus Traditional Types of Games

There are a handful of benefits to playing games on a computer, smartphone, tablet, or on a console-based video game system, including the following:

- You can play anytime and anywhere, even if you're alone and have nobody to compete against. Some games are designed for one player. Others enable you to compete against computer-controlled opponents and other human players via the Internet (so your competitors can be located anywhere in the world).

- Games designed to be played on a smartphone, tablet, or handheld gaming system can be experienced anywhere and provide a fun way to relax and pass time.

- Some games are ideal for playing for just a few minutes at a time, when you have time. Others are designed to keep players entertained for many hours of continuous play.

- Many types of interactive gaming experiences are available, so depending on what you're in the mood for, there's always a vast selection of options.

- Although some games for console-based game systems, and some computer games, tend to be expensive ($30 to $70 each), most games for your smartphone or tablet are free (or initially cost well under $5.00 to purchase the game app). Many offer optional in-app purchases, however, so over time, you will probably wind up spending more money on each game.

- If you already enjoy playing board games, card games, trivia games, puzzle games, or casino games, the interactive game adaptations are authentic, challenging, and fun to play.

- For people who are uncomfortable using technology, like a smartphone or tablet, learning to play just one or two simple games will help you get used to interacting with your mobile device and become accustomed to using its touchscreen. The comfort level you develop playing games on your smartphone or tablet can easily be adapted when you opt to use your mobile device for other tasks.

- No matter what time of day or night it is, thanks to games that work in conjunction with the Internet, you can always find players to interact and play with. Some games allow you to converse with your opponent(s), via text message or using your voice, while you're playing the game, which provides a social experience in addition to an interactive gaming experience.

- Most kids and teens love playing video games. Some games are ideal for playing with your kids or grandkids, as a way to bond with them using technology—even if you're located on the opposite side of the country. Many board games, puzzle games, and word games, for example, have an online component, so if you're both using the same version of the game on your own mobile devices, you can play together via the Internet.

Ways to Experience Interactive Gaming Experiences

There are many ways to experience interactive games on your television set (via a console-based video game system), using your desktop or notebook computer, on your smartphone or tablet, or using a dedicated handheld gaming system.

Computer Gaming

Whether you're a PC or Mac user, thousands of games are available that you purchase outright. You then download the required gaming software/app to experience it on your computer. Most of these games can be purchased online and downloaded directly from the Windows Store (PCs) or Mac App Store (Mac).

In some cases, computer games offer a one-player experience, in which you compete against computer-controlled opponents or the clock to achieve the game's objectives.

Other games enable two or more people to compete, using the same computer or through an online element, which allows multiple people in different locations to experience the same game and compete in real-time against each other.

Some Games Have Ongoing Fees

Whereas some computer games are initially free, or have an upfront cost associated with them, they also may have in-game purchase options that allow you to speed up game play, unlock game play elements, utilize in-game features, or unlock more advanced levels or stages. See the "Watch for In-App Purchases" note later in this chapter for more information.

Online Gaming

An online game is one that typically requires no software to download, because you play it by visiting a specific gaming website via the Internet (using your computer's web browser). Thus, a continuous Internet connection is required.

Some online games are free to play, especially those available through social media networks, like Facebook. Others require you to pay a subscription fee to a gaming service, pay one flat fee to acquire the game, and/or have in-game purchase options associated with them.

Depending on the online game, some can be played solo. Others allow you to compete against one other opponent whom you choose, and some massively multiplayer online games enable you to experience the same game with dozens, hundreds, or even thousands of competitors in real-time via the Internet.

To play most online games, you launch your favorite web browser and visit a specific website. In some cases, however, you need to also download and install special software onto your computer that allows you to access an online gaming network or gaming service via your existing Internet connection.

Smartphone and Tablet Games

Apple's App Store for the iPhone and iPad and the Google Play Store for Android-based smartphones and tablets have many game apps available that you can download and install onto your mobile device in the form of individual apps.

Some of these game apps are for one-player games that require no Internet connection after they've been downloaded. These games typically require you to initially purchase the game app, for between $0.99 and $4.99 (although some cost more), and then you're able to play them as often as you like, with no ongoing or additional changes.

Other game apps are free initially, but have in-app purchases associated with them and/or require a continuous Internet connection so you can compete against other players in real-time.

Console-Based Video Game Systems

A console-based video game system is a device that you connect to your HD television set (and the Internet). On it you can choose from a vast library of games (sold separately) that have been designed for that system. These game consoles have specialized controllers that allow you to control the onscreen action, whether you're competing against computer-controlled opponents, human components located in the same room as you, or people you're playing against via the Internet.

The Nintendo Wii, Sony PlayStation 3, Sony PlayStation 4, Xbox 360, and Xbox One are all examples of popular console-based video game systems that cost between $199.00 and $599.00, plus the cost of individual games, which range in price from $9.99 to $79.00. Games are available at popular retails stores and from online sellers, such as Amazon.com.

You can also purchase used copies of games from retail stores like GameStop (www.gamestop.com), or you can rent games from movie/video game vending machines, such as Red Box (www.redbox.com/games).

There's also a subscription-based service, called GameFly (www.gamefly.com), that allows you to rent one or two games at a time and have them mailed to your home. When you return them, new games that you preselect are sent. As long as you pay the monthly subscription fee, you can keep each game as long as you want before returning it, or purchase the used game at a deeply discounted price.

>>>Go Further

APPLE TV OFFERS A CONSOLE-BASED GAMING EXPERIENCE

The original Apple TV device (released in 2007) can be used to experience on-demand TV shows, movies, and music, and can also be used to view your digital photo collection on your television screen. However, the latest Apple TV device (released in 2015 and priced between $149.00 and $199.00) has an App Store associated with it. From the Apple TV App Store, you are able to download and install a wide range of individual interactive games to play on your HD television set.

You can control these games using the remote control device that comes with the Apple TV unit, use your iPhone or iPad as a game controller, or purchase one or more optional handheld and wireless controllers (one for each player). To learn more about Apple TV's gaming capabilities, visit www.apple.com/tv/games-and-more.

Dedicated Handheld Gaming Systems

A handheld video game system is a standalone device that is designed exclusively to play video games. Although these were extremely popular a few years ago, the latest smartphones and tablets now offer similar technologies that provide very similar gaming experiences.

Like a smartphone or tablet, handheld gaming systems are battery powered and have a built in screen, speaker, and buttons to control the gaming action. Depending on the system, games are added to the gaming system by inserting a game-specific cartridge and/or by downloading the game from the Internet.

Handheld gaming systems range in price from less than $100.00 to $200.00 or more, plus the cost of individual games. These currently include the Nintendo 3DS LX ($199.99), Nintendo 2DS ($99.99), PlayStation Vita ($199.99).

Finding Games for Your Smartphone or Tablet

Because most adults enjoy playing games on their smartphone or tablet, this section focuses on how to find specific games, out of the hundreds of thousands available, that you might personally enjoy. You can play these games on your iPhone, iPad, or Android-based smartphone or tablet.

Both the App Store (iPhone/iPad) and the Google Play Store (Android) have a Games app category. When you select this category, you see a submenu of many types of games. You can also browse through the Top Charts lists that showcase the most popular games, or if you know the type of game you want to find, you can enter a game's title, category, keyword, or search phrase directly into the Search field.

Free Games Typically Feature Ads

When you download and play a game that's offered for free, it often includes advertisements embedded within the game, or you're forced to watch short commercials during game play. For a fee, you can typically purchase an ad-free version of the same game.

>>>Go Further

GAME REVIEWS AND RATINGS

Whether you're looking for games for your PC or Mac from the Windows Store or Mac App Store or you're browsing through game listings within one of the app stores for your mobile device, each game has detailed reviews from people who have played the game. Star-based ratings for each game are also a quick way to determine the quality and entertainment value of a game, especially if it has an abundance of 4 or 5 stars. The number of people who have reviewed the game is displayed in parentheses next to the star rating. If you want to see a more detailed breakdown of how many one, two, three, four, or five stars a specific game has received, from the app's Description screen, tap the Reviews tab.

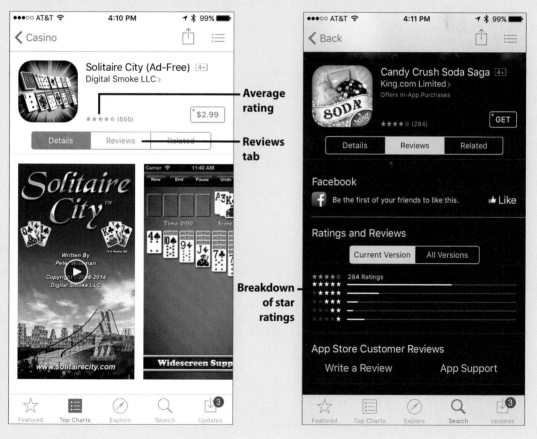

Each game's description screen also includes a detailed description and sample screenshots from the game, which allow you to preview what the onscreen graphics look like.

By investing just two or three minutes to read a game's description, and then checking out a game's star-based ratings and reading a few reviews, you can quickly determine if you'll be interested in playing the game, and if based on other peoples' experiences, the game lives up to expectations.

Avoid games (or any apps for that matter) that have an abundance of one, two, or three-star reviews; plenty of game apps have received hundreds or thousands of five-star reviews that are well worth playing.

Games for iPhone and iPad

To find fun and challenging games on your iPhone or iPad (shown here), make sure your mobile device has Internet access, launch the App Store app, and then follow these steps:

(1) Tap the Featured icon and look at the app listings displayed under the Best New Games or Popular Games heading. You can swipe your finger from right to left to scroll across the listing of game apps under a heading, or tap the See All option to view all apps that Apple has chosen to showcase within that category of games.

Game headings

See All option

iPhone Versus iPad Games

Although all games designed for the iPhone play on an iPad, many games designed to take advantage of the iPad's larger screen do not work on an iPhone. Keep an eye out for games that are specific for your device.

(2) Search specifically for games by tapping the Categories option and then tapping the Games category option.

(3) Tap the type of game that's of interest. You see a screen of app listings for the category you've chosen.

Using the Search Field

If you know the title of the game app you're looking for, or have a specific type of game in mind, such as a **crossword puzzle** or **blackjack** game, type this into the Search field. Within the Search field, you can also enter any keyword or search phrase that will help you find the type of game you're seeking. As you're viewing the search results, tap any app listing to view its description screen.

4 Scroll horizontally to view all app listings under each heading, and scroll down to view all heading options, such as Best New Games, All-Time Games, and Free Games, that fit into the Games subcategory you've selected.

5 Tap any game listing to view its description screen.

6 Read a game's description screen, which includes details about the game app, its average star-based rating, the game's price, a handful of sample screenshots from the game, a text-based description of the game, plus access to the game's reviews.

7 Acquire the game by tapping its Price button. If the game is initially free, you see a Get button instead of the Price button.

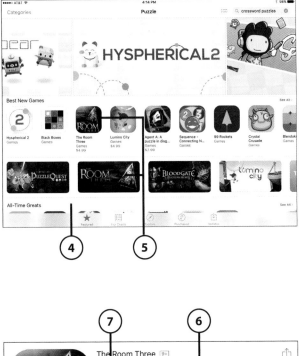

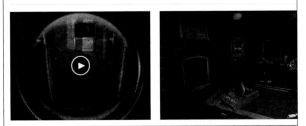

Purchasing Universal Apps

When a game is designed to work on both the iPhone and iPad (meaning it's a universal app), within the Price button for that app you see a + icon. After you acquire that app, you can then download and install it on both your iPhone and iPad (that are linked to the same Apple ID account) for no additional charge, and then play the game on both devices.

Watch for In-App Purchases

Many games for the iPhone or iPad have in-app purchase options, especially if the game is initially offered for free. To determine if this is the case, as you're looking at a game's description screen, scroll down and look for the heading In-App Purchases, and tap it to see a description of what types of in-app purchases are available and how much they cost.

Most free games that offer in-app purchases can be played entirely for free, but are designed to slow down, or somehow encourage you to make in-app purchases to speed up or somehow enhance the game play experience.

8 Tap the Buy icon to confirm your purchase decision. If the game is free, you see an Install button instead of a Buy button.

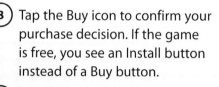

9 If prompted, enter the password that's associated with your Apple ID account, or place your finger on the compatible device's Touch ID sensor (Home button) to scan your fingerprint and confirm your purchase decision. The game app downloads and automatically installs on your device.

Some Patience Required

The download takes between 15 seconds and several minutes to complete, depending on the size of the game and your current Internet connection.

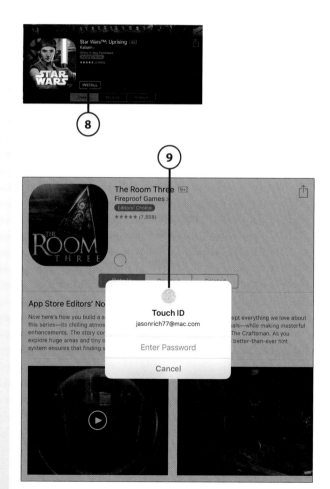

(10) Tap the Open button, or access the Home screen and tap the game's app icon to launch the game and begin playing.

The Room Three [9+]
Fireproof Games >
Editors' Choice
★★★★★ (7,858)

OPEN

Details   Reviews   Related

App Store Editors' Notes

(10)

Finding Games for Your Mac

When using the Mac App Store to find, download, and install games for any Mac computer, the process is very similar to using the App Store for the iPhone and iPad.

Discover the Most Popular Games

To discover the currently most popular games available from the App Store, tap the Top Charts icon, tap the Categories option, tap the Games option, and then tap the All Games option.

Three separate Top Charts—Paid, Free, and Top Grossing—are displayed. Scroll down through each list to view up to 100 of the currently most popular games in the entire Games genre.

To narrow your search, from the Games category submenu tap a specific game genre, such as Board, Card, or Puzzle, to see listings of the top games from only that category.

Games for Android-Based Smartphones and Tablets

The Google Play Store offers an entire section dedicated to showcasing the thousands of games available for Android-based smartphones and tablets. To find, download, and install a game onto your Android-based smartphone or tablet, make sure it's connected to the Internet, launch the Google Play Store app, and then follow these directions:

1. From the main Google Play App Store screen, tap the Menu icon and select the Apps & Games option.

2. Scroll down on the Apps & Games screen to preview listings for featured games that fall under each displayed heading, such as New + Updated Games. Swipe your finger from right to left across the app icons displayed under a specific heading to view all of the listings, or tap the More option that's associated with a particular heading.

3. Alternatively, tap the Top Charts option to reveal charts that showcase the currently most popular games.

4. Alternatively, tap the Games option to see a list of categories.

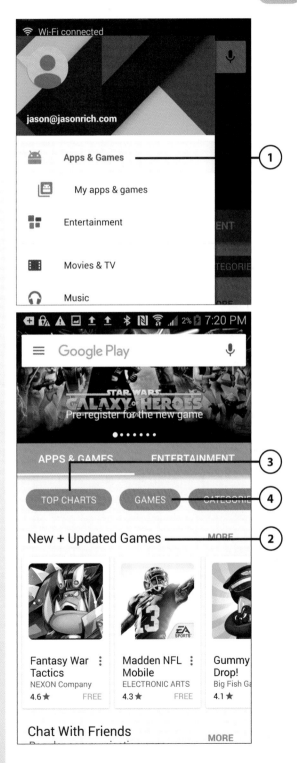

Using the Search Field

If you know the title of the game app you're looking for, or have a specific type of game in mind, such as a **crossword puzzle** or **blackjack** game, type this into the Search field. Within the Search field, you can also enter any keyword or search phrase that will help you find the type of game you're seeking. As you're viewing the search results, tap any app listing to view its description screen.

(5) Tap a game subcategory to reveal a series of related app listings.

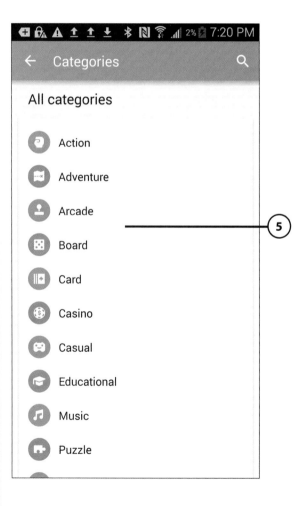

6 Tap a game's title or graphic to view its description screen.

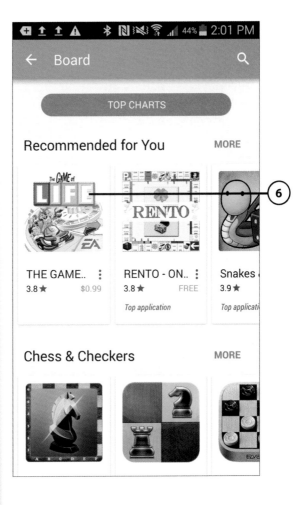

(**7**) Read a game's description screen for details about the game app, its average rating, the game's price, a handful of sample screenshots from the game, a description of the game, and reviews of the game from people who have tried it. Scroll down on this screen to see all the information.

(**8**) Tap the Price button to purchase the game. (If the game is free, you see an Install button instead.) Confirm your purchase decision and allow the app to download and install onto your mobile device.

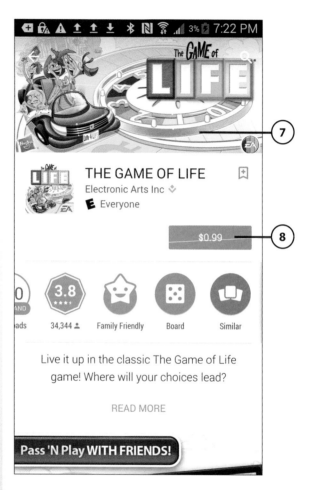

9 After the app is installed, launch it by tapping the Open button within the Google Play Store (shown), or launch it from the Home screen (by tapping on its app icon) in order to start playing.

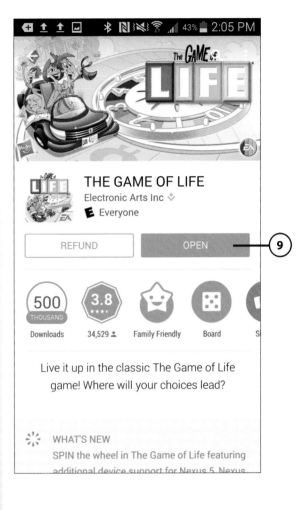

>>>Go Further

WATCH FOR IN-APP PURCHASES

Many games for Android-based mobile devices have in-app purchase options, especially if the game is initially offered for free. If in-app purchases are available, this is mentioned below the Install or Price button associated with the app. Look for the message "In-App Purchases."

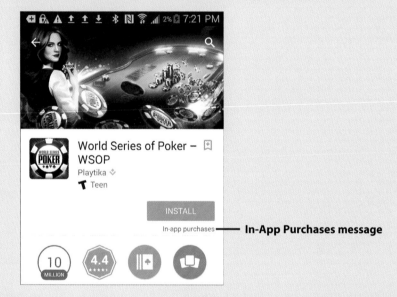

In-App Purchases message

If you tap the Read More option associated with a game listing and scroll toward the bottom of the information screen, the price range of in-app purchases is listed.

Most free games that offer in-app purchases can be played entirely for free, but are designed to slow down, or somehow encourage you to make in-app purchases to speed up or somehow enhance the game play experience.

15 Popular Games for Mobile Devices

The following 15 games are popular, appeal to adults (and/or people of all ages), and offer fun, ongoing, and challenging game play experiences. This, however, is only a small sampling of the types of games offered. Many similar games are also available for your computer, as well as most other gaming platforms.

Quickly Find Any of These Games

To quickly find any of these games, type of the name of the game into the Search field of the app store and then tap the app's listing in the search results. In some cases, a series of games, or the original game and its sequels, will be listed among the search results.

The majority of these games are available for the iPhone, iPad, and/or Android-based smartphones and tablets:

- **Angry Birds**—This popular series of games offers comical, puzzle-like challenges that involve logic, strategy, and problem-solving skills. The goal is to shoot birdlike creatures across the screen using a virtual slingshot to knock down or break through specific barriers. To solve each puzzle (each version of the game has hundreds of separate puzzles), you need to use the right combination of bird types and adjust the shooting angle and speed of each shot to jettison each bird properly. Within the Search field of the app store, type the search phrase **Angry Birds** to find all the games in this series from Rovio Entertainment, but watch out for imposter games. This is a free game (shown here on an Android smartphone) with in-app purchases available.

- **Bingo Bash**—If you love playing bingo, you'll appreciate how this mobile device games brings the excitement of bingo into the palms of your hands, allowing you to play anytime against other people. You can also opt to play one bingo card or multiple cards. This is a free game (shown here on an Android smartphone) with in-app purchases available.

- **Bridge Baron**—Priced at $19.99 (with additional in-app purchases available), this game enables you to compete (based on your skill level) with other players from around the world via the Internet. Various versions of the game are offered, and you can participate in organized competitions as well. Many less costly bridge card games are available from the app store (shown here on an iPhone) or Google Play Store, including apps that offer instruction on how to play bridge.

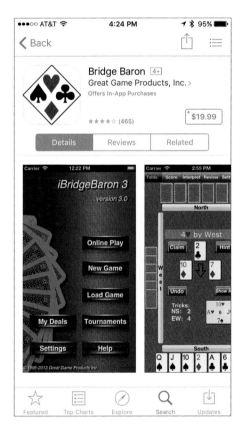

- **Candy Crush Saga**—This is a wildly popular, fast-paced, colorful, puzzle-like game (shown here on an iPhone) that requires quick reflexes, good timing, and strategy. As similar-looking candies appear on the screen, swipe your finger to make three or more of them line up horizontally or vertically to make them disappear. Several versions of Candy Crush from King.com Limited are available. All are free, but offer in-app purchases.

- **DoubleDown Casino**—Shown here on an Android smartphone, this free game (which offers in-app purchases) re-creates the fun and excitement of visiting a casino and playing more than 50 popular slot machines, as well as video poker and table games like blackjack and roulette.

- **Heads Up**—Based on a game created for *The Ellen DeGeneres Show,* this is a fun party game or a good game to play with your kids or grandkids. It's a trivia-like challenge where a word is displayed on the screen, and then one or more players give clues so the person holding the smartphone or tablet against his or her forehead to show others the word can then guess the word before the timer runs out. Eighteen trivia categories are available, and more are constantly being added. This app costs $0.99 and offers in-app purchases. Shown here is the tutorial video shown on the iPhone, which features Ellen DeGeneres teaching users how to play.

- **Mahjong Deluxe**—There are many versions of Mahjong for smartphones and tablets, and all faithfully re-create the centuries-old game. Most versions of this game are free, although some have in-app purchase options.

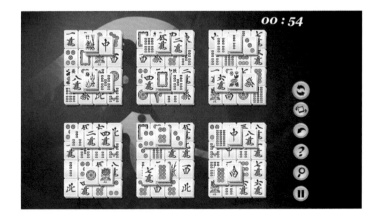

- **myVegas Slots**—This casino simulation allows you to play virtual slot machines for free, plus win real prizes and perks at actual Las Vegas casinos. The game app (shown here on an iPhone) is free, but in-app purchases are available.

- **NYTimes Crossword**—The vast collection of *New York Times* crossword puzzles that are part of the newspaper's archive, as well as each new daily puzzle, are made available on your smartphone or tablet's screen. The app itself is free, but to access most of the puzzles, you'll need to purchase a *New York Times* Crossword Subscription (which, to unlock all puzzles, costs $39.99 per year). Less expensive subscription options, starting at $1.99, are available. Some sample puzzles and bonus "mini" puzzles are offered for free.

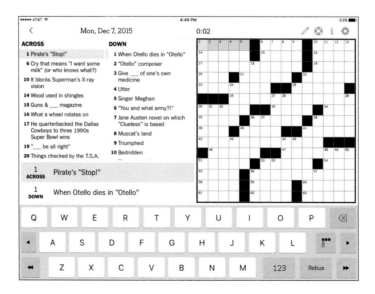

- **Scrabble**—The classic board game has been faithfully transformed into an interactive gaming experience that can be played anywhere, against opponents using the same mobile device, or their own mobile devices that are linked via the Internet. Shown here on the iPad, this version of the game is free, with in-app purchases available.

- **Solitaire Deluxe Social Pro**—Many versions of solitaire are available for the various smartphones or tablets. To find them, enter the word **solitaire** into the Search field of the app store. This particular version is priced at $2.99 and has in-app purchase options available. In addition to offering 16 variations of solitaire, it allows you to access your social media accounts simultaneously, so you can interact with your online friends while you're playing.

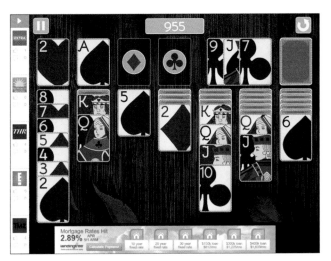

- **Sudoku**—Many versions of Sudoku are available for the various smartphones and tablets. Some are free, others are free with in-app purchases, and some charge for the game app itself. To find these games, enter the word **Sudoku** into the Search field, and then read each app's description to discover one that you'll find appealing. Shown here is the free Sudoku app on an iPhone, from a developer called Mind the Frog.

Because this app is free, ads are displayed on the screen while you're playing.

- **The Room Three**—This is an interactive puzzle/strategy game that follows a detailed storyline. It requires you to explore a virtual environment and solve puzzles to proceed. This unique game app (shown here on an iPhone) is priced at $4.99, features stunning graphics, and will provide many hours of thought-provoking entertainment.

Tap on the screen to access interactive elements and solve puzzles

- **WordBrain**—WordBrain (shown here on an iPhone) displays a grid featuring four or nine seemingly random letters. Within a predetermined amount of time, you must create words from those letters. As you discover words, drag your finger across the letters to spell them out. The game can be played in 15 languages and includes more than 580 levels that get increasingly more difficult as you proceed. What's great about games like this is that you can play for just a few minutes or for hours at a time.

- **Words with Friends**—This is an extremely popular, turn-based game that's similar to Scrabble and is designed to be played against other people (via the Internet). You can simultaneously play separate games against different opponents, in real-time, or as each person has time to play a single turn. This is a great game for adults to play against each other, or for adults to play against their kids or grandkids. Words with Friends (shown here on an Android smartphone) is a free app, but it offers in-app purchases.

Playing Online Games

In addition to playing popular games on your computer, smartphone, or tablet, for example, an ever-growing selection of games are available on popular social media services, such as Facebook (when you access these services from your PC or Mac). Most of these games are free to play on an unlimited basis. All require a continuous Internet connection. Some of these games, like Word with Friends, sync information between all versions of the game, so you can play using the mobile app or on Facebook, for example, using the same account.

To discover online games while using Facebook, use the following steps. These instructions are for using a Mac with the Safari web browser, but the steps are similar if you're using a PC or tablet:

1 Using your computer's web browser, visit www.Facebook.com.

2 Log in to your Facebook account.

3 Click Games in the left menu.

4 From the Games menu, explore listings for the many online gaming options, many of which offer a multiplayer gaming experience (allowing you to complete against other people).

5 Click a game listing that looks interesting. In some cases, you might need to download additional software to play the selected game. Other games can be played within the Facebook web browser window that's already open.

Games Option

(6) Follow the onscreen directions to begin playing the selected game. Shown here is a free version of Zynga Poker (Texas Hold'em Poker).

(6)

Other Online Gaming Services

In addition to Facebook, if you want to play online games from your PC or Mac, you can also set up a free account on one of these online-based gaming services, each of which offers an ever-growing selection of game titles: Pogo (www.pogo.com), Addicting Games (www.addictinggames.com), Games. com (www.games.com), and MSN Games (http://games.msn.com).

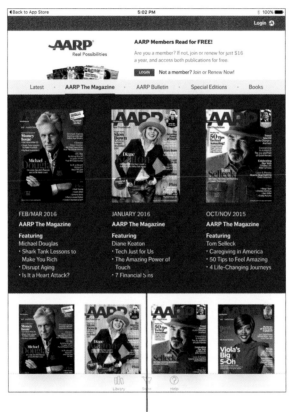

Almost every popular national magazine and major
daily newspaper is now available in digital form.

This chapter introduces you to the world of digital newspapers and magazines, including

→ Finding, downloading, and reading single issues of your favorite magazines and newspapers
→ Subscribing to the digital editions of your favorite newspapers and magazines
→ Subscribing to an online service that offers unlimited access to hundreds of magazines each month for a flat monthly fee
→ Using the News (iPhone/iPad) or Play Newsstand (Android) app that comes preinstalled on your mobile device

Reading Digital Newspapers and Magazines

Once upon a time, printed newspapers were delivered to your front door every morning, in time for you to read while drinking your morning coffee or commuting to work. Back in the day, reading a city's daily newspaper was how most people kept up-to-date on local, national, and international news, sports, weather, and business, financial, and entertainment news. For focused coverage of a topic, you'd subscribe to a national, full-color, weekly or monthly magazine. Although printed major daily newspapers and magazines still exist, their popularity is quickly diminishing because the same information is now readily available via the Internet in a more timely and condensed format.

To keep pace with fast-changing times, virtually every printed newspaper and full-color magazine now offers a digital edition that is accessible in a variety of ways. This chapter explains how you can access the digital editions of publications.

Using the iPhone and iPad with Digital Editions

Just about every newspaper and magazine that publishes a print edition also now offers a proprietary iPhone and/or iPad mobile app that allows you to read each issue of that publication on your mobile device's screen. Visit the App Store to find, download, and install the specific app for each publication you want to read.

The publication-specific app is free. However, through in-app purchases, you typically pay for one issue of the publication at a time or pay a subscription fee for the digital edition of the publication. When you have a subscription, each new issue is automatically downloaded to your mobile device when it is published.

In most cases, the iPhone/iPad mobile app for a newspaper or magazine allows you to read each issue of a publication as it appears in its printed form. However, the digital edition typically also offers bonus interactive content. For example, if you click a photo that's associated with a news story, instead of just a single photo, a series of related photos or video clips display.

The Cost of Digital Publications Vary

In some cases, the digital edition of a newspaper or magazine is free to existing paid subscribers of the printed publication. In addition, some publications offer a trial subscription, or a handful of free issues are included with the app. However, it's also possible to pay for single issues or an ongoing subscription to only the digital edition of many newspapers and magazines. The cost of a digital publication is typically somewhat less than the printed edition, although this varies by publication.

Another option is to use the free Zinio app on your iOS, Android, or Kindle mobile device in order to borrow digital editions of magazines, for free, via your local library.

After you've acquired the publication-specific iPhone or iPad app and have paid for one or more individual issues of the publication (or an ongoing subscription), using the app to read the publication is very similar to reading an eBook. Each page of the publication is displayed on your mobile device's screen. You "turn" the pages with a horizontal finger swipe across the screen from right to left.

Depending on the publication, you may also be able to use a reverse-pinch figure gesture to zoom in on a specific area of a page or tap a specific headline, photo, or hyperlink to access additional content.

Downloading a Publication's App

Literally thousands of individual newspapers and magazines have proprietary iPhone and/or iPad apps that allow you to access and read the digital editions of those publications. Because more content is displayed on the iPad than on an iPhone, the figures in this section are from an iPad.

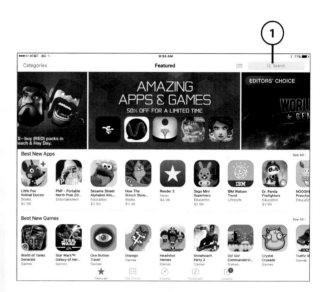

(1) Make sure your iPhone or iPad has Internet access, and then launch the App Store app from the Home screen.

(2) Enter the name of the newspaper or magazine you're interested in reading within the Search field.

A Search Alternative

When you launch the App Store app, tap the Featured icon and then tap the Categories option. Scroll down to the Magazines & Newspapers option and tap it. From the Magazines & Newspapers submenu, choose the type of publication you're interested in, and then browse through the app listings. Tap the app you're interested in and then tap its Get button, followed by its Install button.

(3) From the search results, tap the logo or title of a publication-specific app to access its Description screen.

(4) Tap the Get button. Next, tap the Install button.

(5) Enter your Apple ID account's password at the prompt, or place your finger on the device's Touch ID sensor to scan your fingerprint. The app downloads and installs itself onto your iPhone or iPad.

(6) After the app is installed, an icon for it will appear on your device's Home screen. Tap the app icon to launch it. In most cases, you need to purchase individual issues of that publication or subscribe to the publication from within the app. In some cases, publication content is offered to everyone for free.

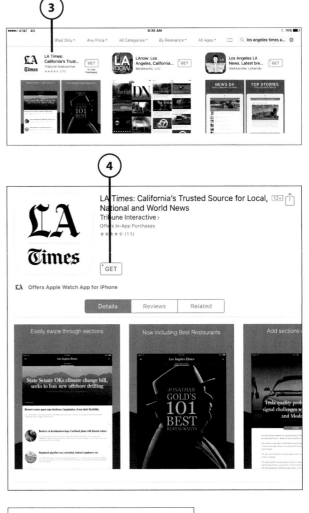

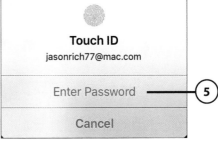

Paying for Publications

When you purchase single issues of a publication from within a mobile app or purchase a subscription, you make an in-app purchase from within the publication-specific app. You pay for the content using the credit or debit card that's linked to your Apple ID account. You also have the option of paying for content using prepaid iTunes Gift Cards.

If you're already a paid subscriber to the print edition of a newspaper or magazine, you may be entitled to receive the digital edition for free. If so, an option for this is presented when you launch the publication-specific app. You typically need to enter the account number that appears on the mailing label attached to a recent issue of the printed publication that you've received.

Read a Digital Publication

After you've acquired the free iPhone/ iPad app for a specific newspaper or magazine, the next step is to launch the app from your device's Home screen so you can get started with reading your digital publications. This example uses the *Entertainment Weekly* magazine app; other apps work in a similar way, although some functions might differ slightly.

(1) After downloading and installing the publication-specific app, launch it from your iPhone or iPad's Home screen (not shown).

(2) If prompted, allow the app to send you notifications, which will alert you when new issues are available or when breaking news stories from that publication are published. Tap the OK button to continue.

"ENTERTAINMENT WEEKLY Magazine" Would Like to Send You Notifications

Notifications may include alerts, sounds, and icon badges. These can be configured in Settings.

Don't Allow   OK   — (2)

(3) Scroll through the app's introductory screens, when applicable. These typically demonstrate key features of the app and explain how to access and read content (not shown).

(4) You have the option to sign in to your account, purchase individual issues of the magazine, or subscribe to the magazine. Tap the Sample This Issue button to download and read a free sample issue. Tap the Buy Issue button to select and purchase one or more single issues, or tap the Subscribe button to purchase a discounted subscription to the publication.

(5) Enter your Apple ID account password or use the device's Touch ID sensor to scan your fingerprint and pay for your content purchase (not shown).

Subscribers Have Unlimited Access to Content

If you already have a paid subscription to a publication and you're entitled to the digital edition for free, sign in to the publication-specific app to see a listing of available issues. Tap the cover thumbnail for the issue(s) you want to download.

After the download process completes, the content is stored within your mobile device, so you can read the publication even if you're not connected to the Internet. However, you might not be able to access certain interactive content or features when you're not connected.

Depending on the publication, you may be able to download and store past issues of a publication, in addition to the most current issue, or you may be limited to which issues are available and when.

6 You see cover artwork for issues of the publication you've purchased (or that are available to you for free). Tap a cover thumbnail to open an issue and begin reading the publication.

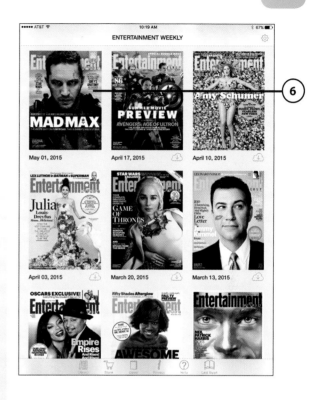

Reading in Portrait Mode

When reading a newspaper or magazine on your smartphone or tablet's screen, hold the device in Portrait mode. Each page of the printed publication will be reproduced on your device's screen. However, within the digital edition, certain elements of each page may be interactive, depending on the publication you're reading. These interactive elements will be showcased in conjunction with an icon for you to tap on. For example, when you tap a photo or an icon associated with a photo, you may gain access to a multi-image slide show or a relevant video clip as opposed to a single photo.

In many instances, you can zoom in or out when viewing a page using a reverse-pinch or punch finger gesture, or by quickly double-tapping on the area of the screen where you want to zoom in or out.

7 Use a horizontal finger swipe from right to left to turn the virtual pages. In some cases, you may see icons labeled Scroll, or that offer other directions for reading or viewing additional content.

Flipping Pages Back

If you want to return to a page you previously read, swipe across the screen from left to right until you reach the page you want.

(8) Tap near the top or bottom margin of the page to access app-specific icons. In this example, icons along the top of the screen allow you to return to the app's Library screen to load additional content, access an interactive Table of Contents for the issue you're reading, return to the previous article you were reading, add an article to your Favorites list for easy access later, or view thumbnails of each page within a publication and quickly scroll around.

(9) Along the bottom of the screen, when you tap on the top or bottom margin, a page slider is displayed, along with icons that allow you to return to the app's Library screen, access the publication's online store, return to the cover for the issue you're reading, read the publication's Privacy Policy, get help using the app, or quickly return to the last article you read.

(10) Tap the Menu or Settings icon to manage your publications.

Automatic Downloading and Deleting

With some publications, you can adjust the app to automatically delete old content when a new issue is loaded and automatically load new issues as soon as they become available.

Scroll icons

Manage or Cancel a Digital Subscription

If you've purchased an ongoing or automatically renewing subscription to a digital publication via an in-app purchase when using a publication's proprietary app on your iPhone or iPad, follow these steps to manage or cancel the subscription:

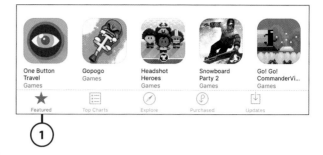

(1) Launch the App Store app from the Home screen of your mobile device, and tap the Featured icon.

(2) Scroll to the bottom of the Featured screen and tap the Apple ID: [*Username*] button.

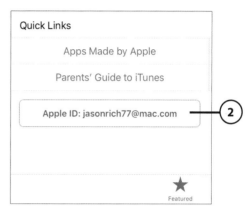

(3) Tap the View Apple ID button, and enter the password that corresponds with your account (not shown).

(4) Scroll to the Subscriptions heading in the Account Settings screen and tap the Manage option. You see a list of your current and expired subscriptions.

(5) Tap a specific listing to manage that subscription (not shown).

(6) The date your subscription ends is displayed. Under the Renewal Options heading, tap the option you want to utilize, or cancel the subscription by turning off the virtual switch that's associated with that subscription's Automatic Renewal option (not shown).

Manage Each Subscription Separately

It is necessary to manage/cancel each autorenewing subscription separately. However, if the subscription is not autorenewing, you do not need to cancel it when your subscription ends. In this case, though, you have to manually renew the subscription to continue receiving new issues of that publication after the subscription lapses. You will receive emails and in-app notices when a subscription is about to autorenew or needs to be manually renewed.

Discover Apple's News App

Apple has launched an app called News, which comes preinstalled on all iPhones and iPads that run iOS 9 or later. Through partnerships with thousands of newspaper and magazine publishers, global news agencies, blog writers, and other content providers, the News app allows you to access a truly personalized newsfeed that gets continuously updated throughout the day, every day.

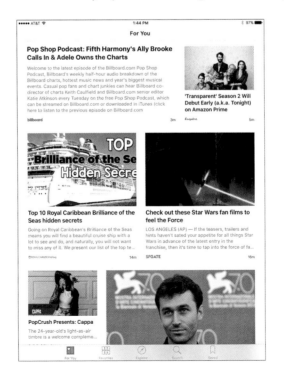

The News app aggregates news from different sources, which means that it collects and displays articles that relate directly to your interests. Each article is displayed with a headline, includes a few sentences from the news story/article, features a photo (when applicable), and showcases when and where the article was originally published. Each time you launch the News app, it automatically accesses the Internet and updates the content to be displayed, so the newest articles are listed first. Best of all, the News app, and all the content that's accessible from it, is available for free. There are no subscription fees.

The News App Requires Continuous Internet Access

To utilize the News app, your iPhone or iPad must have a continuous Wi-Fi or cellular Internet connection because the content is collected in real-time from the Internet and streamed to your mobile device.

Articles that are displayed within the News app are not, by default, stored within your mobile device. However, if there's an article you want to save to read later, tap the bookmark icon associated with the article to save it for later offline viewing.

It's Not All Good

The News App Does Not Offer Unlimited Access to Every Publication

Apple has teamed up with the publishers of well-known newspapers, magazines, and news organizations from around the world, but the News app offers only the articles and content that each content provider opts to share. In other words, the News app does not offer complete access to every article, published within each issue of every publication.

If you want to read the *New York Times* or the *Wall Street Journal* from cover to cover every day, for example, you need to subscribe to the digital edition of those publications.

Set Up the News App

The first time you launch the News app, you will be prompted to enter your Apple ID account username and password before walking through a quick setup process to select one or more channels (news/information sources) that you're interested in having the app follow on your behalf. You can then further customize your newsfeed.

1. Tap the Favorites icon to see a list of channels (news/information sources) the app is following on your behalf.

2. Remove a channel by tapping the Edit option (displayed in the top-right corner of the screen) and then tapping the X icon that appears in the top-left corner of a channel's thumbnail listing (shown here).

3. Tap Done to save your changes.

4. Tap the Explore icon to find new channels you can subscribe to via the News app.

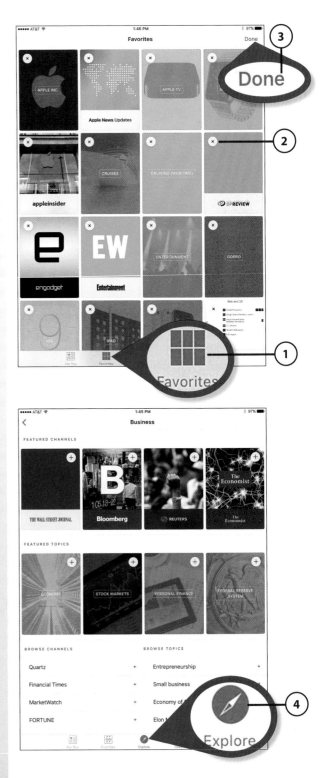

(5) Additional related channels and topics are displayed below the Suggested Channels and Suggested Topics headings. Tap the + icon for any channel or topic listings that you want to add to your personalized newsfeed.

(6) Tap a category below the Browse heading to display a series of related channels and topics you can subscribe to. Tap the + icon associated with each desired listing to add it to your newsfeed.

(7) Tap the Search icon, and type a word or phrase within the Search field. This can be as broad or as specific as you desire.

(8) Tap the + icon associated with a search result to add it to your newsfeed.

(9) Tap the For You icon to display your now personalized newsfeed.

Navigating Your Newsfeed

Each time you launch the News app, as long as your iPhone or iPad has Internet access, it's possible to tap the For You icon to have the app scour the Internet to locate and display relevant content based on how you've personalized the app.

Thus, each time you tap the For You icon, what's displayed is a timely and truly customized digital newspaper that showcases articles and content that the app deems relevant to your interests. The articles are displayed based on their initial publication date, with the newest content displayed first. When an article headline or photo captures your attention and you want to read or view it, tap it.

Tap the Read Original Story Option

In some cases, it will be necessary to have your iPhone or iPad access the entire article you select from the web page where it was originally published. When this is necessary, the Read Original Story message is displayed near the bottom of the screen. Tap this message to view the relevant content.

Tap the Share icon to share the article with other people via text message, email, or social media. Other options are also offered from the Share menu that allow you to import the article into a specific app, such as Notes, or add the article to the app's Reading List.

Tap the Bookmark icon to save the article within the internal storage of your iPhone or iPad so you can quickly access and read it later, even if no Internet connection is available.

Accessing Saved Articles

To access articles you've bookmarked, tap the Saved icon. Then tap the Saved tab that's displayed near the top center of the screen. You see a list of saved articles. Tap an article listing to view it.

Alternatively, tap the History tab to view articles you've previously read but that are not necessarily stored within your mobile device.

Reading Digital Editions with Your Android Device

Available for the more current versions of the Android operating system is a free app called Play Newsstand. This app comes preinstalled on most Android-based smartphones and tablets (or can be acquired from the Google Play Store). With it you can create a customized newsfeed based on content providers, news sources, and subjects that you preselect.

Most individual newspapers and magazines do not have proprietary apps for Android devices. Instead, you're able to subscribe to the digital editions of newspapers and magazines through the Google Play Store and then access and read that content using the Play Newsstand app.

Why Pay for Content?

Because so much free newspaper and magazine content is available to you via the free Play Newsstand app, you may discover there's no need to pay for a digital subscription to a specific newspaper or magazine.

The Play Newsstand app offers free content from thousands of newspapers, magazines, news organizations, and content providers, but does not offer entire issues of specific publications for free. For this, you need to pay for the digital subscription to the publications you're interested in reading from cover to cover.

Play Newsstand Is Also Available for the iPhone/iPad

A version of Google's Play Newsstand app is available, for free, from the iPhone/iPad's App Store. To find and download it, launch the App Store app, and within the Search field, type **Play Newsstand**. From within the app's listing, tap the Get button, followed by the Install button. Enter your Apple ID password or scan your fingerprint using the device's Touch ID sensor to complete the installation.

Use Google's Play Newsstand App

The Play Newsstand app allows you to create and view a customized newsfeed that offers articles and content from a wide range of sources. Each time you launch the app, updated content from preselected sources and content providers is downloaded and displayed in an easy-to-navigate format.

The secondary use of the Play Newsstand app is to view digital issues of newspapers and magazines that you've paid for and/or subscribed to via the Google Play Store. When paid issues of a publication are available to be read within the Play Newsstand app, listings for them will be displayed within the app's Library screen.

1 Launch the Play Newsstand app
from the Homes screen. The first
time you launch the app, you'll
be asked to select topics that
interest you.

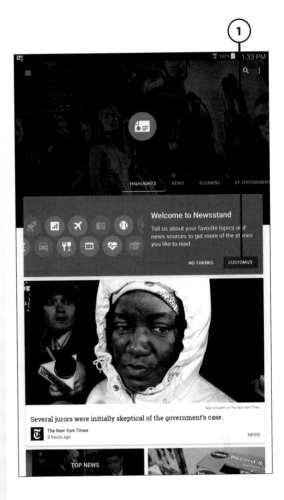

2 Displayed near the top of the screen are the News, Magazines, and Topics headings. Tap each heading to reveal relevant content providers you can subscribe to and access, for free, from within the app. In this example, the News heading was selected.

3 Tap each content listing you want to add to the My Library section. The app begins collecting content from that news source/content provider.

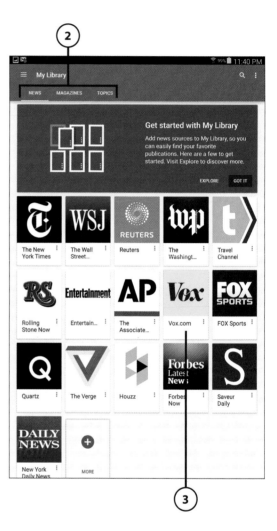

4 If you've paid for one or more issues of a specific magazine via Google Play (or have acquired a digital subscription), tap the Magazines heading to view the content that's been downloaded to the app and that's available for reading. That magazine opens.

5) Use a horizontal finger swipe from right to left to turn the virtual pages. (Return to previous pages by swiping left to right.) Look for icons that appear on the page that tell you about interactive content or to scroll downward, for example.

6) Tap the Topics heading to select specific topics you're interested in. After you select a Topic, the Play Newsstand app searches all its sources and content providers and displays relevant content (in contrast to displaying content from specific preselected content providers).

Narrowing the Focus

Topics are organized by broad categories, such as News, Business, Entertainment, Sports, Technology, and World. However, when you tap any of these listings, you see subtopics, so you can narrow down your Topics to very specific areas of interest.

7) Tap the Search icon to locate content based on a keyword or phrase that you enter into the Search field.

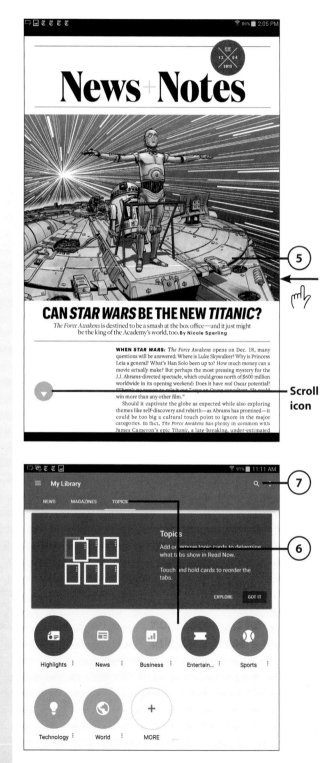

8 Tap any listing on your My Library screen to begin viewing and reading articles and content. Shown here are entertainment-oriented articles from *Entertainment Weekly* magazine accessed via the Play newsstand app.

Refresh Often

Each time you launch the Play Newsstand app, and your mobile device is connected to the Internet, all content within the app is updated. The newest or most current articles and content are displayed first. Content is continuously being published, so you can manually refresh the app at any time by tapping the More icon and then tapping Refresh.

Tap here to use the Refresh command.

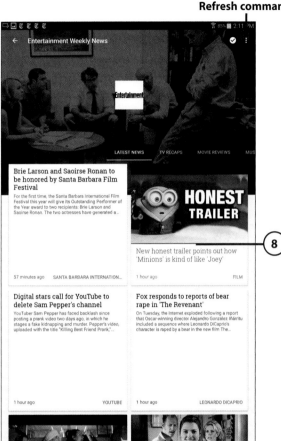

Reading with eBook Readers or Apps

You can use the Kindle eBook readers from Amazon and the Nook eBook readers from Barnes and Noble to access and read digital editions of newspapers and magazines. This is also true if you use the Kindle or Nook mobile app on your computer, smartphone, or tablet.

Both Amazon.com and barnesandnoble.com offer digital newsstands that enable you to purchase individual issues of newspapers or magazines or pay for subscriptions to digital publications. The figure shows the Newsstand section of the Kindle Store that's accessible via the Kindle app or a Kindle eBook reader.

It's Not All Good

Different Versions Means Different Functionality

When you're using the iPhone, iPad, or Mac version of the Kindle or Nook app, you acquire content, including digital editions of newspapers and magazines, by using your web browser and visiting www.Amazon.com to access the Kindle Store (Newsstand) or www.barnesandnoble.com to access the Nook Store (Newsstand). After you purchase content, you can read it using the Kindle or Nook app that's running on your iPhone, iPad, or Mac.

From all other editions of the Kindle and Nook apps, as well as from the Kindle and Nook eBook readers, you can purchase eBooks and digital editions of newspapers and magazines directly through the app.

Using a Kindle or Nook eBook reader or mobile app to read the digital edition of a newspaper or magazine is just like reading an eBook. One page of the publication is displayed on the screen at a time. Note that reading the digital editions of full-color magazines on a Kindle or Nook eBook reader that does not have a full-color screen takes away from the authenticity of the magazine-reading experience.

Subscribing to a Magazine Service

Instead of subscribing to the digital editions of specific newspapers and magazines, and paying for each subscription separately, one option is to pay a flat monthly fee to a service that offers unlimited access to dozens (and in some cases hundreds) of publications. There are also independent companies that serve as digital newsstands, allowing you to acquire single digital issues of magazines or pay for a discounted digital magazine subscriptions.

Three of these services are Issuu, Texture, and Zinio. All have free apps available for the iPhone and iPad (available from the App Store) or for Android-based smartphones and tablets (available from the Google Play Store). Each also offers a web-based reader so you can access and read newspaper or magazine content from your computer's web browser.

Issuu (www.issuu.com) is a service that offers unlimited, free access to an ever-growing lineup of publications. Using this service from your computer or mobile device costs nothing. However, if you want to experience ad-free content from the various publications, you can pay a flat monthly fee of $35.00.

For a fee of between $9.99 and $14.99 per month, the Texture service (www.texture.com) gives you unlimited access to hundreds of popular magazines via a single proprietary app that's available for the iPhone, iPad, or Android-based (shown) mobile devices.

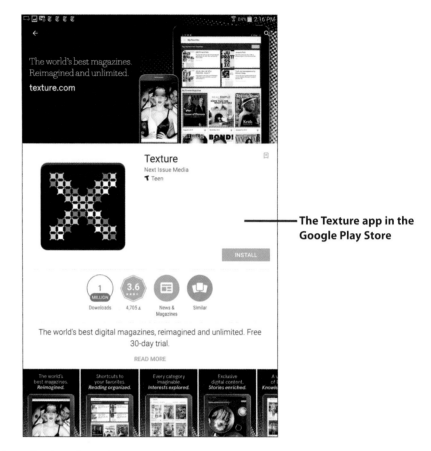

The Texture app in the Google Play Store

There is no need to deal with individual subscriptions or purchasing single issues. For the flat monthly fee, you can access as many of the participating magazines as you want, on up to five different mobile devices that are linked to your Texture account. In addition to the current issue of weekly and monthly magazines, your Texture subscription grants you access to each publication's past issues. From the app's Library screen (shown here on an iPad), tap the cover artwork for the issue of the magazine you want to read.

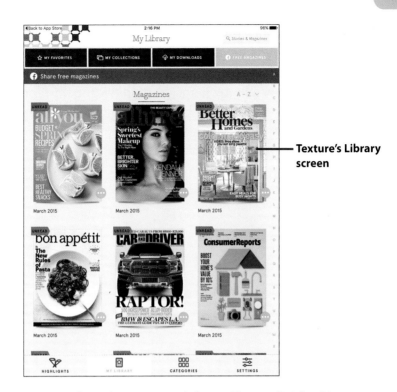

Texture's Library screen

Zinio (www.zinio.com) is a digital newsstand that offers individual issues, as well as discounted digital subscriptions to more than 6,000 well-known publications. By visiting the Zinio website, or using the Zinio mobile app, you can find, purchase, and download publication content and then read it on your computer or mobile device's screen. In many cases, subscriptions acquired through Zinio are offered at a discount of between 20 and 50 percent.

A Directory of Digital Publications

To access a comprehensive directory of digital newspapers and magazines—many of which can be read from your computer, smartphone, tablet, or eBook reader—visit www.onlinenewspapers.com.

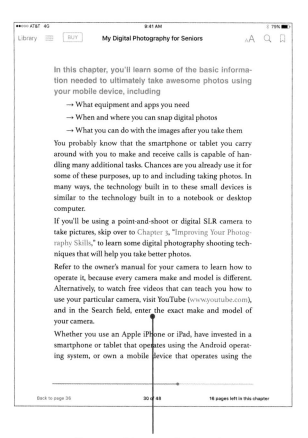

In this chapter, you'll learn some of the basic information needed to ultimately take awesome photos using
your mobile device, including

→ What equipment and apps you need

→ When and where you can snap digital photos

→ What you can do with the images after you take them

You probably know that the smartphone or tablet you carry
around with you to make and receive calls is capable of handling many additional tasks. Chances are you already use it for
some of these purposes, up to and including taking photos. In
many ways, the technology built in to these small devices is
similar to the technology built in to a notebook or desktop
computer.

If you'll be using a point-and-shoot or digital SLR camera to
take pictures, skip over to Chapter 3, "Improving Your Photography Skills," to learn some digital photography shooting techniques that will help you take better photos.

Refer to the owner's manual for your camera to learn how to
operate it, because every camera make and model is different.
Alternatively, to watch free videos that can teach you how to
use your particular camera, visit YouTube (www.youtube.com),
and in the Search field, enter the exact make and model of
your camera.

Whether you use an Apple iPhone or iPad, have invested in a
smartphone or tablet that operates using the Android operating system, or own a mobile device that operates using the

Use your tablet as an eBook reader.

This chapter shows you how to acquire and read books published in a digital format. This includes

- → Using a dedicated eBook reader
- → Learning where and how to acquire eBooks to read
- → Customizing your reading experience
- → Using your smartphone or tablet as an eBook reader

Reading eBooks

Like so many other forms of entertainment, books are now available in digital format. Thus, instead of holding a printed book in your hands, you can view that same content on a digital device's screen.

Books that are published in digital form are called *eBooks*. Most books these days are published in printed and eBook form, but someday digital books might completely replace printed books. As this publishing technology has evolved, it has opened up an opportunity for many people—such as aspiring or up-and-coming writers and independent publishing companies—to inexpensively create and distribute content.

As a result, you can now find all sorts of fiction and nonfiction books that major publishing houses never would have published in printed form.

Carry Your Own Library with You

One of the benefits to eBooks is that they can be stored as digital files within an eBook reader or a smartphone, tablet, or computer that uses an eBook reader app. As a result, it's possible to carry with you hundreds of full-length books so that they're accessible anytime and virtually anywhere. Also, when your eBook reader has access to the Internet, millions of eBook titles are available at your fingertips.

Using eBook Reader Devices

An eBook reader is a battery-powered device that's designed to be held comfortably in your hands. It displays the pages of eBooks on its screen in an easy-to-read format that replicates the printed page of a book. The two most popular eBook readers are offered by Amazon.com and Barnes and Noble.

An Amazon eBook reader is called a *Kindle*, and an eBook reader available from Barnes and Noble is called a *Nook*. Both companies offer a variety of models, which range in price from around $50.00 to $300.00. The following figure shows the Kindle Voyage ($199.00) model, which has a noncolor, 7" display.

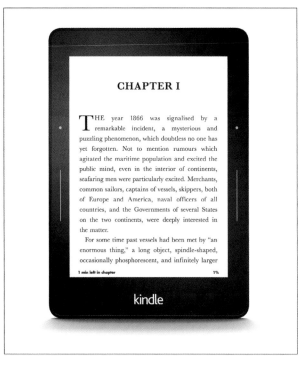

©**Amazon**

The Kindle and Nook eBook readers each have their own file formats, so an eBook designed to be read on a Kindle can't be installed onto a Nook (or vice versa). You acquire eBooks for your reader from the device's respective website: www. amazon.com/Kindle-eBooks or www.barnesandnoble.com.

However, virtually all eBook readers these days also support an industry-standard file format, called ePub, and most are also compatible with documents published in the PDF file format. Thus, many other online-based sources of eBooks are available. See the "Other eBook Stores" sidebar at the end of the chapter for more information about other sources for eBooks.

Selecting an eBook Reader

A variety of standalone Kindle and Nook eBook readers are available from Amazon.com and Barnes and Noble, respectively. Each model offers a different collection of features and functions that allow users to customize their reading experience. Before purchasing an eBook reader, give some consideration to the features that are important to you so that you get the device that best suits your needs and preferences.

Some of the differentiators that you should consider before deciding on an eBook reader include the following:

- **Battery life**—Depending on a variety of factors, the rechargeable battery built in to most eBook readers is designed to last between several days and several weeks per charge. Battery life is impacted by the type of screen the device has, how it connects to the Internet, and what other technologies are built into the device (and how those technologies are used). For example, using built-in speakers to listen to audiobooks drains the battery faster than plugging in and using headphones to listen to audiobooks. In general, eBook readers with full-color touchscreens have the shortest battery life.

- **Internal storage capacity**—How much internal storage an eBook reader has determines how many eBook titles you can store within the device at any given time. Most eBook readers have enough internal storage to hold at least several hundred full-length eBooks.

- **Internet connectivity**—All eBook readers have Wi-Fi connectivity built in. Thus, whenever the device is located within the signal radius of a Wi-Fi hotspot or home wireless network, it can connect to the Internet to access an online eBook store. Some eBook readers also offer a cellular data connection, which means they can access the Internet using a compatible cellular network and aren't limited by the signal radius of a Wi-Fi hotspot.

- **Other functionality**—Beyond allowing users to acquire and read eBooks, some eBook readers have the capability to play audiobooks, stream audio content (including music) from the Internet, store and play music files, and store and display digital photos. Others offer functionality that's similar to a full-featured tablet, which means you can install apps to further expand functionality.

- **Price**—The prices of eBook reader models range between $50.00 and $300.00. The more features and functionality a eBook reader has, the more expensive it is. Instead of spending several hundred dollars for a standalone eBook reader, however, many people opt to acquire an iPad or Android-based tablet that can be used as an eBook reader but can also handle many other functions. However, if all you want to do is read eBooks, an inexpensive Kindle or Nook eBook reader is a viable option.

- **Screen type and size**—Like tablets, eBook readers are available with different size screens. Some of the least expensive eBook readers have noncolor screens. In some cases, eBook readers have special screen technology that allows text to be displayed (also without color) in any lighting situation, with no screen glare or reflection. There are also many eBook readers with full-color, touch-screen displays, just like a tablet.

Advantages of Full-Color Screens

Full-color screens are sometimes difficult to read in direct sunlight, but one advantage is that they're able to display the pages of digital newspapers and magazines in full color, so what you see on the screen replicates the printed pages of your favorite publications.

- **Size and weight**—The size and weight of an eBook reader is important. When you're reading a book, you'll typically be holding the device for long periods of time. Thus, you want the eBook reader to be comfortable in your hands and have a display that's easy to read. Some people prefer smaller screens and lightweight devices, whereas others prefer looking at a larger screen that better replicates the size of a printed page within a book.

Shopping for an eBook Reader

Kindle eBook readers are sold online, directly from Amazon.com. They're also available from popular retail stores, such as Best Buy, Target, and Walmart. Nook eBook readers are sold online from BN.com, as well as from Barnes and Noble bookstores and other retail stores that sell consumer electronics.

You Need to Purchase an eBook Only Once

After you acquire or purchase an eBook from Amazon.com, BN.com, iBook Store, or the Google Play Store (or any other service that sells eBooks), you can download and install the book onto any compatible computer, smartphone, tablet, or eBook reader that's linked to the same account. You need to purchase an eBook title only once, but you can store and read it on multiple computers and/or devices.

The eBook reader device or app you use automatically keeps track of your virtual bookmarks and syncs this information between your computers and mobile devices, so you can start reading an eBook on one device and then continue on another, picking up exactly where you left off.

Shopping for eBooks

After you've purchased an eBook reader, you'll then need to populate it with eBooks to read. To do this, allow the device to connect to the Internet so that you can visit the compatible online bookstore. The icon for accessing the online bookstore is on the main menu screen of the eBook reader you're using. What this icon looks like and where on the screen it's located varies depending on whether you're using a Kindle or Nook eBook reader and which model device it is.

Prices for eBook titles are set by each book's publisher, but typically they're about the same price as a hardcover or softcover book (and sometimes less). In many cases, you can download and read a free sample of the book before you commit to making a purchase. The length of the samples vary, but often you get a single chapter. To help you decide which eBooks to read, all the online eBook stores publish star-based ratings, as well as detailed reviews of each title.

When you visit a specific eBook store, finding individual book titles is relatively easy. You have several options for doing this:

- Within the Search field of the eBook store, enter the title of the book, an author's name, a subject, or any keyword or search phrase that will help you find what you're looking for.

- Select an eBook category, such as Fiction & Literature, Nonfiction, Mysteries & Thrillers, Biographies & Memoirs, Business & Personal Finance, Cookbooks, Humor, Parenting, Reference, Romance, or Travel, and then browse through the offerings.

- View selected eBook titles being promoted and showcased by the eBook store you're visiting.

- View a list of bestsellers, which is typically based on the sales of eBooks on that service. In some cases, you can also access the current *New York Times* bestseller list(s).

The listing for each eBook includes a detailed description of that book, reviews, and, in some cases, a free sample.

An Account Is Required

After you decide which online-based eBook store(s) you want to shop from, you need to set up a free account with that service. The account will be linked to your credit or debit card so you can quickly purchase eBooks with a few taps on the screen without having to reenter your name, billing address, and credit card details each time you want to make a purchase.

Instead of paying for purchases using a credit or debit card, you can also use prepaid gift cards from Amazon.com, BN.com, iTunes (for use with iBook Store), or Google Play on their respective services.

Customize Your eBook Reading Experience

After you've downloaded and installed one or more eBooks onto your eBook reader or into the eBook reader app on your smartphone, tablet, or computer, you're able to fully customize your reading experience for each book.

In most cases, some of the things you can easily adjust are the background color and brightness of the screen, the font used to display text, the font size of the text, and the action that's required to turn the virtual page. The eBook reader or mobile app will then automatically reformat the text to accommodate your customizations.

The eBook reader or eBook reader app will also keep track of virtual bookmarks. Whenever you stop reading, a virtual bookmark is automatically created. The bookmark is synced to your online account. You can then pick up exactly where you left off when you reopen that eBook, even if you open it on a different device.

In addition, many of the eBook readers enable you to look up text, highlight text, and/or create your own virtual notes as you're reading. This is all saved within the eBook file. The Table of Contents and often the Index within the eBook are also interactive. You can tap or click a keyword, chapter number, or chapter title to jump right to that text.

Reading eBooks Using iBooks

The iBooks app comes preinstalled with iOS 9 on all iPhones and iPads. A version of this eBook reading software is also available for the Mac and available from the Mac App Store (if it's not already preinstalled on your computer). iBooks is used to acquire, download, manage, and read eBooks you acquire from Apple's iBook Store, and also to read eBooks published in the ePub or PDF file format.

Audiobooks Are Also Available from iBook Store

In addition to offering one of the world's largest collections of eBooks, Apple's iBook Store offers audiobooks that are compatible with the iBooks app. When browsing through the book titles within iBook Store, tap the Books or Audiobooks tab near the top of the screen to choose between eBooks and audiobooks.

More information about listening to audiobooks from your smartphone, tablet, computer, and/or eBook reader is covered in Chapter 12, "Listening to Audiobooks."

Acquire eBooks from iBook Store

Follow these directions to find and acquire eBooks from Apple's iBook Store.

(1) Make sure your iPhone, iPad, or Mac is connected to the Internet (not shown).

Read Without Being Connected

You need an Internet connection to browse and acquire eBooks, but you don't have to be connected to read them.

(2) Launch the iBooks app from the Home screen of your iPhone or iPad.

(3) Tap the Featured icon to see the books that iBook Store is currently spotlighting.

(4) Tap the Featured icon and then tap the Categories option. Then tap one of the displayed category options to browse that category.

Browse the Correct Area

Be sure to tap the Books tab that's displayed near the top center of the screen (rather than the Audiobooks tab) to browse through available eBooks.

(5) Tap the NY Times icon to browse a list of fiction and nonfiction bestsellers, based on the current *New York Times* bestsellers list.

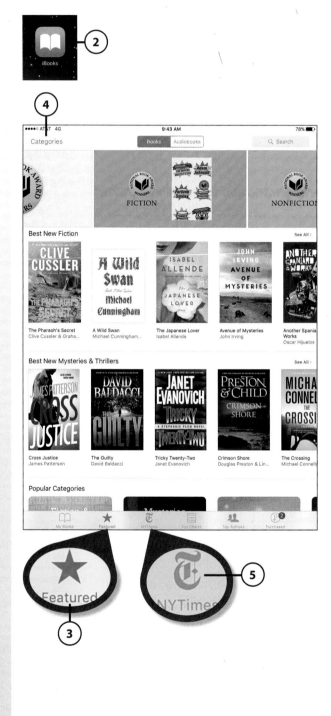

6) To find an eBook based on a specific title, author, subject, or keyword, enter what you're looking for within the Search field and then tap one or more of the Search result listings.

7) Tap the Top Charts icon to view a list of popular Paid and Free eBooks.

Refining the Top Charts List

To view a Top Charts list for a specific category, tap the Categories option, choose a category, and then browse through the displayed listings.

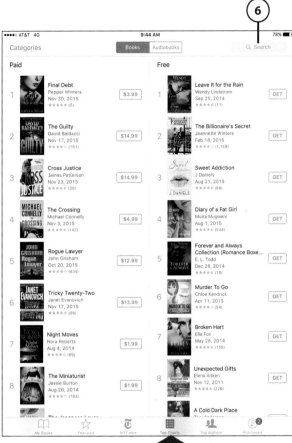

8 Tap the Top Authors icon to view an alphabetical listing of bestselling and popular authors whose work is available from iBook Store. Tap an author's name, and then tap the listing for any author's individual eBooks that you're interested in.

Sorting Author Listings

While you're viewing the Top Authors screen within iBook Store, you can sort listings by Paid or Free eBooks, as well as by All-Time Bestsellers, Release Date, or Name. To search for eBooks by author within a specific category, tap the Top Authors icon followed by the Categories option. Select a category from the menu and then browse through the authors listed.

iBooks on the iPhone

When you use the iBooks app on the iPhone, displayed along the bottom of the screen are the My Books, Featured, Top Charts, Search, and Purchased icons. To access the *New York Times* bestsellers lists, tap the Top Charts icon and then scroll down on the screen.

Works of selected author

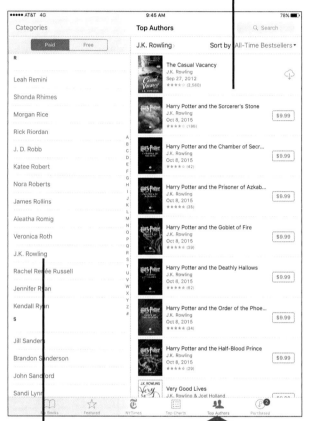

Author listing

(9) After you've selected a particular eBook title, you see details about that title, such as its average rating, a description, reviews, a Price button, and a Sample button. There's also a Share icon, which reveals a Share menu with options for sharing details about an eBook title with others. To read the eBook's description, tap the Details tab.

(10) Tap the Reviews tab to see a breakdown of the ratings a book has received. Scroll down on this screen to read reviews of the eBook written by other iBook Store customers.

Star-Based Ratings

Anyone who reads an eBook acquired from iBook Store can provide a star-based rating and write a full review of the title. An eBook's star-based rating can be between one (worst) and five (best) stars. Each book's listing includes its average rating, along with the total number of ratings it has received (displayed in parentheses).

eBook Description Screen **(9)**

Reviews Tab **(10)**

(11) Tap the Sample button on a book's page to download a free sample of the title. The content is downloaded to the iBooks app, and then it's listed as a Sample within the My Books section of the app.

(12) To purchase an eBook, tap its Price button. If the eBook is being offered for free, you see a Get button instead of a Price button. When prompted, enter the password that's associated with your Apple ID account or place your finger on your iPhone or iPad's Touch ID sensor (Home button) to scan your fingerprint and continue with the purchase. Within 10 to 30 seconds, the eBook is downloaded to your iPhone, iPad, or Mac.

Read and Manage eBooks

After you've launched the iBooks app on your iPad, iPhone, or Mac, use these steps to start reading an eBook or to manage the titles in your library:

(1) Tap or click the My Books icon to display the *Library screen*, a virtual bookshelf that showcases all the eBooks you've acquired and that are ready to read on the device you're using.

(2) Tap the Select option to select titles to move or delete.

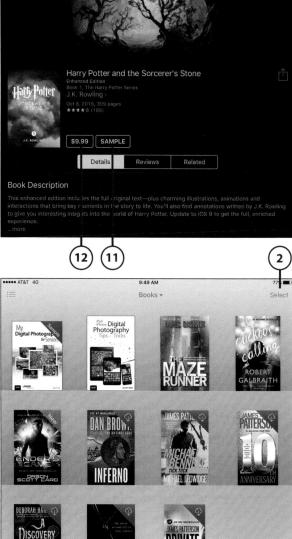

Watch for the iCloud Icon

When viewing iBook's Library screen, an iCloud icon in the top-right corner of a book cover thumbnail means you have previously acquired that eBook, and it's stored within your iCloud account, but it has not been downloaded to the mobile device or computer you're currently using. Tap or click the iCloud icon (when your mobile device or computer has Internet access) to download that eBook.

(3) Tap titles one at a time to select them. Selected titles are indicated with a white check mark in a blue circle.

(4) Tap Move to relocate the selected books to a separate folder.

(5) Tap Delete to remove the selected titles from the computer or mobile device you're using.

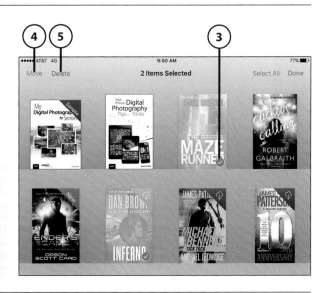

Gone but Not Forgotten

All eBooks acquired from iBook Store are automatically and permanently saved within your iCloud account. When you delete a book from a device, you can download it again later without paying for it a second time.

To do this using iBooks on an iPad, for example, launch the iBooks app, tap the Purchased icon near the bottom-right corner of the screen, and then tap the Books and All tabs that are displayed in the top-center of the screen. You see a listing of all eBooks you own. Tap the iCloud icon associated with any eBook listing to re-download it onto the device you're using. There is no additional charge to do this since you already own the content.

Alternatively, tap the My Books icon (located in the bottom-left corner of the screen), and then select the All Books option from the pull-down menu at the top-center of the screen. You own the books that have an iCloud icon within the cover thumbnail, but those books are not installed on the device you're using. Tap the iCloud icon for an eBook to download it to the device you're currently using.

6 Tap the View icon to switch from the virtual bookshelf view of the Library screen to a more detailed listing that you can then sort.

7 Tap a tab that's displayed near the top-center of the screen, below the pull-down menu title, to sort and display the eBooks stored within your computer or mobile device by Most Recent, Titles, Authors, or Categories.

8 Tap the View icon, which now looks like a cluster of six boxes, to return to the Bookshelf view.

Customize Your Reading Experience

Use these steps to customize your reading experience:

(1) Tap or click the thumbnail of the book cover for the book you want to open. The book opens on your iPhone, iPad, or Mac.

(2) Tap the aA icon to adjust the screen's brightness, increase or decrease the font size, choose the font, choose a theme (which impacts the color scheme of the background and text), and turn on/off the virtual switch associated with the Scrolling view. See the nearby "Customization Options" sidebar for more information about these settings.

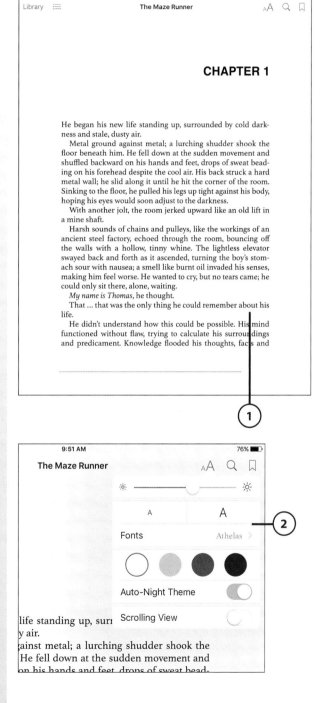

>>>Go Further

CUSTOMIZATION OPTIONS

Upon tapping the aA icon after opening an eBook, place your finger on the Brightness slider to drag it left or right to adjust the screen's brightness.

Tap or click the a icon to decrease the font size of the text, or tap the A icon to increase the font size. Each time you tap or click one of these icons, the font size decreases or increases by one point size, so it may be necessary to tap or click the icon repeatedly to achieve the font size you desire.

Tap or click the Fonts option to access a menu of available fonts, and choose which font you'd like to use for all the text displayed within the currently open eBook.

The iBooks app has several built-in themes. Tapping one of the colored dots changes the theme, which impacts the background color and font color that's displayed on the screen. The default option is a white background with black text. Which option you choose is a matter of personal preference; consider the lighting conditions where you'll be reading when you're choosing your theme. When reading in a dark room, for example, some people prefer a dark background color with white text.

When you turn on the virtual switch associated with the Auto-Night Theme, iBooks automatically adjusts the theme to make the onscreen text from the eBook easier to read whenever you're reading in a dark or dimly lit area.

The default action for turning a page in iBooks is a horizontal swipe. Turn on the virtual switch associated with the Scrolling View option to instead have the book display as a single page that you scroll through vertically.

(3) Tap or click the Search icon and then use the keyboard to enter a word or page number so you can jump to that content or page.

(4) Tap the Bookmark icon to manually add a virtual bookmark to a page.

(3)

••••• AT&T 4G   9:52 AM   76% ⬛

Library ☰   The Maze Runner   ᴀA Q 🔖

twice."
Teresa put her hands through the bars, rested her forearms against the concrete sill. "Just one a night? Why?"
"I don't know. He also said it had to do with ... trials. Or vari-

(4)

(5) Tap the Table of Contents icon and then tap the Bookmarks tab to see a list of saved bookmarks. Tap any listing to jump to the bookmarked page.

Automatic Bookmarks Versus Manual Bookmarks

A bookmark to save the place where you leave off reading is automatically created each time you close or exit out of the iBooks app or leave the eBook you're reading. You can set a manual bookmark to save a particular page that includes a passage of text you might want to return to later.

(5)

Library	Resume	iPad and iPhone Digital Photography Tips and Tricks

Contents | Bookmarks | Notes

1. Prepare Your iPhone or iPad to Take Awesome Photos — 29
🔖 Today

There's a Lot More You Can Do with t...s You Take Using Your iPhone or iPad — 35
🔖 Today

What You Need to Get Started as a Mobile Digital Photographer — 44
🔖 Today

Edit and Enhance Your Images — 262
🔖 Today

Camera App Alternatives — 433
🔖 Today

Quickly Email Up to Five Images at a Time to Specific People — 584
🔖 Today

Accessing an Interactive Table of Contents

Besides accessing the Bookmarks tab through the Table of Contents icon, you can also access the Contents and Notes tabs. Tap or click the Contents tab to view an interactive Table of Contents for the open eBook. Tap a chapter or section listing to jump to the appropriate page.

Tap or click the Notes tab to view notes you've typed into the margins of an eBook as you're reading. Using the Notes feature (described shortly), you can add virtual sticky notes to the margins of eBook pages.

To return to the open eBook and continue reading, tap or click the Resume option. To exit out of the eBook and return to iBooks' virtual bookshelf screen, tap or click the Library option.

6 With a tablet or smartphone, rotate the device to landscape orientation to display two pages on one screen. Note that each page displays less content than you see on a screen in portrait orientation.

7 Turn the page by swiping your finger from right to left to advance to the next page, or from left to right to return to the previous page. Instead of a swipe motion, you can also tap the right or left margin of a page (not shown).

8 Displayed along the bottom of the screen is information about the page of the eBook you're currently viewing, how many pages compose the entire eBook, and how many pages remain in the current chapter you're reading. Depending on the eBook you're reading, the author's name, the eBook's title, and/or the chapter title may appear at the top of each page.

9 Place and hold your finger on a word to reveal a pop-up menu. This menu includes the Copy, Define, Highlight, Note, Search, and Share command tabs. Tap the appropriate tab based on the feature you want to use. If you're using iBooks on a Mac, press and hold down the Control key on the keyboard and simultaneously click the mouse on a word.

(10) Tap Library to return to the iBooks' virtual bookshelf screen. When you do this, a bookmark for the page you last read is automatically saved. From the Library screen, it's possible to open and begin reading another eBook.

Another Way to Quit

When you're using an iPhone or iPad, you can also exit a book by pressing the Home button. The iBooks app closes, and you return to the device's Home screen. A virtual bookmark for the last page you read is automatically saved.

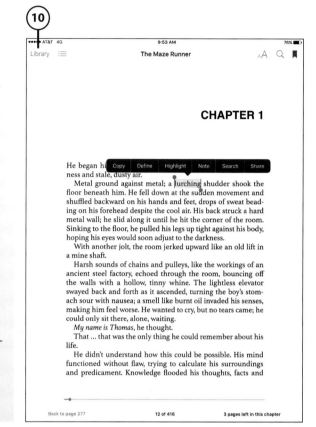

>>>*Go Further*
SELECTING TEXT AND USING COMMANDS

When you place and hold your finger on a single word in an eBook, the word is highlighted in blue, and you see a set of pop-up commands. You can extend the highlighted area by dragging the blue dots associated with the highlighting left, right, up, or down. On a Mac, press and hold down the Control key at the same time you click on a word that appears within the eBook.

Tap or click Copy to copy the selected content into the virtual clipboard. You can then Paste that content into another app.

When one word is selected and highlighted, tap or click Define (when your computer or mobile device has Internet access) to look up the definition of that word.

Tap or click Highlight to use a virtual highlighter. You can then tap or click the Highlight icon to select an Underline Text option or choose among virtual highlight colors.

Tap or click Note to compose a text-based note that will appear as a virtual sticky note within the margin of the page. You can then go back and read those notes anytime. (See the "Accessing an Interactive Table of Contents" sidebar earlier in this chapter for more information.)

Tap or click Search to search the entire eBook for the occurrences of a specific word or phrase that you enter into the Search field.

By tapping the Share tab, you can easily share the selected text with other people (when your mobile device or computer has Internet access). You can use a text message, AirDrop, email, Facebook, or Twitter. You can also use Share to export the selected text into the Notes app.

Reading eBooks Using Android Mobile Devices

The Play Books app that comes preinstalled on most Android-based smartphones and tablets enables you to find and acquire eBooks from the Google Play store and then read those eBooks on your mobile device's screen.

(1) Launch the Play Books app from your device's Home screen.

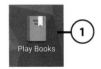

(**2**) Tap the Menu icon.

(**3**) Tap Shop. The Books area of the Google Play Store opens.

Internet Access Is Initially Required

To shop for and acquire eBooks from the Google Play Store, your smartphone or tablet requires Internet access. However, after you have downloaded eBooks to your device, you no longer need an Internet connection to read them.

4 Browse through available books by scrolling through the listings displayed under the various headings, such as Recommended for You or Load Your New Library. Alternatively, tap one of the section tabs that appear along the top of the screen.

5 Tap the Search icon, and enter a book's title, author's name, subject, or any keyword related to the type of book you're looking for.

6 Regardless of which browsing option you choose, you see a listing of available books. Tap any eBook listing to see a detailed description screen for that book.

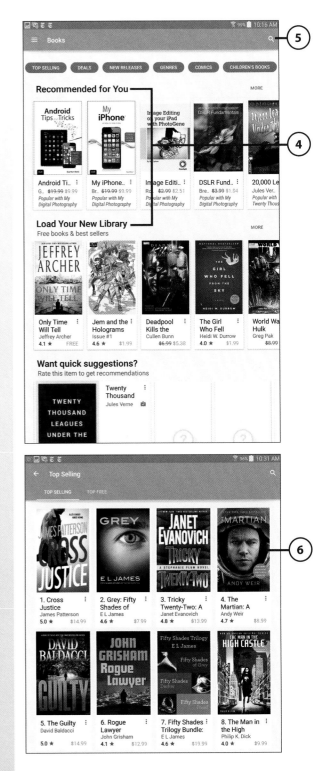

7 Read a detailed description of the book, read its reviews, see its star-based ratings, download a free sample of the book (by tapping the Free Sample button), or purchase the book by tapping its Buy button (which also displays the eBook's price).

Some eBooks Are Free

If a specific eBook is being offered for free, you see an Add to Library button rather than a Price button. Tap this button to download the free book and add it to your personal library.

8 You see a pop-up window confirming the eBook's price and title. Tap the Continue button to proceed with your purchase. The credit or debit card that's linked to your Google Play account is charged, and the eBook downloads to the device you're using. You can also use a prepaid Google Play Gift Card to pay for eBook purchases (not shown).

9 Tap the app's Menu button, and select the My Books option. You see the My Library screen (not shown).

10 Tap the book cover thumbnail for the eBook you want to open. The first page of the eBook is displayed on the screen.

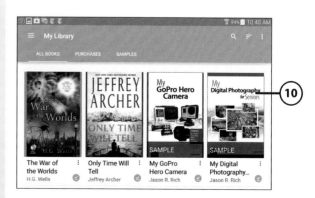

11 Swipe right to left to turn the pages of the book, or tap the right margin. To move one page back, swipe from left to right or tap the left margin.

12 Tap near the center of the page to see the options for customizing your reading experience.

13 Tap the Search icon to reveal a Search Field. Within this field, enter any word or phrase to see a list of occurrences of it within the open eBook.

14 Tap the Table of Contents icon to reveal the table of contents for the book.

In this chapter, you'll learn some of the basic information needed to ultimately take awesome photos using your mobile device, including

→ What equipment and apps you need
→ When and where you can snap digital photos
→ What you can do with the images after you take them

You probably know that the smartphone or tablet you carry around with you to make and receive calls is capable of handling many additional tasks. Chances are you already use it for some of these purposes, up to and including taking photos. In many ways, the technology built in to these small devices is similar to the technology built in to a notebook or desktop computer.

If you'll be using a point-and-shoot or digital SLR camera to take pictures, skip over to Chapter 3, "Improving Your Photography Skills," to learn some digital photography shooting techniques that will help you take better photos.

Refer to the owner's manual for your camera to learn how to operate it, because every camera make and model is different. Alternatively, to watch free videos that can teach you how to use your particular camera, visit YouTube (www.youtube.com), and in the Search field, enter the exact make and model of your camera.

Whether you use an Apple iPhone or iPad, have invested in a smartphone or tablet that operates using the Android operating system, or own a mobile device that operates using the Windows Mobile operating system, all these devices can handle a wide range of tasks from virtually anywhere.

Of all the features and functions your device likely has, its digital camera is by far one of its most useful and fun pieces of technology. In fact, some smartphones and tablets actually have two separate cameras built in to them—one in the front and one in the back. Depending on which app you use to operate these cameras, they can be used to make and receive video calls, shoot video, or take digital photos.

Shown here is the front of an iPhone 6, which has a tiny camera located in the top-center of the device.

The back of the iPhone 6 also has a camera, along with a flash, which is shown here.

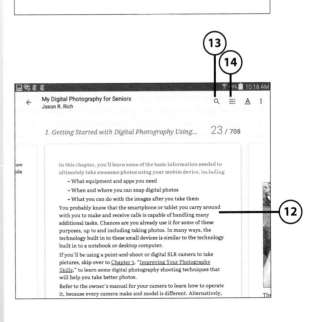

(15) Tap the Chapters tab to display a detailed and interactive Table of Contents for the open eBook. You can then tap any chapter title or section title, for example, to jump to the appropriate page within the book.

(16) Alternatively, tap the Bookmarks tab to reveal a list of manually saved bookmarks, or tap the Notes tab to view a list of notes you've created and previously added to the eBook.

(17) Tap the A icon to customize the formatting of the eBook. The formatting menu opens.

(18) Adjust the theme (color scheme), screen brightness, font, font size, paragraph justification, and line spacing. As you make changes to this menu, the open eBook automatically reformats itself on the screen.

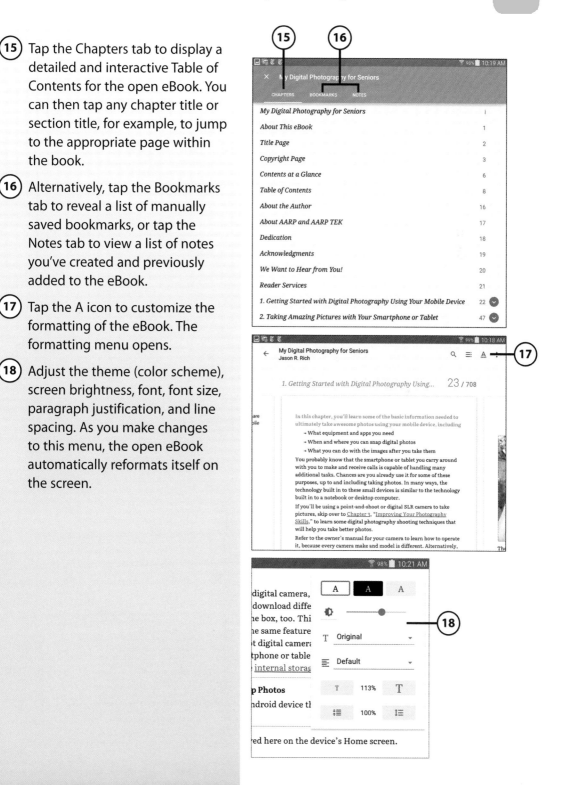

19 Tap the More Menu icon (three horizontal dots) to see more formatting options.

20 Tap a command to reset the eBook's formatting to its original settings, access the About This Book screen, share details about the eBook with other people, manually create a bookmark, or adjust additional app-related settings.

21 Displayed along the bottom of the screen is a page slider. Place your finger on this slider and drag it to the right to move forward within the book quickly and scan the pages as you go (not shown).

22 Tap the left-pointing arrow icon, or tap anywhere on the virtual page, to return to reading and make the icons disappear.

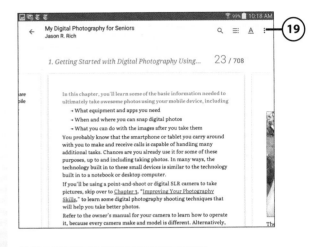

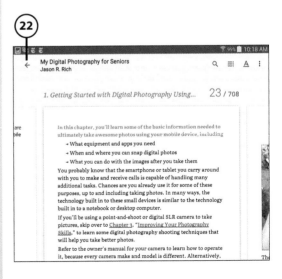

Play Books Is Available for iOS Mobile Devices and Computers Too

A version of the Google Play Books app is available for the iPhone and iPad from the App Store for free. If you want to read eBooks acquired from the Google Play Books eBook store on your PC or Mac, depending on the computer you're using, you might be required to download the free Adobe Digital Editions software. You'll find this software here: www.adobe.com/solutions/ebook/digital-editions.html.

Reading eBooks Using the Kindle App or Device

The way the Kindle app operates depends on which type of device you're using. If you use the Kindle app on an Android-based tablet or smartphone, you can also shop for eBooks from Amazon.com directly from the app. However, if you're using the Kindle app on your iPhone or iPad, you need to use your computer or mobile device's web browser to access Amazon.com's website (www.amazon.com) and then shop for eBooks from the website. After you purchase the eBooks through the browser, you can manage and read them using the Kindle app. You can also import into your iPhone or iPad eBooks purchased on other Kindle devices (or devices running the Kindle app) that are already stored within your Amazon account.

Find Books Using the Kindle App on an iPhone or iPad

After you launch the Kindle app on your iPhone or iPad, tap the Book Browser icon (which looks like the Amazon "A" logo) to access the Book Browser feature of the online bookstore. You can download a sample of the book or download the entire eBook if you're a Kindle Unlimited subscriber. Otherwise, to purchase an eBook from Amazon for use with the Kindle app, you need to use any web browser and visit the Amazon.com website directly.

When you launch the Kindle app for the first time, you need to sign in to the app using your Amazon username and password. If you don't have an Amazon account, you need to create one and link a major credit card or debit card to the account to easily pay for purchases.

One Amazon Account

If you already have an Amazon account that you use for online shopping or to access Amazon Prime Video or Amazon Music, you can use the same account with the Kindle app. You need only one Amazon account. To make eBook shopping a faster process, be sure to turn on the Amazon 1-Click feature for your Amazon account. This will allow you to purchase, download and install an eBook with a single click, and not have to manually enter credit card information each time you place an order.

To do this, visit www.amazon.com, sign into your account, and then tap or click the Your Account option (located near the top-right corner of the website). From the Your Account screen, tap or click the 1-Click Settings option to turn on this feature and customize it from the Manage Addresses and 1-Click Settings screen.

When you sign in to the Kindle app for the first time, it will introduce you to the Amazon eBook Store and ask you to select categories of books that interest you so that the app can recommend books. If you prefer, though, you can jump right to the Kindle Store and begin shopping for eBooks.

Read Kindle eBooks on Your PC or Mac

There's also a free Kindle eBook reader app available for PCs and Macs. Search for **Kindle app** in the Windows Store from your PC or the Mac App Store from your Mac. These apps work very much like the Kindle app for mobile devices, as well as any of the Kindle eBook readers.

Subscribe to Kindle Unlimited

For a flat monthly fee of $9.99 you can subscribe to Kindle Unlimited, which gives unlimited access to more than one million eBooks and audiobooks offered by Amazon. Visit www.amazon.com/gp/feature.html?docId=1002872331 for more information.

Find and Acquire eBooks

The following steps use an Android-based tablet as an example, but the procedure is the same regardless of what type of device you're using with the Kindle app.

(1) If you're using a Kindle eBook reader, turn on the device and make sure it's connected to the Internet. If you're running the Kindle app on a compatible computer, smartphone, or tablet, make sure it's connected to the Internet, and then launch the app (not shown).

(2) Tap or click the Menu icon.

(3) Tap or click the Store option. The Kindle Store opens.

(4) Use the Search field to quickly find any eBook by entering its title, an author's name, a subject, or any keyword.

(5) Alternatively, browse through the listings of features or recommended eBooks, or tap one of the Category options. Scroll down to see additional category headings.

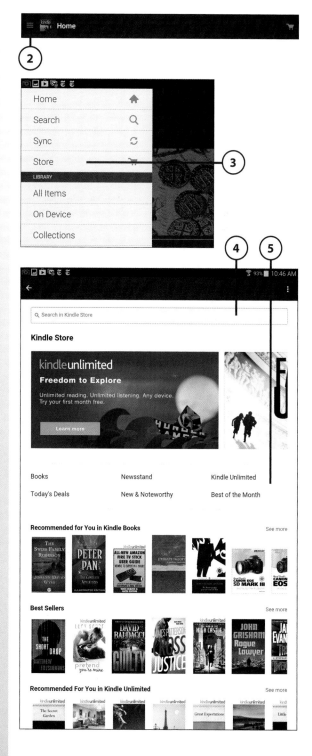

6) Tap a book cover's thumbnail image to reveal a detailed description for that eBook.

7) Read a detailed description of the book, read its reviews, glance at its star-based ratings, download a free sample, add the book to your wish list, or purchase or acquire the book by tapping or clicking the Buy Now button.

8) After you tap or click the Buy Now button, the price of the eBook will be charged to the credit or debit card you have linked with your Amazon account. If an eBook is free, you see a Read for Free button rather than the Buy Now button.

Using Gift Cards

You also have the option of using a pre-paid Amazon Gift Card to pay for eBook purchases from the Kindle Store.

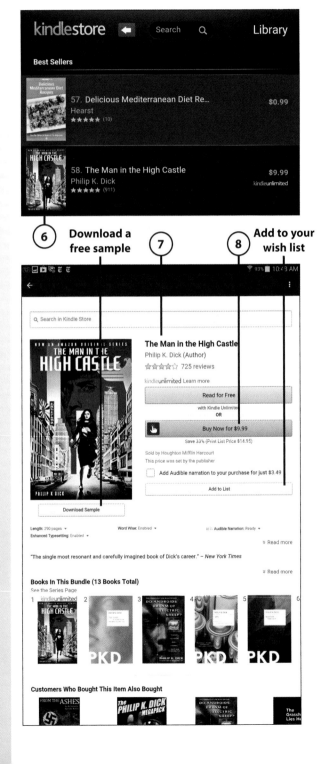

6) Download a free sample

7)

8) Add to your wish list

9 You see the purchase confirmation screen, and the new eBook is downloaded to the device you used to make the purchase. A copy of the eBook is permanently stored in your Amazon account, so you can later retrieve it from any compatible computer or device that's linked to your Amazon account.

10 Tap Read Now to immediately begin reading the newly purchased book. Alternatively, tap the left-pointing Back icon or the More icon, and then select the Home option to return to the main Kindle screen.

11 Tap a book cover on the Library screen to open the eBook and begin reading.

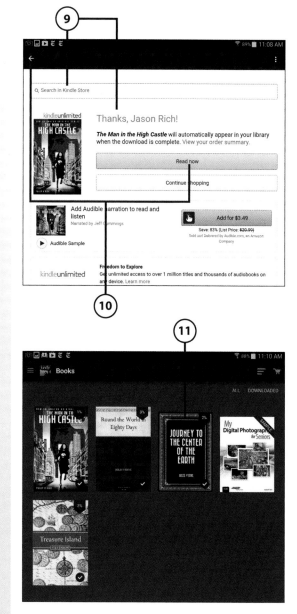

Read eBooks

This example shows how to read an eBook on an Android-based tablet, but the instructions are very similar regardless of the type of device you're using.

(1) Turn on the Kindle eBook reader, or if you're using the Kindle app on your smartphone, tablet, or computer, launch the app (not shown).

No Internet Connection Required

Remember, after one or more eBooks that you want to read are loaded into the app or on the Kindle reader, you no longer need an Internet connection to read those eBooks.

(2) Tap or click the Menu icon.

(3) Tap or click Books under the Library heading.

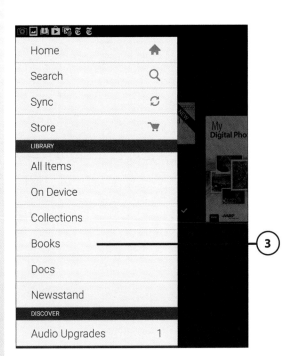

4 Tap or click the book cover for the eBook you want to read. The eBook opens to the first page.

5 Swipe from right to left across the page to advance to the next page, or tap somewhere on the page's right margin. To move back one page, swipe from left to right across the page, or tap the page's left margin.

6 Tap near the top of the page to make a series of command icons appear that are used to customize your eBook reading experience and manage the eBook that's open.

7 Tap the Share icon to recommend the book to other people by sending them an email or text message, or by posting details about the book on social media (such as Facebook or Twitter). This option is not available when using the the iOS edition of the Kindle app on an iPhone or iPad.

8 Tap the X-Ray icon to reveal tabs that allow you to access Notable Clips, details about characters (People), definitions of terms used within the book (Terms), and display images from the book, if applicable (Images).

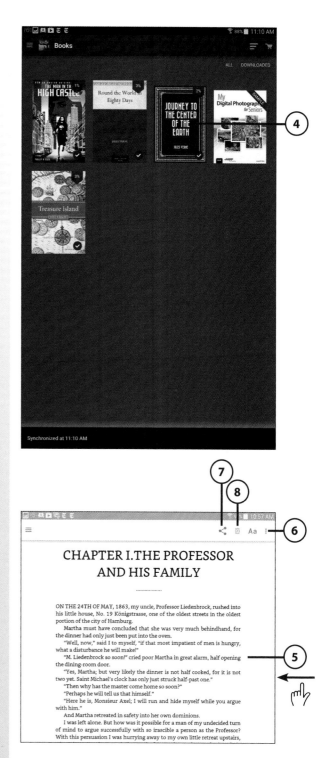

>>>Go Further

USING THE MENU

Tap the Menu icon to see a number of options for navigating the book and getting more information.

Menu icon —

Go To —

Sync —

Interactive table of contents —

Return to the Library screen

About This Book

Search

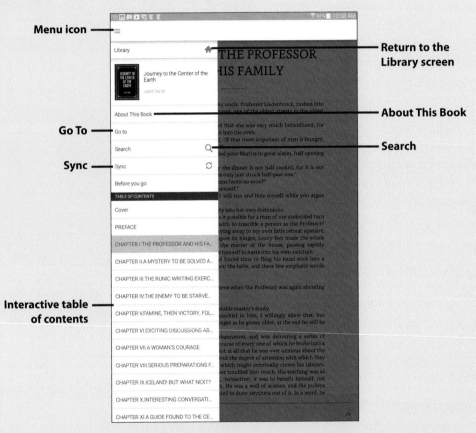

Tap About This Book to view a brief synopsis of the book, view its star-based ratings, and access other details about the open eBook.

To jump to a specific page within the eBook, Tap Go To. Within the Enter Page pop-up window, enter the page number you'd like to jump to. Tap Search to find occurrences of a specific word or phrase within the book.

To sync the open eBook, as well as your bookmarks, notes, and other related information with your Amazon account, and then be able to access it using any Kindle eBook reader or the Kindle app running on any other computer or mobile device that's linked to your Amazon account (and that's running the Kindle app), tap the Sync option.

Use the Sync with Audio option (when available) to purchase and download the audiobook edition of the open eBook, and listen to a professional narrator read the book to you. This option only appears if an audiobook edition of the open book is available from Amazon.

To see an interactive summary of popular highlights within the open eBook, including page number references where each highlight can be found, tap or click the Popular Highlights option. This feature is also available only in some eBook titles.

At the bottom of the menu is an interactive table of contents. Tap any chapter or section title or number to jump directly to the corresponding page within the open eBook.

To return to the main Bookshelf (Library) screen, tap the Home Library icon. A virtual bookmark is automatically created to mark the last page you read.

9 Tap the Aa icon to customize your reading experience. Use the options to adjust the screen brightness, font size, font, background color, margins, and line spacing used to display the text within the eBook.

10 Tap the More menu icon to access a secondary menu with additional options. (This menu option is not available within the iOS edition of the app for the iPhone/iPad.)

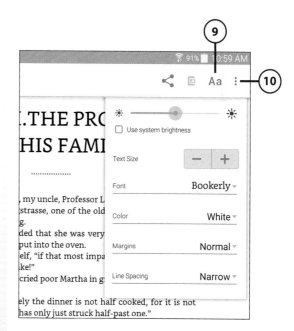

11 Tap or click an option to visit the Kindle Store, create and edit notes within the margins of the open eBook, manually add a virtual bookmark to a page, share your progress while reading the book, and access definitions of words used within the book.

Word Runner

The Kindle eBook readers and apps offer what Amazon calls the Word Runner feature, which is available from the More menu. This feature allows you to read faster by keeping your eyes focused near the center of the page as the eBook reader/app displays one word or sentence at a time, at a pace that you adjust using an onscreen slider. Word Runner is not yet available in the iPhone/iPad version of the app.

12 Place and hold your finger on a single word to highlight it and see a pop-up menu. Drag the end markers to change the size of the highlighted area. If you're using the Kindle app on a computer, right-click the word.

Word Definitions

When you highlight a single word, a Dictionary window pops up to give you a definition of the word.

13 Tap a color to change the color of the highlight on the word or words.

14 Tap the Note icon to compose a text-based note.

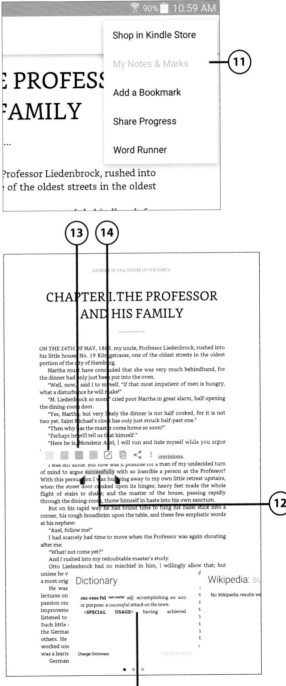

Selected word's definition

(15) Tap the Copy icon to copy text to the device's clipboard (to be pasted into another app).

(16) Tap the Share icon to share the selected text with others.

(17) Exit the eBook you're reading by tapping or clicking the Menu icon and selecting the Home Library option. You can also press the Home button on your mobile device to close the app and return to its Home screen (not shown).

Audiobooks and Digital Publications

You can use your Kindle or Nook eBook reader (as well as the Kindle and Nook apps) to acquire, download, and read digital editions of magazines and newspapers. In many cases, you can also download and listen to audiobooks. Read more about this in Chapter 10, "Reading Digital Newspapers and Magazines," and Chapter 12.

(16)

JOURNEY TO THE CENTER OF THE EARTH

CHAPTER I. THE PROFESSOR AND HIS FAMILY

....

ON THE 24TH OF MAY, 1863, my uncle Professor Liedenbrock, rushed into his little house, No. 19 Königstrasse, one of the oldest streets in the oldest portion of the city of Hamburg.

Martha must have concluded that she was very much behindhand, for the dinner had only just been put into the oven.

"Well, now," said I to myself, "if that most impatient of men is hungry, what a disturbance he will make!"

"M. Liedenbrock so soon!" cried poor Martha in great alarm, half opening the dining-room door.

"Yes, Martha; but very likely the dinner is not half cooked, for it is not two yet. Saint Michael's clock has only just struck half-past one."

"Then why has the master come home so soon?"

"Perhaps he will tell us that himself."

"Here he is, Monsieur Axel; I will run and hide myself while you argue .... ominions.

I was left alone. But how was it possible for a man of my undecided turn of mind to argue successfully with so irascible a person as the Professor? With this persuasion I was hurrying away to my own little retreat upstairs, when the street door creaked upon its hinges; heavy feet made the whole flight of stairs to shake; and the master of the house, passing rapidly through the dining-room, threw himself in haste into his own sanctum.

But on his rapid way he had found time to fling his hazel stick into a corner, his rough broadbrim upon the table, and these few emphatic words at his nephew:

"Axel, follow me!"

I had scarcely had time to move when the Professor was again shouting after me:

"What! not come yet?"

And I rushed into my redoubtable master's study.

Otto Liedenbrock had no mischief in him, I willingly allow that; but unless he v d

Dictionary   Wikipedia: su

He was   i
lectures on   No Wikipedia results we
passion on   suc·cess·ful /sek'sesfal/ adj. accomplishing an aim   s
improveme   or purpose: a successful attack on the town.   v
listened to   <SPECIAL   USAGE>   having   achieved   n
Such little   i
the German   t
others. He   i
worked und   i
was a learn   Change Dictionary   Full Definition
German

(15)

Reading eBooks with the Nook App

When your Nook eBook reader is connected to the Internet, you can shop for eBooks from BN.com. On Windows computers or with the Android-based mobile app, you can shop for eBooks from BN.com directly from within the Nook app. When you're using a Mac, iPhone, or iPad, you need to use your computer or mobile device's web browser to visit www.bn.com to download books to the device you're using.

Find and Acquire eBooks

These steps demonstrate finding and acquiring an eBook on an Android tablet, but the steps are very similar on other devices.

(1) Turn on your Nook eBook reader or launch the Nook app on your computer or mobile device. From the launch screen, tap the Sign In button to sign in to your BN.com/Nook account. An Internet connection is required to browse and acquire eBooks (not shown).

(2) Tap or click the Menu icon on the Library screen.

(3) Tap or click Shop.

Shopping on an iOS Device

If you're using an iPhone or iPad with the Nook app, you need to browse and acquire eBooks from BN.com by visiting www.bn.com via your computer or mobile device's web browser.

(4) Tap the Books tab and then tap one of the Category buttons. Alternatively, scroll down to view the Nook Books Top 100 or other listings of eBooks sorted in various ways.

(5) Tap the Search icon and, within the Search field, enter a book's title, author's name, subject, or any keyword or phrase that will help you find what you're looking for. When you find a title you're interested in, tap its cover to view a detailed description of that eBook.

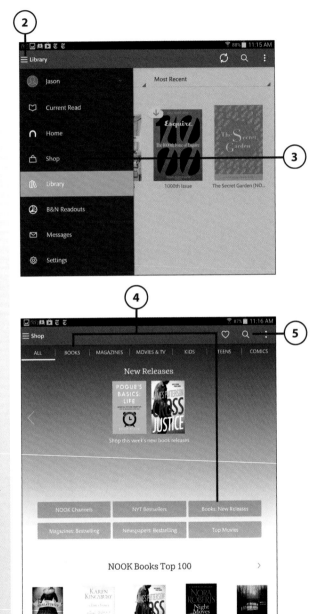

(6) Tap the Price button to purchase the eBook, or tap the Free Sample button to download and read a free sample of the selected eBook.

(7) Tap the Confirm button. The purchase price of the selected eBook is charged to the credit or debit card that's linked to your BN.com/Nook account.

Using Gift Cards

You can also use a prepaid Barnes and Noble Gift Card to pay for purchases.

(8) The eBook is downloaded to your Nook eBook reader or to your smartphone, tablet, or computer and appears on the Library screen (not shown).

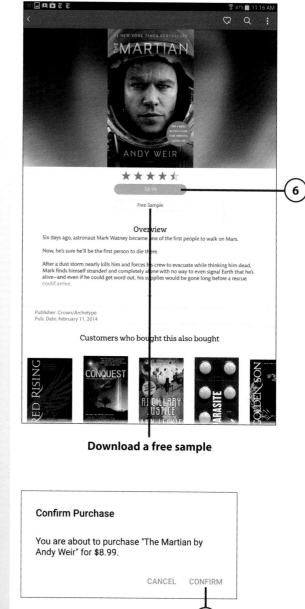

Download a free sample

Confirm Purchase

You are about to purchase "The Martian by Andy Weir" for $8.99.

CANCEL   CONFIRM

(7)

Read eBooks

The following steps use an Android-based tablet as an example, but the procedure is the same regardless of what type of device you're using with the Nook app.

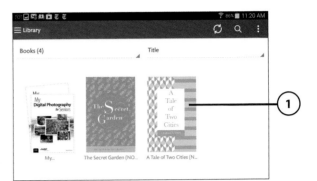

1. From the Nook's Library screen, tap the cover for the book you want to open and read. The book opens to the first page.

2. To move to the next page, swipe horizontally from right to left, or tap the right margin of the page. To go back one page, swipe from left to right, or tap the left margin of the page.

3. Tap near the top center of the screen to see command icons.

4. Tap the Menu icon to access a variety of options, including the capability to view the currently open eBook, return to the Home screen, visit the online BN.com eBook store, view and manage your Library, or adjust app-specific settings.

A Tale of Two Cities

I. The Period

It was the best of times,
it was the worst of times,
it was the age of wisdom,
it was the age of foolishness,
it was the epoch of belief,
it was the epoch of incredulity,
it was the season of Light,
it was the season of Darkness,
it was the spring of hope,
it was the winter of despair,

we had everything before us, we had nothing before us, we were all going direct to Heaven, we were all going direct the other way— in short, the period was so far like the present period, that some of its noisiest authorities insisted on its being received, for good or for evil, in the superlative degree of comparison only.

There were a king with a large jaw and a queen with a plain face, on the throne of England; there were a king with a large jaw and a queen with a fair face, on the throne of France. In both countries it was clearer than crystal to the lords of the State preserves of loaves and fishes, that things in general were settled for ever.

It was the year of Our Lord one thousand seven

4 of 380

I. The Period

It was the best of times,
it was the worst of times,
it was the age of wisdom,
it was the age of foolishness,

5 Tap the Table of Contents icon to access an interactive table of contents for the open eBook. At the top of the window, tabs for Contents, Highlights & Notes, Bookmarks, and Lookups are displayed. Tap the feature you want to access.

6 Tap the Share icon to share details about the eBook with other people.

7 Tap the Aa icon to adjust the onscreen font size, font, background color and font color (theme), margins, and line spacing. Alternatively, turn on the virtual switch for Publisher Defaults to set the eBook reading experience to how the publisher intended it.

86% 11:22 AM

| CONTENTS | HIGHLIGHTS & NOTES | BOOKMARKS | LOOKUPS |

ood or for evil, in the superlative de-

86% 11:22 AM

Font Options

| - A | +A |

Georgia >

Aa Aa Aa Aa Aa Aa

Margins   Line Spacing

Publisher Defaults: ⬤——

— Publisher Defaults switch

Per

best of t
orst of
ge of wi
e of fool
poch of
ch of inc
eason of Light,
son of Darkness,
oring of hope.

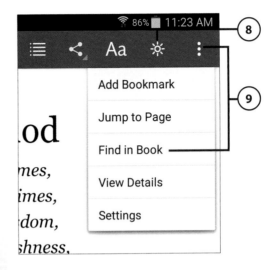

8 Tap the Brightness icon to adjust the screen's brightness using a slider that appears on the screen. Dragging the slider with your finger to the right increases the brightness of the screen.

9 Tap the More icon to manually add a virtual bookmark to the page you're currently reading, jump to a specific page within the eBook, use the Search tool to find occurrences of a word or phrase, view details about the book, or adjust the app's settings.

10 Place and hold your finger on a word to see its definition.

11 Tap one of the colored circles to select a highlight color for text. All of the text that's selected will become highlighted in the selected color.

12 Send the selected text to someone or post it on social media by clicking the Share icon.

13 Tap the Dictionary icon to look up a selected word and view a more detailed definition, use the Google search engine to do an Internet search related to the selected word, or look up the word online using Wikipedia. After tapping on the Dictionary icon, you see icons for the Dictionary, Google, and Wikipedia in the top-right corner of the screen.

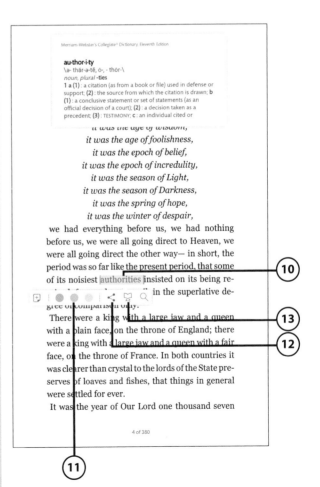

(14) Tap the Search icon to find and view all uses of the word (along with page number references) that appear within the eBook that's currently option.

(15) Add a virtual sticky note to the page you're reading by tapping the Note icon and then typing your note within the pop-up window. Tap the Save button to store your note and display an icon for it within the margin of the eBook's page that's currently displayed.

(16) Exit the currently open eBook and return to the Library screen by tapping the Menu icon and then the Library option. Alternatively, press the Home button on a smartphone or tablet (not shown).

Selected word's definition

Merriam-Webster's Collegiate® Dictionary, Eleventh Edition

au·thor·i·ty
\ə- thär-ə-tē, ȯ-, - thȯr-\
noun, plural **-ties**
1 a (1) : a citation (as from a book or file) used in defense or support; **(2)** : the source from which the citation is drawn; **b (1)** : a conclusive statement or set of statements (as an official decision of a court); **(2)** : a decision taken as a precedent; **(3)** : TESTIMONY; **c** : an individual cited or

it was the age of wisdom,
it was the age of foolishness,
it was the epoch of belief,
it was the epoch of incredulity,
it was the season of Light,
it was the season of Darkness,
it was the spring of hope,
it was the winter of despair,
we had everything before us, we had nothing before us, we were all going direct to Heaven, we were all going direct the other way— in short, the period was so far like the present period, that some of its noisiest authorities insisted on its being received, for good or for evil, in the superlative degree of comparison only.

There were a king with a large jaw and a queen with a plain face, on the throne of England; there were a king with a large jaw and a queen with a fair face, on the throne of France. In both countries it was clearer than crystal to the lords of the State preserves of loaves and fishes, that things in general were settled for ever.

It was the year of Our Lord one thousand seven

4 of 380

>>>Go Further

OTHER EBOOK STORES

Aside from the eBook stores already covered in this chapter, many independent online eBook stores offer eBooks formatted in the industry-standard ePub or PDF file format, which you can read on any eBook reader or with any eBook reader mobile app.

Some of these online-based eBook stores sell eBooks, whereas others offer vast collections of copyright-free eBooks that are available free of charge. Some of these alternative sources for eBooks include All You Can Books (www.allyoucanbooks.com), Booksends (http://booksends.com), eBooks.com (www.ebooks.com), GoodReads eBooks (www.goodreads.com/ebooks), and Free eBooks (www.free-ebooks.net).

You can find additional sources for acquiring eBooks by visiting any Internet search engine, such as Google, Yahoo!, or Bing, and entering the phrase **eBooks** into the Search field.

If you're interested in publishing your own eBooks, within the search field of any search engine, enter the phrase **eBook Publishing**, or visit an eBook publishing service such as BookBaby (www.bookbaby.com), Blurb (www.blurb.com/ebooks), or Lulu (www.lulu.com/create/ebooks).

Most local libraries lend eBooks for free, while Project Gutenburg (www.gutenberg.org) offers a collection of more than 50,000 eBook titles that are available to download free in the Kindle and ePub file formats. Upon visiting the Project Gutenburg website, books can be found by entering a keyword, title, author's name, or topic into the Search field, or titles can be displayed based on popularity. Click on the Recent Books option to see a listing of eBook titles sorted by release date.

You can listen to audiobooks on your computer,
smartphone, tablet, or eBook reader.

In this chapter, you'll learn all about how to find, purchase, and then enjoy listening to audiobooks. Topics covered include how to

→ Use the Audible.com service to enjoy audiobooks on your computer, smartphone, tablet, or eBook reader
→ Acquire and listen to audiobooks using iBooks on a Mac, iPhone, or iPad
→ Acquire and listen to audiobooks on Android-based mobile devices
→ Acquire and listen to audiobooks on a Kindle or Nook eBook reader

Listening to Audiobooks

In addition to making books available as eBooks, publishers also make some books available as audiobooks. To produce an audiobook, the publisher hires an actor (or in some cases several actors), and within a recording studio, has that actor read a book, word for word. In some cases, additional music, sound effects, and other production elements are added to make the audiobook sound more like an old-style radio drama.

The benefit to listening to an audiobook, as opposed to reading a book, is that you can engage in another activity at the same time. For example, you can listen to an audiobook while driving, cooking, taking a walk, passing the time on a long airplane ride, or relaxing just before bed.

An audiobook that you listen to on your computer, smartphone, tablet, or eBook reader is supplied as a digital audio file, which you purchase and download from the Internet. The audio file is just like a digital music file. It gets stored within your computer's hard drive (or the internal storage of your mobile device), and is then played using a specific app.

When the Internet Is Needed

Although an Internet connection is required to acquire and download audiobooks, no Internet connection is needed to play them. Because audiobooks are distributed as digital audio files, they can be played on any device that's capable of playing digital audio, including a digital music player or a streaming device that connects to your television set.

Typically, an audiobook is an unabridged version of the printed book it's based upon. Thus, for longer length books, an audiobook can require 10 to 20 hours (sometimes longer) to listen to. However, using a specialized app for listening to audiobooks, you can start and stop the playback process at anytime. When you pause playback, a virtual bookmark is automatically created, so when you restart the audiobook player, you can pick up where you left off.

Audiobooks Are Available on Multiple Devices

Depending on which audiobook app you use and where you acquire your audiobooks from, any book in your personal audiobook library can be enjoyed on your computer, smartphone, tablet, and/or eBook reader. You can easily switch between computers and mobile devices, and your virtual bookmarks automatically sync via the Internet.

The price of an audiobook varies greatly, but is often about the same price as a hardcover book. After you purchase an audiobook, you own it, and it becomes part of your personal audiobook collection. There are, however, ways to save money on audiobooks or pay a flat monthly fee and have access to a service's entire library of audiobooks on an unlimited basis.

The type of equipment you use to listen to audiobooks determines from where you can acquire your audiobooks, although you typically have multiple options. For example, Audible.com offers apps for listening to audiobooks that are available for PCs, Macs, and all popular smartphones, tablets, and the Kindle eBook readers.

Using Audible.com

Audible.com is a service owned by Amazon.com that offers one of the world's largest selections of audiobooks (with more than 180,000 titles to choose from), as well as the apps needed to enjoy audiobooks on almost any computer or mobile device. Audible.com has its own online audiobook store (www.audible.com) from which you can shop for individual audiobook titles.

The same as a printed book or an eBook, the price of an audiobook varies and is set by the publisher. However, in addition to being able to purchase individual audiobooks for their list price, Audible.com offers a membership plan where you can pay a flat monthly fee of $14.95 and acquire any one audiobook per month, and then receive a 30 percent discount on additional purchases during that month.

Two Membership Options

Instead of paying $14.95 per month to acquire one audiobook and receive a 20 percent discount on all additional purchases, you can pay $22.95 per month to acquire two audiobooks per month, plus receive the 20 percent discount on your additional purchases.

You can cancel your Audible.com membership at any time, or you can "bank" your audiobook credits. So, if you don't select an audiobook for one or two months, you can acquire them later and will not forgo your credits, as long as your membership remains active.

If you already have an Amazon.com account, you can use that same username and password for Audible.com, and your membership fee or individual purchases will be charged to the credit or debit card you have linked to your Amazon.com account.

To begin using Audible.com, you first need to set up a free account using any web browser and by visiting www.audible.com. Click the Get Your Free Audiobook button. You provide your name, billing address, phone number, email address, and credit/debit card details, and create a password for your account.

Upon setting up a free account, you're provided with one free audiobook credit so you can select, download, and begin enjoying any one audiobook immediately. At this point, you can add a monthly membership plan to your account or simply purchase future audiobooks one at a time, for their listed price.

After you've created your Audible.com account (or use your existing Amazon.com account details), the next step is to acquire the free Audible audiobook player app that's needed for your computer or mobile device. It comes preinstalled on all Kindle eBook readers and some other mobile devices.

To do this, visit www.audible.com/mt/Apps, and follow the link associated with the type of computer or mobile device you'll be using. You can also visit the app store for your computer or device. Download and install the Audible app, just as you would any other free app.

When using the Audible app from your PC, Android-based smartphone or tablet, or a Kindle eBook reader, you can shop for audiobooks (from Audible.com) and then listen to those audiobooks directly from the Audible app. However, if you're using a Mac, iPhone, or iPad, you need to shop for audiobooks directly from the Audible.com website and then download and listen to your audiobook acquisitions from the Audible app.

Shop for Audiobooks via Audible.com

From the Audible.com website, which you can access from the web browser on your computer (shown here) or any mobile device, begin shopping for audiobooks by clicking or tapping the Sign In button to log in to your account. Then follow these steps to find and acquire audiobooks:

(1) Browse through the featured audiobook titles on the Audible. com home page.

(2) Another way to browse through the more than 180,000 audiobook titles is to click the Browse Audible option that's displayed near the top center of the screen. Tap or click one of the categories to find relevant audiobook listings.

3 Alternatively, type a specific title into the Search field if you know what you're looking for. You can also search by author name, subject matter, or keyword.

4 Click an audiobook title to view its description.

5 Read an audiobook's description, which includes its author, who it's narrated by, its price, length (in hours and minutes), and average star-based rating. A text-based description of the book is also provided. Scroll down on this screen to read commentary about the book from critics, as well as reviews from fellow customers.

6 Click the Play Audio Sample to stream a short sample of the audiobook to your computer or mobile device, so you can preview it prior to purchasing it.

7 Click the Add to Cart button or the Xpress Pay option. If you have an Audible Membership with available credits in your account, this will be displayed near the top of the browser window. During the checkout process, you can apply the available credit to acquire the audiobook you've selected. Otherwise, you can use the credit/debit card information you have linked with your Audible.com/Amazon.com account. It's also possible to use prepaid Amazon gift cards to pay for Audible.com purchases.

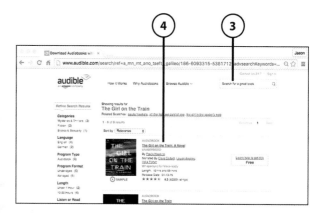

Four Types of Reviews

Aside from the typical star-based rating, which will be between one (worst) and five (best) stars, you can read what recognized book critics had to say about the book (when applicable) by scrolling further down the screen.

Audible also allows you to read text-based reviews that other Audible.com customers have written. You can also click through to reviews of the printed book that have been published on Amazon.com.

(8) After you've purchased an audiobook, it's automatically added to your online-based Audible.com Library. Any Audible app you use, on any computer or mobile device, accesses this library via the Internet and gives you full access to your audiobooks (not shown).

(9) When you're ready to listen to one of your acquired audiobooks, launch the Audible app on your computer or mobile device (this example uses the iPad), and tap or click the My Library option. Follow the directions in the next section to download and begin listening to one of your acquired audiobook titles.

It's All Yours

Upon purchasing any audiobook title from Audible.com, you own that audiobook. It will be stored online within your Audible Library, so you can download it to any or all of your computers or mobile devices that have the free Audible app installed and that are linked to your Amazon/Audible account.

However, if after listening to a portion of a purchased audiobook, if you decide you want to return it, visit www.audible.com/purchase-history from any web browser, find the listing for the audiobook you want to return from your list of purchases, and click the Return button. You will instantly receive a credit to your account that you can redeem for a different audiobook selection.

Listen to Audiobooks Using the Audible App

In addition to the vast selection of audiobook titles that Audible offers, one reason to purchase audiobooks from this service is that it offers an easy-to-use, yet full-featured app that makes listening to your audiobooks a pleasure.

Follow these directions to begin using the Audible app on your mobile device (shown here on an iPhone). The operation of the app is similar on all computers and mobile devices, although the location and appearance of some icons, menus, features, and functions varies.

1. Connect headphones or an external speaker to your computer or mobile device, unless you plan to use its internal speakers to listen to the audiobook (not shown).

2. Launch the Audible app. If you're using a computer, launch the app just as you would any other application.

3. Tap the I'm Already Using Audible button to sign in to the app. You do this only once. If you don't yet have an Audible account, tap the I'm New to Audible button and then follow the prompts to create an account.

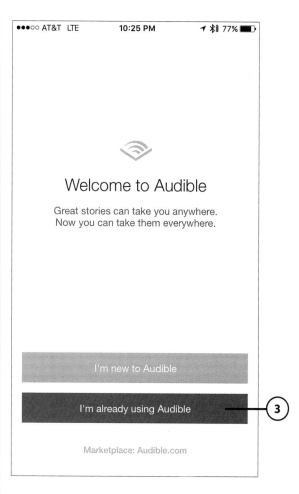

(4) When prompted, enter the email address associated with your Audible account, as well as your password (not shown).

Account Credentials

Remember, you can use your Amazon. com account information as well.

(5) Tap the My Library icon. A listing of your acquired (purchased) audiobooks from Audible displays.

Books in the Cloud

If you tap the Cloud tab, listings with a downward-pointing arrow in the lower-right corner of the cover artwork are audiobooks that you own but have not downloaded to the computer or mobile device you're using. Tap the book cover to download the audiobook file to your mobile device. An Internet connection is required to do this.

(6) Tap the title or cover artwork to begin listening to it. Continue to the next section for more information.

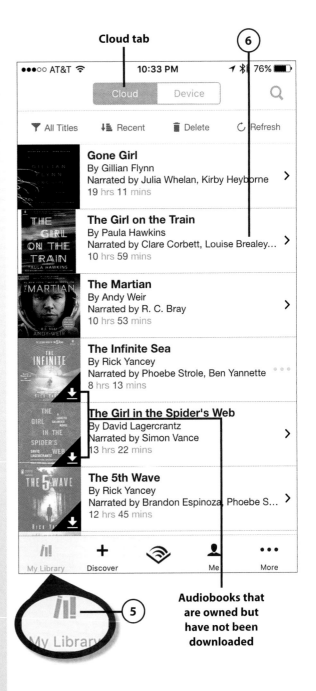

Cloud tab

●●●○○ AT&T 📶   10:33 PM   📍 ⚹ 76% 🔋

Cloud   Device   🔍

▼ All Titles   ⬇ Recent   🗑 Delete   ↻ Refresh

Gone Girl
By Gillian Flynn
Narrated by Julia Whelan, Kirby Heyborne
19 hrs 11 mins   >

The Girl on the Train
By Paula Hawkins
Narrated by Clare Corbett, Louise Brealey...
10 hrs 59 mins   >

The Martian
By Andy Weir
Narrated by R. C. Bray
10 hrs 53 mins   >

The Infinite Sea
By Rick Yancey
Narrated by Phoebe Strole, Ben Yannette
8 hrs 13 mins   • • •

The Girl in the Spider's Web
By David Lagercrantz
Narrated by Simon Vance
13 hrs 22 mins   >

The 5th Wave
By Rick Yancey
Narrated by Brandon Espinoza, Phoebe S...
12 hrs 45 mins   >

📊 My Library   ➕ Discover   📡   👤 Me   ••• More

My Library

(5)

Audiobooks that are owned but have not been downloaded

Using Audible's Onscreen Controls for Listening to Audiobooks

From the Play screen of the Audible app, you can control the audio volume (using a slider) and fast forward or rewind using the Time slider. Simply place your finger on the slider and drag it left to rewind or to the right to fast forward.

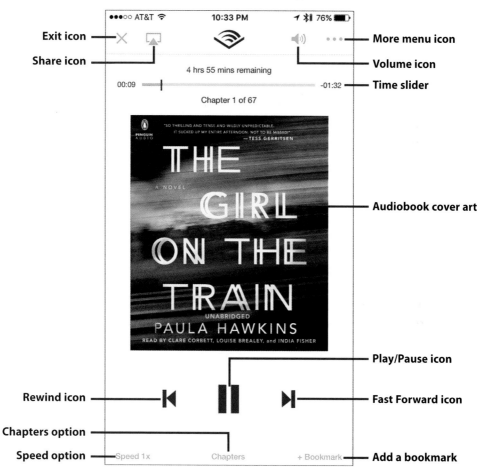

Another option to fast forward or rewind is to tap the Fast Forward or Rewind icons. Tap one of these icons to jump forward or backward to the beginning or end of the current chapter, or press and hold the icon to skim through the current chapter while fast forwarding or rewinding.

Tap the Pause icon to pause the audio. The icon changes to a Play icon. Resume playing the audio by tapping the Play icon. To increase the playback speed, tap the Speed 1X option.

Jump to a different chapter within the audiobook by tapping the Chapters option, which opens a table of contents, and then tap the chapter number you want to listen to.

Table of contents

Manually add a virtual bookmark as you're listening to an audiobook by tapping the +Bookmark option.

When you tap the More menu (…) icon, you see more options.

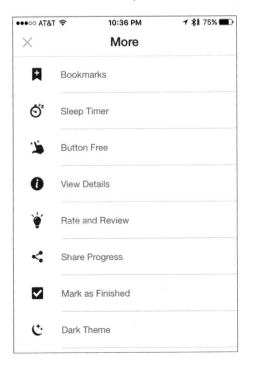

The following options are on the More menu:

- **Bookmarks**—View a list of previously saved bookmarks, and then jump to that bookmarked location and begin listening from that point by tapping one of the listings.

- **Sleep Timer**—Set the Audible app to play the audiobook for a predetermined amount of time (between 5 minutes and 60 minutes, or until the end of the current chapter) and then shut down and stop playing the audiobook.

- **View Details**—View information about the audiobook you're listening to. From here, you can read a description of the book, as well as reviews it has received. An Internet connection is required to use this feature.

- **Rate and Review**—You can compose your own text-based review for the audiobook you're listening to, and give it a star-based rating. An Internet connection is required to use this feature.

- **Share Progress**—From within the Audible app, you can share details about the audiobook you're listing to via social media. An Internet connection is required to use this feature.

- **Mark as Finished**—When you mark an audiobook as Finished, this is denoted within your library. It makes it easier to keep track of the books you've listened to. When you mark a book as finished, you see the word "Finished" below the audiobook title, and the corresponding progress meter is fully filled in.

- **Light Theme**—Adjust the appearance of the Audible app's screen, based on the lighting conditions in the room or your personal taste. If you're using the app in a dark room, for example, you can choose a darker color scheme.

To exit the Play screen, tap the X icon at top-left corner of the screen. You return to the My Library screen. From the My Library screen, you can sort, view, access, and delete audiobooks stored on the computer or mobile device you're using, as well as access your online-based Audible account to download additional audiobook files.

By tapping on the Discover icon that's displayed at the bottom of the screen, you can access the Audible.com online service (an Internet connection is required) to learn about additional audiobook titles available. Depending on which version of the Audible app you're using, however, you may or may not be able to acquire the audiobooks from within the app.

Tap the Me icon to review details about your Audible account and audiobook listening history. Tap the News icon to learn about new audiobook titles available from Audible.com. This information is presented in an online newsletter format.

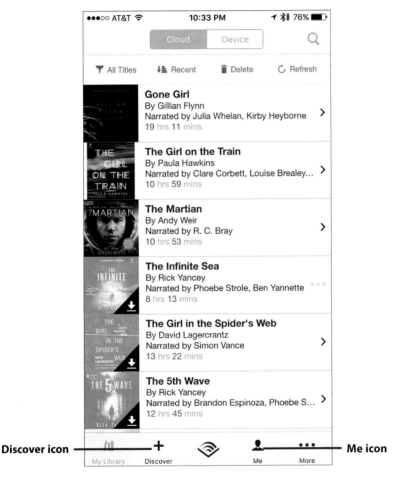

Discover icon — My Library | Discover | Me | More — Me icon

To adjust app-specific settings, tap the Settings icon. Some of these settings enable you to further customize your audiobook listening experience.

Using iBooks with Audiobooks

As a Mac, iPhone or iPad user, the iBooks app, which is primarily used for acquiring and reading eBooks (see Chapter 11, "Reading eBooks"), can also be used to listen to audiobooks that you purchase from Apple's online-based iBook Store. The audiobooks you acquire from iBook Store, however, are formatted to be played exclusively using the iBook app running on a Mac, iPhone, and/or iPad.

Shop for Audiobooks Using the iBooks App

To shop for audiobooks via the iBooks app (shown here on an iPad), launch the app from the Home screen, and follow these steps:

1. Tap or click the Featured icon to browse through audiobook offerings.

2. Tap or click the Audiobooks tab.

3. Scroll through the listings to see what's available, and tap a listing for an audiobook that catches your interest.

4. Alternatively, to narrow down your search to a specific category of audiobooks, tap the Categories option.

5. Tap or click a category you'd like to browse. A selection of related audiobook titles displays that fit into that category, based on its subject matter.

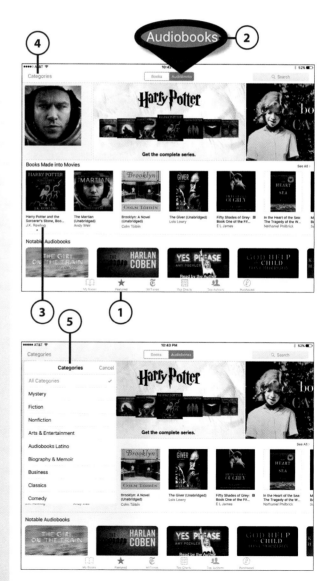

(6) Enter a book title, author name, or keyword within the app's Search field. Tap one of the search results to view that title's description screen.

Look Below the Audiobooks Heading

When using the iBooks app's Search tool to find audiobooks, as you're viewing the search results, be sure you have tapped or clicked the Audiobooks tab. Otherwise, when you tap a listing, you'll be directed to the eBook edition of that title.

(7) When you're not looking for something specific and are interested in what's popular, tap or click the Top Charts icon. Then, from the Top Charts screen, tap the Audiobooks tab to see a listing of the top Audiobooks.

(8) Tap or click a book cover or title to see that audiobook's description page.

Choose a Top Charts Category

To narrow your search as you look at a Top Charts listing, be sure to tap or click the Categories option, and then choose a category so that you see Top Charts lists of audiobooks based on that specific category.

Audiobooks tab

9 Read the audiobook's description, including its title, author, publisher, length, average star-based rating (and the number of ratings it has received), and narrator.

10 Tap the Preview button to stream a short sample of the audiobook, and listen to it before making your purchase decision.

11 Tap the Reviews tab to view the title's star-based ratings chart, as well as text-based reviews written by other iBook Store customers.

12 If you decide to purchase the audiobook, tap the Price button. Then tap the Buy Audiobook button. When prompted, enter your Apple ID account password, or place your finger on the iPhone or iPad's Touch ID sensor (Home button), when applicable, to scan your fingerprint and confirm your purchase decision.

13 After you confirm the purchase decision, the audio file for the purchased audiobook is downloaded to the Mac, iPhone, or iPad you're using. You can find it listed in the Library screen of the iBooks app (not shown).

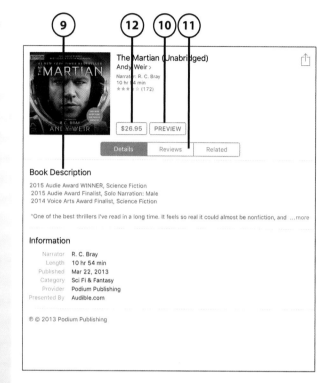

Purchases Are Automatically Stored Within Your iCloud Account

Whenever you purchase an audiobook, that purchase is automatically stored online within your iCloud account. It then becomes instantly accessible from any Mac, iPhone, iPad, or other compatible device that's linked to your iCloud account. It's also available to anyone in your family that's linked to the iCloud Family Sharing account (if you're using this optional service).

In other words, you need to purchase an audiobook only once to be able to listen to it on any Mac, iPhone, iPad, or compatible device that's linked to your iCloud account. In addition, all your virtual bookmarks related to each audiobook automatically sync between your computers and mobile devices.

Listen to Audiobooks Using the iBooks App

After you've acquired audiobooks from the iBook Store via the iBooks app, to manage and begin listening to any of these purchases, follow these steps:

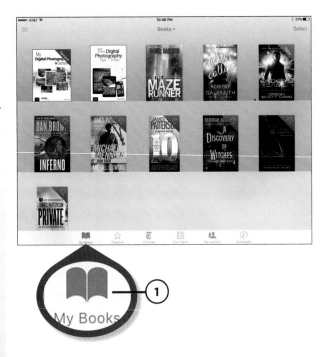

1. Launch the iBooks app and tap My Books.

Free Audiobooks

Project Gutenburg (www.gutenberg. org/wiki/Gutenberg:The_Audio_Books_ Project) offers an ever-growing collection of digital audiobooks that can be downloaded from the organization's website for free. To view an alphabetical listing of available audiobooks sorted by author's name or title, visit the organization's website, and click on the List of Human-Read Audiobooks option.

(2) Tap the drop-down menu heading and select the Audiobooks option. You see a listing of the audiobooks you've acquired from the iBook Store.

(3) Tap the Listing icon to select how the books will be sorted on the Bookshelf. You can sort by titles, authors, or categories.

(4) If an iCloud icon appears in conjunction with a listing, this means that you own that audiobook but have not downloaded it onto the Mac or mobile device you're using. Tap the iCloud icon to download the audio file (not shown).

(5) Tap a book's listing or cover artwork to begin listening to it. You can then control the playback of the audiobook using the displayed onscreen controls.

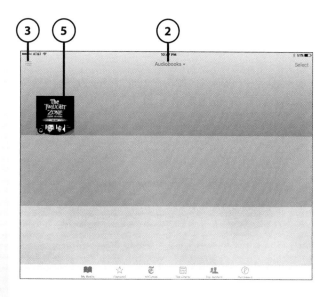

Playing Audiobooks Using the iBooks App

After you tap an audiobook listing from the Library screen of the iBooks app to begin playing it, the app's Play screen is displayed. In the center of this screen is the cover artwork for the audiobook.

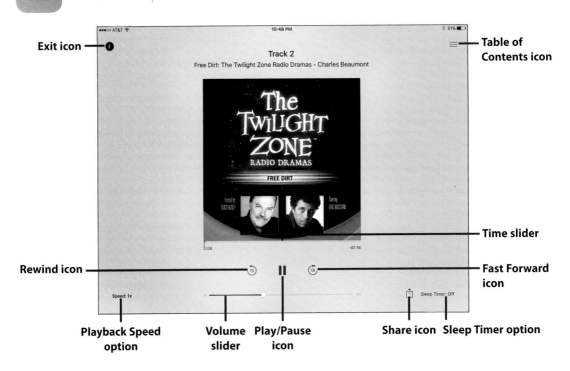

Exit icon

Table of Contents icon

Rewind icon

Fast Forward icon

Time slider

Playback Speed option

Volume slider

Play/Pause icon

Share icon   Sleep Timer option

Displayed immediately below the cover artwork is the Time slider. Swipe your finger to the right to fast forward or to the left to rewind as you're listening to an audiobook. By tapping either the Forward 15 or Rewind 15 icons, you can fast forward or rewind by 15 seconds.

Tap the Play/Pause icon to play the audio or pause it. Below the Play icon is the app's Volume slider. Move it to the right to raise the audio volume or to the left to lower the volume.

In the lower-left corner of the screen is the Playback Speed option. Tap this to increase or decrease the audio playback speed. To share details about the audiobook you're listening to, tap the Share icon.

Tap the Sleep Timer and, from the displayed menu, set how long the audio will play before it automatically turns itself off.

Sleep Timer	
Off	✓
5 minutes	
10 minutes	
15 minutes	
30 minutes	
45 minutes	
1 hour	
When current track ends	

— **Set Sleep Timer duration**

To view an interactive Table of Contents for the audiobook and quickly jump to a specific chapter or section, tap the Table of Contents icon and then tap a chapter or section listing.

To exit out of the Play screen and return to the app's Library screen, tap the < icon that's displayed in the top-left corner of the screen.

Using Your Android Device

Using any Android-based smartphone or tablet, you can use the Audible mobile app (available from the Google Play Store) to download and listen to audiobooks. Another option is to download and install the free Kindle or Nook app (see the next section), and then acquire audiobooks from Amazon.com or BN.com, respectively. All of these apps work in a very similar way when it comes to shopping for and then listening to acquired audiobooks.

From the Google Play Store (shown here on an Android tablet), type **Audiobooks** into the Search field to discover a handful of other third-party apps that allow you to acquire audiobooks from various sources and listen to them on your Android-based mobile device.

Search field ——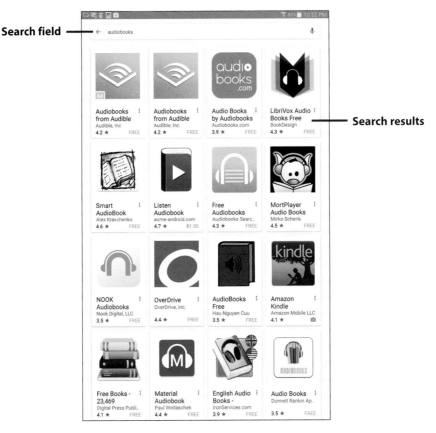

—— Search results

Using a Kindle or Nook eBook Reader or Mobile App

You can also use the Amazon Kindle and Barnes and Noble Nook eBook readers to download and listen to audiobooks. (See Chapter 11 for more information about these devices.)

When using a Kindle eBook reader, you need to acquire your audiobooks from Amazon.com's Kindle Store. When using a Nook eBook reader, you need to acquire your audiobooks from barnesandnoble.com's Nook Store. This is also true if you're using the free Kindle or Nook app on your computer, iPhone, iPad, or Android smartphone or tablet.

A Perk of Using the Kindle

For people who enjoy listening to audiobooks, one perk of using a Kindle eBook reader or the Kindle app from Amazon is that you can subscribe to the Kindle Unlimited service. For a flat fee of $9.99 per month, you have access to as many eBooks and audiobooks as you'd like from the service's collection. You're able to keep this content stored on your computer or mobile device for as long as you maintain your Kindle Unlimited membership.

In other words, instead of purchasing audiobooks, you're technically borrowing them until you're no longer a Kindle Unlimited subscriber. However, if you plan to listen to an audiobook only once, this is a low-cost way to gain access to a vast and ever-growing audiobook library without having to separately purchase each audiobook title.

When using the Kindle or Nook eBook reader or mobile app, launch the app and access the bookstore to browse for audiobooks. The process of finding and acquiring audiobooks using a Kindle or Nook eBook reader or the mobile app is very similar to acquiring eBooks from these apps (which is discussed in Chapter 11).

Another Perk of the Kindle App

One feature of the Kindle app is that if you purchase an eBook, you can tap on the Audio Upgrades option in the app's main menu and then acquire the audiobook edition of the same title at a deeply discounted price.

After the audiobook is downloaded, stored, and viewable within the app's Library screen, you can tap its title or cover artwork, and the app's audio playback controls are displayed. These are similar to the Audible or iBooks app and offer much the same functionality.

The Benefit of Shopping from Amazon.com or BN.com

When you acquire audiobooks from Amazon.com in the Kindle format, you can then listen to them on any Kindle eBook reader or any computer or mobile device that has the Kindle app installed and that's linked to your Amazon account. This includes your PC, Mac, iPhone, iPad, or any Android-based smartphone or tablet.

Likewise, when you shop for audiobooks from BN.com that are compatible with the Nook, you can listen to this content from any Nook eBook reader or Nook app that's running on your PC, Mac, iPhone, iPad, or any Android-based smartphone or tablet that's linked to your BN.com account.

You can take most forms of digital entertainment
on the go using your smartphone or tablet.

This chapter's focus is on how you can manage and experience various forms of digital entertainment on the go using your smartphone and table. This includes the following:

→ Accessing TV shows and movies distributed by your cable/satellite service provider from your mobile device

→ Recording programs remotely and then accessing content from your TiVo DVR using your mobile device

→ Using your smartphone in your vehicle

Taking Digital Entertainment on the Road

You already know that eBook readers allow you to read eBooks and digital publications on the go, and that you can use your smartphone or tablet to store or stream TV shows, movies, and music that can be experienced virtually anywhere. Then, when you're at home, you can use different technologies to connect to your HD television set, enabling you to truly customize your digital entertainment experience in your living room, den, or TV room, for example.

Thanks to the Internet and the technology built in to mobile devices, the distinction between what forms of digital entertainment can be experienced at home and what you can do while on the go is extremely blurred.

Accessing TV Shows and Movies

If you subscribe to a cable or satellite TV service and have a cable or satellite receiver box connected to your HD television set at home, you're no longer limited to watching TV shows and movies on only that one television set. For no additional fee, using the proprietary app that's offered by your cable TV or satellite service provider (such as Xfinity TV Go, if you're a Comcast Xfinity subscriber), you can do several things, including the following:

- Stream a program or movie as it's airing on television directly to your Internet-connected smartphone or tablet. This works with programming offered by a handful of networks that support live streaming via the Xfinity TV Go app or a similar app. (A continuous Internet connection is required.)

- Stream a vast selection of on-demand programming, from most networks and channels offered by Xfinity, starting 24 hours after the programming airs on television, and watch that programming anywhere via the Xfinity TV Go app (or a similar app). (A continuous Internet connection is required.)

- Download selected shows, from participating networks and channels, store that content on your mobile device, and then watch it anytime later, even if no Internet connection is available.

- Within your home, use your Internet-connected mobile device to watch any live programming that airs on any channel or network you typically receive on your television set (via your cable/satellite receiver box). This feature enables you to watch TV in any room of your home, even when no television set or cable or satellite receive box is present.

What's possible using the mobile app that's offered by your particular cable or satellite TV service provider varies. It's important, however, that you install the proper app onto your mobile device. Choose the app that's offered by your cable or satellite TV service provider. It's available, for free, via the App Store (iPhone/iPad) or Google Play Store (Android).

Within the Search field of the app store you use, enter the name of your cable or satellite TV service provider. Some of the more popular apps, from various cable or satellite TV service providers, include the following:

- **Cox Cable**—COX TV Connect
- **DirectTV**—DirectTV app
- **DishTV**—Dish Anywhere
- **Spectrum TV**—Spectrum TV App
- **Time Warner Cable**—TWC TV or My TWC
- **Xfinity**—Xfinity TV Go
- **Verizon FIOS**—FIOS Mobile

If you're not a cable or satellite TV service subscriber, you have the option of downloading the proprietary app for a specific television network and then streaming shows and programming from that channel or network via the Internet, directly to your mobile device.

Virtually every major television network has its own app. Some, however, limit how many episodes of specific shows are available for streaming at any given time. When episodes are made available varies as well. A few networks stream shows via their app at the same time they air on television (allowing you to watch them live, from anywhere, using your mobile device). Others wait 24 hours before making the latest episode of a series or other programming available for streaming.

Most TV Networks Apps Offer Streaming for Free

The majority of television networks and nonpremium cable channels offer their apps and programming for free. Some, however, have begun to charge a flat monthly fee (less than $10 per month), to have full access to all of that network's programming, including all episodes from past series.

Premium cable channels that you typically pay extra for, such as HBO and Showtime, offer the capability to stream programming via their respective mobile app for no additional charge if you're already a paid subscriber (through your cable/satellite TV service provider). If you're not, you can pay a separate flat monthly fee for unlimited access to each premium cable network's programming, via its proprietary mobile app.

Use the Xfinity TV Go App

The various mobile apps offered by cable or satellite TV service providers vary, but the following basic directions for using the Xfinity TV Go mobile app (shown on an iPad) should be similar to most other apps.

The Internet Is Required

To stream or download any programming using the mobile app from your cable or satellite TV service provider, a continuous Internet connection is required. However, if you've chosen to download content, after that programming is stored within your mobile device, the Internet connection is no longer needed to later watch that programming.

(1) Download and install the Xfinity TV Go mobile app from the App Store (iPhone/iPad) or Google Play Store (Android) (not shown).

(2) From the Home screen, launch the app.

(3) Sign in to the app using the user-name (email address) and pass-word that's associated with your Comcast/Xfinity account. You need to do this only once. The app stores your log-in information and automatically signs you in each subsequent time you launch the app (not shown).

(4) Tap the command icon for the category you want to explore. Options are Featured, TV Series, Movies, Live, Family/Kids, Networks, and Downloads. (See the sidebar, "The Xfinity TV Go App's Main Functions," for infor-mation about what each of these command icons is used for.)

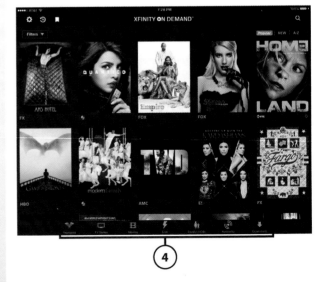

(5) Tap the TV show, movie, or programming you want to watch.

(6) When you tap a listing for a TV series, you see a list of available seasons and episodes. Tap the listing for the episode you want to watch.

(7) Tap the Play button to begin streaming the selected episode from the Internet to your mobile device.

(8) When the option is available, tap the Download button to download and store the program within your mobile device so you can watch it anytime later.

Download Time Varies

The amount of time a program takes to download depends on the speed of your Internet connection. In some cases, it might take a little while for the file to download.

9 Tap the middle of the screen to use the onscreen controls to play/pause, fast forward, rewind, and turn on/off closed captioning. After a few seconds, these icons disappear.

Programs Aren't Always Commercial Free

Keep in mind that if the TV episode or movie you select originally aired on a channel or network that includes commercials, commercials will also be included within the programming you watch (stream or download) using the mobile app.

10 Tap the Additional Episodes icon when a show is playing to view listings for other episodes available from that series (when applicable).

11 Tap the Playlist icon to view a listing of shows you've saved to watch later.

12 Tap the Bookmark icon to save the particular episode or movie you're watching to quickly be able to come back to it later.

13 Tap the Done option to return to the app's previous screen.

THE XFINITY TV GO APP'S MAIN FUNCTIONS

Displayed along the bottom of the screen are a handful of command icons for controlling the features and functions built in to the Xfinity TV Go mobile app.

Tap the Featured icon to see listings for featured TV shows, movies, and other programming that you can stream for free.

Tap the TV Series icon to see listings for current and popular TV series that are available for streaming. After you tap a series listing, a separate screen displays all the episodes available from the current and past season(s), when applicable.

Tap the Movies icon to see a listing of movies that are available for free, and on an on-demand basis, using the Xfinity TV Go mobile app.

Tap the Live icon to select a channel or network that you want to stream to your mobile device and watch live. The selection of channels that are available for live streaming is much smaller than the channel lineup you pay for as part of your Xfinity cable TV service.

Tap the Family/Kids icon to see a selection of kid-friendly TV shows and movies offered by the various channels and networks that compose your channel lineup when watching your television at home.

Tap the Networks icon to search for specific shows or movies to watch, sorted by television network. Tap a specific network to then see a listing of programming that's available.

If you've used the Download feature to download and store programming on your mobile device (instead of streaming it), listings for the content that's stored within the app are displayed when you tap the Download icon. Tap any listing to begin watching the saved programming.

Use the Xfinity TV Go's Search tool to find any programming offered by the app. Within the Search field, enter the title of a TV show or movie, the name of an actor, or any keyword or search phrase that will help you find what you're looking for.

Remotely Accessing Your TiVo DVR

If you have a TiVo DVR (digital video recorder) connected to your television set at home, you probably use it to record and later watch all your favorite television shows and movies. TiVo makes it very easy to record a single episode of a show or automatically record all episodes of your favorite show(s).

Learn More About TiVo DVRs

TiVo DVRs are sold at retail stores, such as Best Buy, Target, and Walmart. You can learn more about them, and purchase them online, from the TiVo website (www. TiVo.com).

Beyond taking advantage of TiVo's features while you're sitting in front of your television set, you can use the TiVo mobile app to program your TiVo DVR remotely and then stream programs you've recorded directly to your mobile device (via the Internet), so you can watch that content from anywhere.

DVR Functionality May Already Be Built In to Your Cable or Satellite TV Receiver Box

Although TiVo is the only major company that manufactures standalone DVRs that can connect to any HD television set, many cable or satellite TV service providers offer DVR functionality (the capability to record shows) built in to some of their respective cable or satellite TV receiver boxes. Often, however, there is an extra charge to purchase or rent these cable or satellite TV receiver boxes with built-in DVR functionality. In some cases, but not all, these DVR boxes can also be programmed, accessed, and controlled using the cable service provider's mobile device app, and they offer some similar functionality to the TiVo DVRs.

The free TiVo app handles multiple tasks. With it you can do the following:

- Use it as a virtual remote control for the TiVo while you're watching TV at home. Use it to change channels, fast forward, pause, or rewind while you're watching a show, or you can program your TiVo to record specific programming.

- Use it to remotely program your TiVo DVR from anywhere.

- View a comprehensive programming schedule for all the TV channels and networks you receive on your TV set (via your cable/satellite TV service provider).

- Use the TiVo Bolt (or another TiVo model with streaming capabilities) to stream any programming you've recorded on your TiVo DVR and watch it on your mobile device. A continuous Internet connection is required.

- Transfer (wirelessly download via the Internet) shows you've recorded on your TiVo DVR to your mobile device and store them there so you can later watch them anywhere without an Internet connection. This feature does not work with all programming because of copyright issues. If this feature is not available for a selected program, the mobile app doesn't offer the Download option.

- Manage multiple TiVo devices within your home at once from the mobile app.

- Access various streaming services that you subscribe to, such as Amazon Prime Video, Hulu, Netflix, and YouTube.

Additional Equipment May Be Required for Streaming

If you have one of the older TiVo models, you need to purchase the optional TiVo Stream accessory ($129.99, www.tivo.com/shop/detail/tivo-stream) to stream programming from your TiVo DVR to your mobile device. You connect it directly to the modem or Internet router within your home. However, if you've purchased the TiVo Bolt ($299.00–$399.00, www.tivo.com/bolt), streaming technology is built directly into it.

An ongoing paid subscription to the TiVo service ($149.00 per year) is also required to utilize any TiVo DVR and its streaming capabilities. A one-year subscription to the TiVo services comes with the TiVo Bolt DVR.

Use the TiVo Mobile App

The TiVo mobile app is available for the iPhone, iPad, and Android smartphones and tablets.

To use the TiVo mobile app, follow these steps:

(1) Download and install the free TiVo app from the App Store (iPhone/iPad) or Google Play App Store (Android) (not shown).

(2) Make sure your mobile device has Internet access. If you're at home, connect your smartphone or tablet to the same home wireless network as your TiVo DVR (not shown).

(3) Launch the app from your mobile device's Home screen.

(4) Sign in to the app using your TiVo account username (email address) and account password (not shown).

(5) Use the pull-down menu to select which TiVo device you want to access and control. (This applies only if you have multiple TiVo devices connected to different TV sets within your home.) Use the mobile app to control or manage one TiVo device at a time, and switch between devices at any time.

(6) Tap the What to Watch icon to see TiVo's recommendations based on shows you've previously watched and programming you've recorded.

7 Select a show or movie and then tap the Info icon to display a detailed description of that programming, including an interactive cast list (credits). Tap an actor, producer, or director's name, for example, to quickly find listings for their other work that you can access on-demand and watch.

8 Tap the Guide icon to see an interactive programming schedule for all channels you receive on your television set (via your cable TV service provider). You can scroll around the screen to select a specific day and time, or view listings for a specific channel or network's shows. This interactive guide provides listings up to two weeks in advance.

9 Tap the My Shows icon to view a listing of all programming that has been recorded and is currently stored within your TiVo DVR.

Choose Between Programming on Your TiVo or iPad

After tapping the My Shows icon, you can view recorded programming that's stored on your TiVo DVR (but that has not been transferred to your iPhone or iPad) by selecting the default On DVR tab. However, to see recorded programming that has been transferred to and is now saved on your iPhone or iPad, tap the On iPhone or On iPad (shown) tab.

To transfer a show from your TiVo to your mobile device, tap the My Shows option, select a recorded show by tapping its listing, and then tap the Download button while your mobile device is connected to the Internet. After the file has been transferred, you can watch that programming offline.

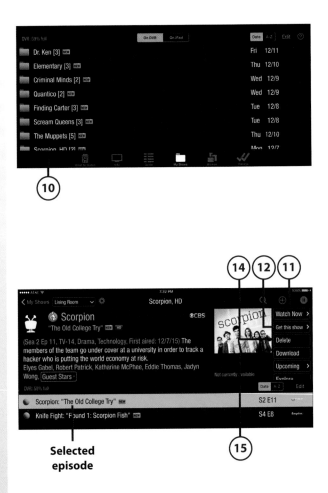

(10) Tap a listing to see a description screen for that stored programming.

(11) Tap the Watch Now option to watch the show on your TV set or stream it to your mobile device.

(12) Tap Get This Show to record additional episodes of the show.

(13) Tap OnePass to manage the OnePass associated with the show (which allows TiVo to record all or specific episodes of the show. In some cases, this option is part of the menu. Otherwise, tap the Get This Show option, and the first option within the submenu is Create a OnePass.

(14) Tap Delete to remove the selected episode of the selected/series from your TiVo DVR.

(15) Tap the Download option (when available) to transfer the show from your TiVo to your mobile device, so you can watch it later.

Selected episode

16 Tap on the Upcoming option to view details about upcoming episodes (when applicable).

17 Tap Explore to view an interactive Credits/Cast list, or tap the More option (not shown) to access additional options (such as the capability to share details about a selected program on social media).

18 Tap the Browse icon to find programming that's sorted and displayed under headings along the left side of the screen.

19 Alternatively, tap the Search icon and then enter what you're looking for into the Search field.

20 Tap the Manage icon to manage your TiVo's To Do list and OnePasses to see and manage what shows and programming it is already programmed to record during the next two weeks. Tap any listing to change the recording options for a listed show or program.

21 Tap the Remote Control icon (if you're sitting in front of your television set that has a TiVo DVR connected to it) to see a virtual version of your TiVo's remote control.

Browse
headings

22 Use the controls on the virtual remote to control the TiVo the same as you would use the actual remote.

>>>Go Further
PLANNING AHEAD

When you're leaving your home (and the Internet connection within your home), it's important to plan ahead and determine what types of digital entertainment you will want access to while you're away. Next, determine whether you need to download content to your mobile device in advance, or if you'll be able to utilize your mobile device's Internet connection while you're out and about to access specific types of digital entertainment content.

For example, if you know you're about to spend many hours on an airplane that does not have Internet access, you need to download and store digital entertainment content that you want to access.

Meanwhile, if you'll be driving in your car, and your mobile device has Internet access via a cellular data (3G/4G/LTE) connection, you will be able to access and stream many forms of digital entertainment, but not all services work with a cellular data connection. Some require a continuous Wi-Fi Internet connection, which probably is not available within your vehicle. In general, you can download or stream music (from any service) to your mobile device. You can also download (or stream) other types of content that utilize smaller file sizes, like eBooks or audiobooks.

Although some streaming video services, such as Netflix, work with a cellular data connection, most don't. For example, to download a TV show or movie from the iTunes Store via your mobile device, you need a Wi-Fi Internet connection.

Experiencing Digital Entertainment in Your Vehicle

As quickly as the technology built in to television sets, smartphones, and tablets is changing and evolving, the same is true for technology that's built in to cars. In the past, cars came with an AM/FM radio preinstalled, and some included a CD or cassette player.

Today's vehicles still offer an AM/FM radio, but most also offer satellite radio (refer to Chapter 7, "The Evolution of Radio: Beyond AM and FM"). Many also offer an in-dash infotainment system, which includes an interactive screen and the capability to link your smartphone to the vehicle to stream content from the Internet. Every vehicle manufacturer has a different way of incorporating integration with various smartphone features. Apple and Google are working closely with most of the world's car manufacturers to incorporate smartphone compatibility into new cars.

If your vehicle has an in-dash infotainment system, chances are that you can connect your smartphone to your vehicle via a wireless (Bluetooth) connection or a cable. Then, from the car's in-dash screen, you can control specific apps that are installed on your smartphone. This allows you to listen to digital music (including audiobooks and audio podcasts) that are stored within your smartphone via your car's stereo system. You can also access your smartphone's cellular Internet connection to stream music from services like Apple Music, Pandora, Spotify, or iHeartRadio.

Stream Any Radio Station While in Your Car

Using the TuneIn Radio (free) or TuneIn Radio Pro ($9.99) mobile app that's available for the iPhone and Android smartphones, you can use your mobile device's Internet connection to access and then listen live to any of more than 100,000 radio stations from around the world. The TuneIn Radio Pro app also offers play-by-play programming from every MLB and BPL game, plus unlimited access to a library of more than 40,000 audiobooks.

When your smartphone is linked with your vehicle, it's possible to easily stream this programming from the Internet to your smartphone, and then from your smartphone, send it directly to your vehicle's in-dash infotainment system or stereo so you can listen to it via your car's speakers.

TuneIn Radio offers an alternative to satellite radio and does not have a broadcast signal that's limited by a geographic region. As long as your smartphone has Internet access via a 3G/4G/LTE connection, you can stream programming from any of the radio stations this app is compatible with.

Some in-dash infotainment systems allow you to run other smartphone apps and access specific smartphone features and functions while you're driving. By pressing a button that's built in to your steering wheel or dashboard, you can issue voice commands to your smartphone.

Thanks to your smartphone's Internet connection, your vehicle can access GPS and navigation information, weather and traffic information, and allow you to safely access text/instant messaging, email, and social media accounts without having to take your eyes off the road.

In some cases, if your vehicle has video monitors in the backseat, you can play TV shows and movies that are stored within your mobile device (or that are being streamed using your smartphone's Internet connection) to entertain your backseat passengers.

>>>*Go Further*

SOME VEHICLES HAVE THEIR OWN INTERNET CONNECTION

A growing number of new cars offer optional 4G LTE Internet access built in to the vehicle. For a monthly fee of between $15.00 and $50.00, your vehicle can have its own 4G cellular Internet connection, allowing its own in-dash infotainment system to access the Internet without using your smartphone's Internet connection.

This same 4G LTE Internet connection is able to create an in-vehicle Wi-Fi hotspot that your various mobile devices and video game systems can access while you're in the car. To determine if your new vehicle offers a 4G LTE Internet option, contact your dealer or car manufacturer.

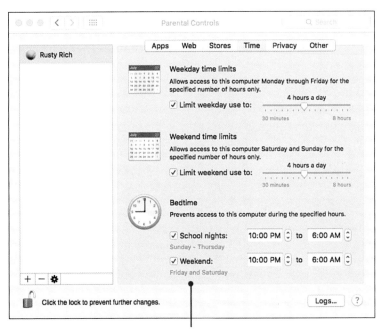

Use parental controls and restrictions to block
inappropriate content from your kids or grandkids.

This chapter shows you how to set up Parental Controls and Restrictions on computers, mobile devices, and other technologies to prevent your kids or grandkids from accessing content that is not appropriate for them. You'll discover

→ Ways to make an Internet-enabled computer safer for a child or teenager to use

→ Ways to add parental controls to a smartphone or tablet to prevent a child or teenager from accessing inappropriate content

→ How to prevent young people from watching inappropriate television shows and movies on a TV set

→ Advice about monitoring the video game–playing habits and the digital entertainment consumption of kids and teens

Using Parental Controls to Protect Your Kids and Grandkids

Your kids or grandkids are probably more technologically savvy than you are. However, you have the advantage because you are older, more experience, and most likely smarter and in possession of more common sense than they are.

There is a vast and ever-growing assortment of digital entertainment content readily available to us all, but not all of it is age appropriate or otherwise suitable for younger people. For example, there are graphically violent TV shows, movies, and videos games, as well as music and other content with strong and offensive language that you may not want your loved ones exposed to.

So, even if you don't fully understand the technology your kids or grandkids are using to access all the different forms of digital entertainment, you do have the wherewithal to monitor the content they're exposed to, and limit the availability of inappropriate content using a variety of tools that are at your disposal.

It is the responsibility of parents and grandparents to determine what types of content are appropriate for their own children or grandchildren and to set limits in terms of how much content, and what types of content, kids and teens are exposed to day to day. This has certainly become much more of a challenge as the choices for entertainment have expanded. Yet there is an arsenal of easy-to-use tools available to you help monitor, limit, and control the digital entertainment content your child or grandchild experiences.

Setting Firm Limits and Expectations

One of the best things you can do for your child or grandchild is to set limits in terms of their digital entertainment consumption, and make it very clear what they can and can't do. For example, set limits for how much time per day they can spend watching TV, playing video games, and/or surfing the Internet, and allow these activities only after they have finished their homework and completed their other responsibilities.

As the adult, you should have full access to every single account used by your child or grandchild that's used to purchase or access content on any computer, video game system, smartphone, and/or tablet they have access to. This includes email accounts and the device(s) they use for text messaging and to surf the Web.

Make it clear what activities are permissible, and what's not, and make having full access to their various computers, video game systems, smartphones, and tablets a privilege that is contingent on their willingness to adhere to your guidelines and rules. Let them know that you will be randomly checking all their accounts, monitoring what they're doing online, and investigating how they're using their mobile devices.

For most kids and teens, it's enough to set these limits and then enforce them. However, if you feel it's necessary, you have the ability to activate the parental control features on the various technologies that allow you to limit what's possible and to closely monitor their activities, even when you're not physically looking over a child's shoulder.

You should, however, make a habit of periodically looking over your children's or grandchildren's shoulders as they're watching TV, playing video games, using their computer, surfing the Internet, and/or using their mobile device. Ask them to show you specifically what they're doing.

Another smart strategy is to prevent younger kids from having computer, video game, and/or Internet access in their bedroom. Keep the technology accessible only in a public room, so your child/teen knows that an adult can walk in at any time. This also helps to prevent access to this content after bedtime.

It's Not All Good

None of the Parental Control Tools Are Foolproof

Although can use parental control tools to block certain types of content from your kids or grandkids or limit their activities when using specific computers, smartphones, tablets, or video game systems, none of these solutions are foolproof.

For example, if you lock down a computer or restrict access to specific content on a video game system, chances are your child knows he can simply go to a friend's house, use the friend's computer or video game system, and access whatever content he wants.

Plus, setting the parental controls on equipment involves creating a password or PIN (Personal Identification Number) that you, as the parent or grandparent create. If your child or grandchild discovers your password/PIN, he or she can unlock the restrictions and locks you have placed on the equipment.

To safeguard against this outcome, choose passwords/PINs they won't easily be able to figure out, and don't allow them to watch you entering this information. Also, change the parental control passwords/PINs often.

Setting Parental Controls

Depending on the type of computer, mobile device, or gaming system your child or grandchild will be using, the steps for setting up the parental controls vary. Keep in mind, it's your responsibility to set up this functionality on each piece of technology separately and then to monitor how your child or grandchild use the technology that's at their disposal.

Set Mac Controls

To set the parental controls and restrictions on a Mac, follow these steps:

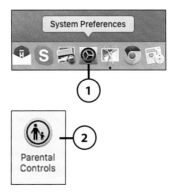

(**1**) Click System Preferences in the Dock. Alternatively, choose the System Preferences command from the Apple menu.

(**2**) Click Parental Controls.

(**3**) Select Create a New User Account with Parental Controls, or Convert This Account to a Parental Controls Account as appropriate, and then click Continue. This example is for creating a new account.

(**4**) Select the age of your child in the Age pull-down menu.

(**5**) Enter your child's full name.

(**6**) Type an account name. This will be used as the name of the Home Folder, where that user's data and files will be stored. Feel free to use the default account name that the computer generates for you.

(**7**) Create a password to be used by you to access the account. Reenter the password to confirm it when prompted.

(**8**) Click Create User.

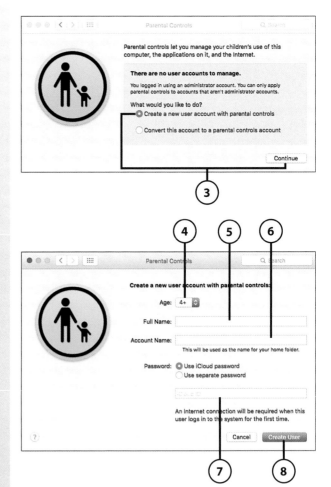

9 Click each command tab along the top of the screen to customize the locks and restrictions for that category.

10 Tap the Time tab, for example, to set what days your children or grandchildren can use the computer, and how much time during those days they'll have computer (and potentially Internet) access.

11 Click the Lock icon to require that a password be entered before the Parental Controls settings can be changed.

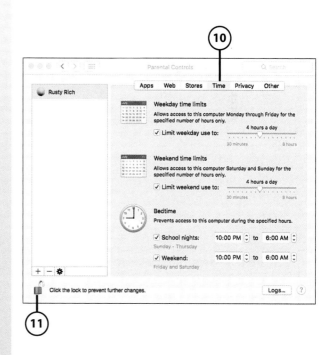

(12) Place a check mark in the check box associated with Manage Parental Controls from Another Computer if you want to be able to make adjustments to this computer's parental control settings remotely.

(13) Repeat these steps on each Mac that your child or grandchild will have access to (not shown).

Don't Forget to Adjust iTunes Store Settings

Be sure to also adjust the iTunes software-related Parental Control settings, which help to determine what content your child or grandchild can access. See the section "Set iTunes Store Parental Controls" later in this chapter.

Set Controls for Windows 10

PCs that are running the Windows 10 operating system also have parental controls built in that allow parents to lock down access to specific features, functions, and content. To access and set these controls, follow these steps:

(1) Make sure your computer has Internet access, and access Settings from the desktop or Start menu (depending on how your computer is set up).

2 Click Accounts.

3 Click Family & Other Users.

4 Click the + Add a Family Member option.

(5) Click the Add a Child option and then enter the email address associated with the child's Microsoft Account. If the child doesn't already have an email address, you can set one up for free using AOL, Gmail, or Yahoo!.

(6) Click Next.

(7) Click Confirm to continue (not shown).

(8) An email message will be sent to your email address confirming the newly created account. A separate invitation gets sent to your child's email account (not shown).

(9) Open the email address to your child/grandchild by logging into her email account and accept the invitation. A web page on the Microsoft website opens.

(5)

×

Add a child or an adult?

Enter the email address of the person you want to add. If they use Windows, Office, Outlook.com, OneDrive, Skype, or Xbox, enter the email address they use to sign in.

⦿ Add a child

Kids are safer online when they have their own account

◯ Add an adult

rusty@mypalrusty.com ×

The person I want to add doesn't have an email address

Next   Cancel

(6)

Microsoft Family   Today at 1:44 PM   MF
To: jasonrich77@yahoo.com
Jason invited you to join their family

▓ Microsoft

Jason would like you to join their family as a child.

When you accept, the adults in your family can help you stay safe online while still giving you the freedom to explore and do things on your own.

Accept Invitation

This invitation will expire in 14 days.

(9)

(10) Click the Yes button.

(11) Visit the Help Keep Your Kids Safer Online web page of the Microsoft website (https://account.microsoft.com/family).

(12) Sign back in to your Microsoft account, if applicable, using your own Microsoft Account username and password (not shown).

(13) Click the Family tab and then click the newly created account listing for your child or grandchild.

(14) From the Recent Activity screen, you now have access to the child's account. For example, if you turn on the virtual switch associated with Activity Reporting, you can keep tabs on everything your child does on the computer when he's logged into his account (not shown).

(15) Under the Recent Activity heading, click each additional option—Web Browsing; Apps, Games & Media; Screen Time; Purchase & Spending; Find Your Child; and Xbox Privacy Settings—to customize settings for each option.

(16) For example, click Screen Time to control how much time your child can spend using the computer. Start by turning on the virtual switch that's associated with this option, and then for each day of the week, set the hours your child can use the computer, and then how many hours per day total she can use the computer.

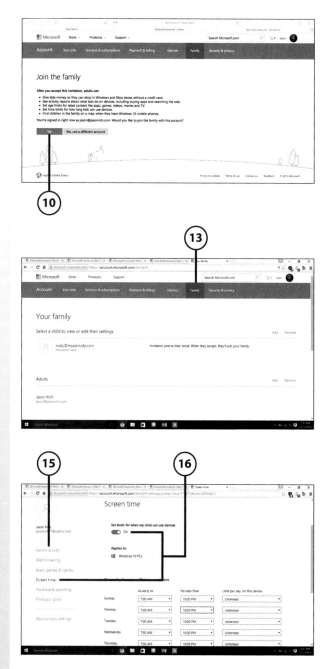

(17) Close the web browser window when you're done setting options. The controls you added to your child's account go into effect immediately.

>>>Go Further

CONSIDER INSTALLING OPTIONAL PARENTAL CONTROL SOFTWARE

For between $20.00 and $50.00, you can purchase optional parental control software from a handful of third-party companies.

Within the Search field of any web browser, enter the phrase **parental control software** to discover easy-to-set-up programs, such as McAfee Safe Eyes ($49.95, www.internetsafety.com/safe-eyes-parental-control-software.php), NetNanny ($39.99, www.netnanny.com), and Norton Family Premier ($19.99, http://us.norton.com/norton-family-premier).

Be sure to load the software onto each computer your child/grandchild will be using or have access to.

Set iTunes Store Parental Controls

Although each iTunes account is linked to a debit or credit card, and you probably control the card on your child or grandchild's account, it's also possible to use prepaid iTunes Gift Cards (available at many stores) to acquire content. So, your children can go to any retail store, purchase an iTunes gift card using cash (such as their allowance), redeem the card from their iTunes account, and use it to acquire content.

If you want to prevent your child or grandchild from being able to watch Rated PG or Rated-R movies, age inappropriate TV shows, or music with explicit lyrics, you probably want to set up the parental controls on your computers that run the iTunes software, as well as on the iPhone, iPad, and/or iPod touch.

Set Controls from a Computer

(1) Launch the iTunes software on any Mac or PC computer. Click the Sign In button.

(2) Sign in to your child or grand-child's Apple ID account, using the email address that's associated with her Apple ID and her password (not shown).

(3) On a Mac, access the iTunes pull-down menu that's located in the top-left corner of the screen. If you're using the iTunes software on a Windows PC, press Control+B to access the iTunes menu bar, and then choose the Edit option.

(4) Select Preferences.

(5) Click the Restrictions icon.

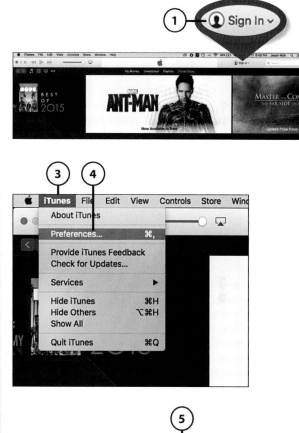

6 Add check marks to any options under the Disable heading that you want to deactivate, so your child or grandchild won't have access to those features.

7 Leave the Ratings For default option set to United States, if you're within the United States. Otherwise, change to the appropriate country.

8 Add a check mark to the Music with Explicit Content check box to block your child or grandchild from listening to music that contains explicit lyrics.

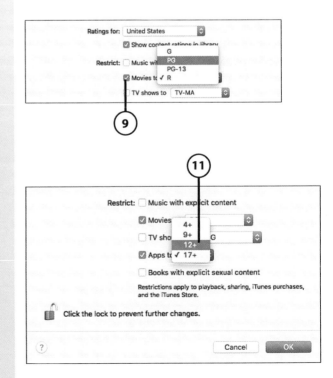

9 Add a check mark to the Movies To check box, and then access the pull-down menu to determine what movie ratings are permissible.

10 Add a check mark to the TV Shows To check box, and then access the pull-down menu to determine what TV ratings are permissible (not shown).

11 Add a check mark to the Apps To check box and then access the pull-down menu to determine what app ratings are permissible. If you select the 12+ option, they will be able to access apps with a 4+, 9+, or 12+ rating, but not a 17+ rating. (These ratings are based on age appropriateness.)

12 Add a check mark to the Books with Explicit Sexual Content check box if you want to prevent your child or grandchild from downloading or accessing eBooks with a sexual theme or content.

13 When you're done adjusting options, click the lock icon and enter the system administrator password that's associated with the computer you're using to save your changes and put the parental controls into effect.

14 Click OK to close the dialog box.

Set Controls on an iOS Mobile Device

1 From the iPhone, iPad, or iPod touch's Home screen, launch Settings.

2 Tap General.

3 Tap Restrictions.

(4) Tap Enable Restrictions.

(5) Set a four-digit passcode. Do not give this code to your child or grandchild.

(6) Reenter the newly created passcode when prompted. Do not forget this passcode (not shown).

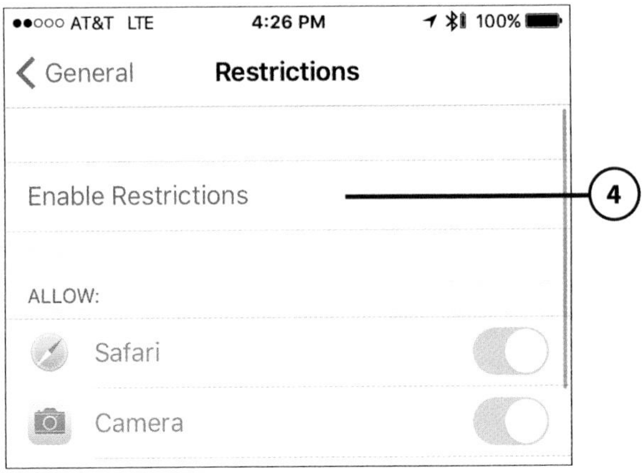

●●ooo AT&T LTE   4:26 PM   ⊀ ✶ 100% 🔋

❮ General   **Restrictions**

Enable Restrictions   —— (4)

ALLOW:

  🧭 Safari   ⚪

  📷 Camera   ⚪

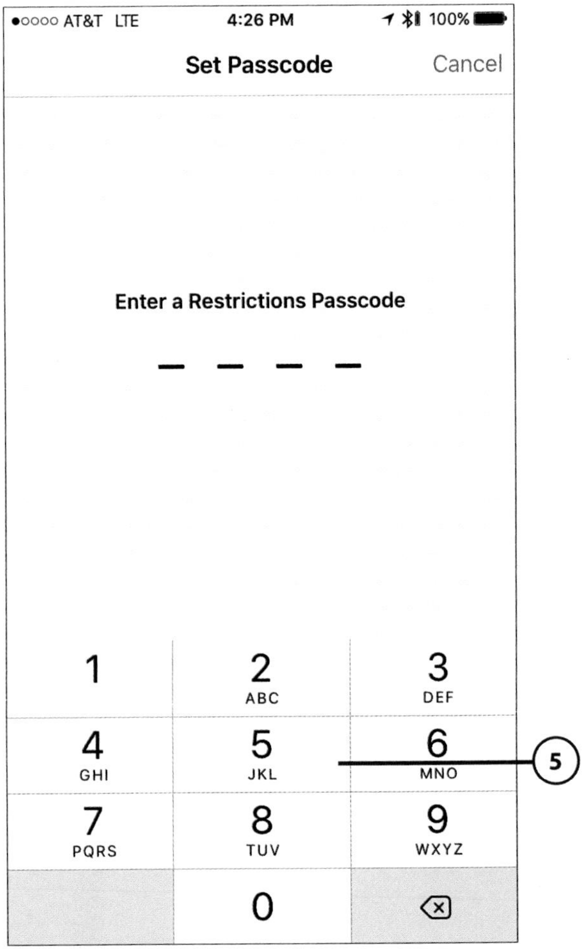

●oooo AT&T LTE   4:26 PM   ⊀ ✶ 100% 🔋

Set Passcode   Cancel

Enter a Restrictions Passcode

— — — —

1	2 ABC	3 DEF
4 GHI	5 JKL	6 MNO —— (5)
7 PQRS	8 TUV	9 WXYZ
	0	⊗

⑦ Turn off the virtual switch for any feature you do not want your child to have access to. Swipe up to scroll down the page to see all the options available.

Restrict Access to Features and Functions

When you turn off the virtual switch for any function or service listed within the Restrictions menu, your child or grandchild will not be able to access or use that feature. For example, if you turn off the virtual switch associated with iTunes Store, the child will not be able to access the online-based iTunes Store to acquire music, movies, TV shows, ringtones, or music videos.

```
••○○○ AT&T  LTE        4:27 PM        ⚡ ✻⃒ 100% ▰
❮ General        Restrictions


  Disable Restrictions


  ALLOW:

  🧭  Safari                           ⬤
  📷  Camera                          ⬤
  🎤  Siri & Dictation                 ⬤——⑦
  📹  FaceTime                        ⬤
  📡  AirDrop                         ⬤
  ▶  CarPlay                         ⬤


  🎵  iTunes Store                    ⬤
  🎶  Apple Music Connect             ⬤
  📖  iBooks Store                    ⬤
  🎙  Podcasts                        ⬤
```

(8) Below the Allowed Content heading, tap Ratings For to select your country or region. If you're from the United States and registered the mobile device within the USA, the default option will be United States.

(9) Tap Music, Podcasts & News, and then turn off the virtual switch for the Explicit option (not shown) if you want to prevent your child or grandchild from accessing music, podcasts, or news stories that contain explicit language. This applies only to content acquired from the iTunes Store that will be listened to (or viewed) using the Music, Podcasts, or News apps.

(10) Tap Movies.

(11) Select what ratings are permissible. Add a check mark to all movie ratings that are permissible. This applies only to movies purchased or rented from the iTunes Store that will be watched using the Videos app.

(12) Tap TV Shows.

●○○○ AT&T LTE   4:27 PM   ◀ ✳↕ 100% ▰

‹ General   **Restrictions**

(Ⓐ) In-App Purchases   ⬤◯

ALLOWED CONTENT:

Ratings For   United States › — **(8)**

Music, Podcasts & News   Explicit › — **(9)**

Movies   All › — **(10)**

TV Shows   All › — **(12)**

Books   All ›

Apps   All ›

Siri   All ›

Websites   All ›

PRIVACY:

Location Services   ›

Contacts   ›

●●○○ AT&T LTE   4:28 PM   ◀ ✳↕ 100% ▰

‹ Restrictions   **Movies**

ALLOW MOVIES RATED

Don't Allow Movies

G   ✓

PG   ✓ — **(11)**

PG-13   ✓

R

NC-17

Allow All Movies

13 Select what TV show ratings are permissible on that device. This applies only to TV shows that are acquired from the iTunes Store that will be watched using the Videos app.

14 Tap Books and then turn off the virtual switch associated with the Explicit Sexual Content option (not shown) if you want to prevent your child or grandchild from reading or accessing eBooks (acquired from Apple's eBook Store) that have explicit sexual content.

15 Tap Apps.

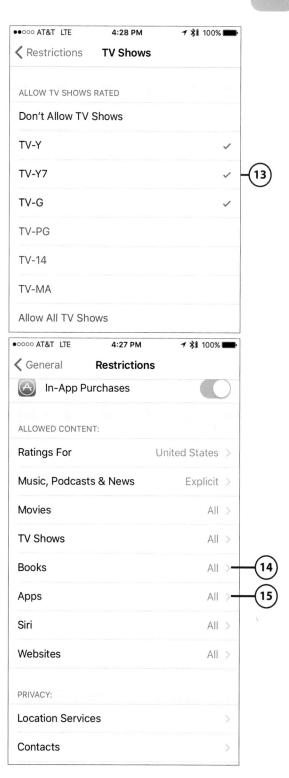

(16) Select what app age ratings are permissible on the mobile device. Tap all options that are allowable for your child or grandchild. This applies to all apps acquired from the App Store.

(17) Tap Siri to determine whether Siri can be used, and if so, the types of information Siri can access.

(18) Tap Websites.

●●●○○ AT&T LTE　　　4:28 PM　　　✈ ✲▮ 100% ▬▬

❮ Restrictions　　**Apps**

ALLOW APPS RATED

Don't Allow Apps

4+　　　　　　　　　　　　　　　✓

9+　　　　　　　　　　　　　　　✓　—(16)

12+　　　　　　　　　　　　　　✓

17+

Allow All Apps

●○○○○ AT&T LTE　　　4:27 PM　　　✈ ✲▮ 100% ▬▬

❮ General　　**Restrictions**

(A)　In-App Purchases　　　　　⬤◯

ALLOWED CONTENT:

Ratings For　　　　　　United States ❯

Music, Podcasts & News　　　Explicit ❯

Movies　　　　　　　　　　　All ❯

TV Shows　　　　　　　　　　All ❯

Books　　　　　　　　　　　　All ❯

Apps　　　　　　　　　　　　All ❯

Siri　　　　　　　　　　　　All ❯ —(17)

Websites　　　　　　　　　　All ❯ —(18)

PRIVACY:

Location Services　　　　　　　　❯

Contacts　　　　　　　　　　　　❯

19 Determine what websites your child or grandchild will be able to access using the Safari web browser. Your options include All Websites, Limit Adult Content, and Specific Websites Only. If you select the Specific Websites Only option, you see a list of kid-friendly websites; add other websites to the list by tapping Add a Website and entering the website's URL.

●●○○○ AT&T LTE   4:29 PM   ⍋ ⁎ 100% ━━

❮ Restrictions   **Websites**   Edit

ALLOWED WEBSITES

All Websites

Limit Adult Content

Specific Websites Only   ✓ **19**

Allow access only to the websites below.

ONLY ALLOW THESE WEBSITES:

Apple — Start   ›

CBeebies (by BBC)   ›

Discovery Kids   ›

Disney   ›

HowStuffWorks   ›

National Geographic - Kids   ›

PBS Kids   ›

Scholastic.com

20 Under the Privacy heading, tap each option, one at a time, to determine how specific iPhone, iPad, or iPod touch functions can be accessed by your child or grandchild (not shown).

21 Under the Allow Changes heading, tap each option, one at a time, to determine whether your child or grandchild will be allowed to adjust certain settings that allow account-related information to be changed. If the child is under the age of 16, prevent any changes from being made to all options listed under this heading.

22 Tap the two options listed under the Game Center heading to determine whether your child or grandchild is allowed to play multiplayer games on the mobile device, and if so, who they can play these games with.

23 When you're done adjusting the options on the Restrictions menu, exit out of this submenu by tapping the General option, or press the Home button to save your changes.

24 Repeat these steps on each iPhone, iPad, or iPod touch mobile device that your child or grandchild will have access to (not shown).

23

●●●○○ AT&T LTE   4:29 PM   ⬈ ✱⬇ 100% ▬▬▶

❮ General   **Restrictions**

Microphone   ❯

Twitter   ❯

Facebook   ❯

Advertising   ❯

ALLOW CHANGES: **21**

Accounts   ❯

Cellular Data Use   ❯

Background App Refresh   ❯

Volume Limit   ❯

GAME CENTER: **22**

Multiplayer Games   ⬤

Adding Friends   ⬤

Keep the Passcode Safe

Don't forget the Restrictions passcode you created. If you forget the code, you will not be able to regain full access to the iPhone, iPad, or iPod touch you're using without first erasing all of its contents, and then setting it up as a new device. Most important, never give this passcode to your child or grandchild.

Turn On iCloud Family Sharing's Ask to Buy Feature

If you set up the iCloud Family Sharing feature, the adult who sets up this account can then activate the Ask to Buy feature. Anytime your child or grandchild wants to make any purchase or acquire content from the iTunes Store, App Store, or Apple's iBook Store, you receive a text message asking for your approval, before they can access the requested content (unless they use a prepaid iTunes Store Gift Card to acquire that content).

To learn more about iCloud Family Sharing and how it works with content purchased and acquired from the iTunes Store, visit https://support.apple.com/en-us/HT201060.

Set Controls on an Android Device

If your child or grandchild has access to an Android smartphone or tablet, you need to add a third-party app to the device to set parental controls.

The following is information on how to use the Kids Place–Parental Controls app, which is available for free (with in-app purchases available), from the Google Play Store:

1. Make sure your Android smart-phone or tablet is connected to the Internet (not shown).

2. Launch the Google Play Store.

③ Type **Kids Place** (or **parental controls** to find another app) into the Search field.

④ Tap the listing for Kids Place or whichever parental controls app you're interested in to see the app's description screen.

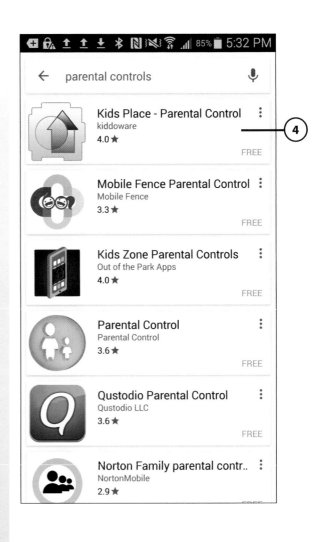

5 Read the description and reviews for the app and take a look at the sample screenshots and/or preview video. If you want to install the app, tap the Install button.

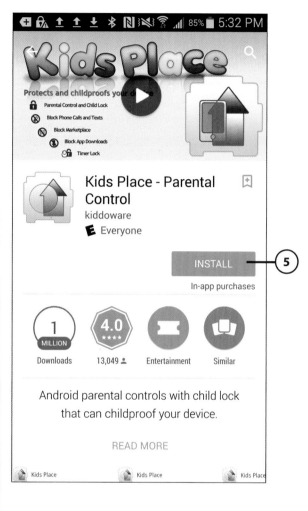

(6) Tap the Accept button to continue.

(7) The app downloads and automatically installs onto the Android smartphone or tablet you're using.

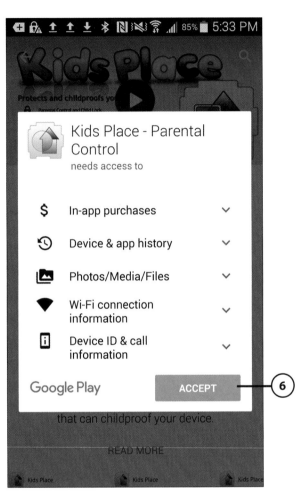

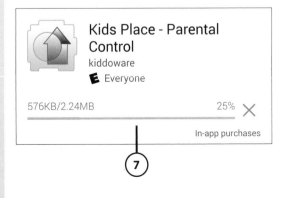

8 Tap the Open button to launch the app after the installation process is complete (which takes about 15 seconds). You can also launch the app by tapping its icon on the Home screen (not shown).

9 Tap the Accept button on the License screen.

License

END-USER LICENSE AGREEMENT AND PRIVACY POLICY

This End-User License Agreement ("EULA") is a legal agreement between you and General Solutions and Services, LLC (operating under Kiddoware brandname). By installing, copying, or otherwise using the SOFTWARE PRODUCT, you agree to be bound by the terms of this EULA. This license agreement represents the entire agreement concerning the program between you and General Solutions and Services, LLC (referred to as "licenser"). If you do not agree to the terms of this EULA, do not install or use the SOFTWARE PRODUCT.

IMPORTANT NOTE:
Kids Place Parental Control app is created for parents and does not ask

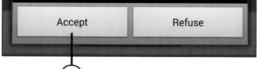

Accept   Refuse

9

10 Read the tips for how to effectively use the app, and then tap Set PIN to create a four-digit pin that you use to control the app's settings. Do not share this PIN with your kids or grandkids.

11 You have the option to lock the Home button and select which installed apps your kids/grandkids will have access to. Tap Select Apps for Kids Place, and then scroll through each app listed on the screen. Tap an app's icon if you want your child to have access to that app. Tap Done to continue.

Kids Place

Quick Tips:

· Go to "Settings > Manage Apps" to add apps your kids use to Kids Place.

· To exit Kids Place select "Exit" from the main menu.

· Go to "Settings > Parental Controls" to change lock settings.

· Checking the "Lock home button" setting makes Kids Place more secure by changing Android home temporarily. *Recommended*

· Checking the "Auto restart apps" setting causes a launched app to restart within a few seconds of it terminating. If your child accidentally exits an app this setting can come in handy.

Set PIN ▶

10

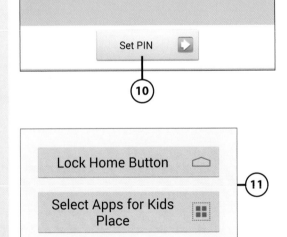

Lock Home Button ⌂

Select Apps for Kids Place ▦

11

(12) From the app's main menu, tap on each option, one at a time, to adjust specific settings related to what apps, content, and mobile device features your child or grandchild will have access to, and also when and how much time they can spend using the mobile device.

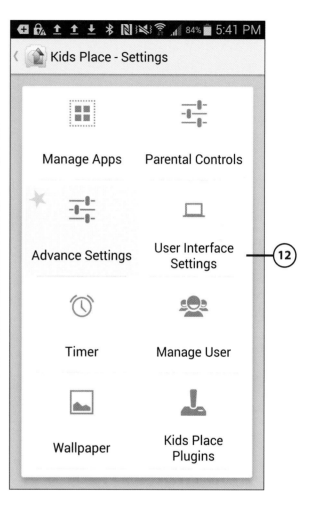

(13) Your child/grandchild will see a customized version of the Home screen that displays only permitted app icons and functions. To exit Kids Place and regain full access to the mobile device, tap the Exit button and enter your parental passcode PIN.

Exit button

Set Controls on Other Devices

If you subscribe to a cable or satellite TV service and have a receiver box connected to your television set, or if you have a console-based video game system and/or DVR connected to your television set, each of these devices also has parental controls associated with it that you can set to limit what programming and content your children/grandchildren can watch or have access to.

In some cases, you can also determine when they can watch television and/or can play games (between what hours), and for how long (number of hours per day) they can watch/play each day.

How to set the parental controls related to your cable/satellite TV services, video game systems, DVR, and/or streaming device varies, based on the service you subscribe to and the equipment that's connected to your television set. In general, you turn on the television set and press the Menu button on the remote control device (or game controller) that was provided with the equipment. From the device's main menu, scroll down to the Parental Controls option, select and highlight it on your TV's screen, and press the Select/OK button. Then follow the onscreen prompts to set your parental control password or PIN and adjust each available setting.

Set Parental Controls Once on Each Device

The parental controls on each device that's connected to your television set need to be set separately. This needs to be done only once per device, and you can adjust settings later at any time.

Separate parental controls are also available from streaming services, such as Amazon Prime Video, Hulu, Netflix, and YouTube/YouTube Red. For example, from the Manage Profiles screen of Netflix, click a child/teen's account. From the Edit Profile menu, click the pull-down menu associated with the Allowed TV Shows and Movies option to set limits as to what that person can watch based on content ratings.

After you set the parental control password/PIN for a specific device, be sure you do not share this with your kids or grandkids, or they'll be able to override whatever controls you set.

10 Web Surfing Tips That'll Keep You Safe

Throughout this book, you have discovered many ways the Internet can be used to give you immediate, on-demand access to a wide range of digital entertainment. The same Internet can also be used for many other purposes, such as surfing the Web to visit various web pages; sending and receiving emails; online shopping; and online banking.

In general, using the Internet is fun, safe, and a straightforward process. However, there are criminals lurking in cyberspace who want to take advantage of others, and you need to know how to keep yourself safe.

The following 10 strategies will help you avoid becoming a target of an online crime or scam and help you protect yourself against becoming a victim of identity theft as you use the Internet in your everyday life.

How to Identify Identity Theft

If you think you've become a victim of identity theft, it's essential that you take action immediately by reporting the problem to your bank(s), credit card issuer(s), and the credit reporting agencies (Equifax, TransUnion, and Experian). Visit this website for tips on how to do this: www.identitytheft.gov/sample-letters.html.

To learn more about how to determine if you've become an identity theft victim, visit the Consumer Federal Protection Bureau's website at www.consumerfinance.gov/askcfpb/1359/how-can-i-spot-identity-theft.html.

You can find additional tips for protecting yourself from identity theft at www.annualcreditreport.com/protectYourIdentity.action.

Use Secure Passwords

One of the downsides of surfing the Web and handling tasks online is that for many websites you visit, it's necessary to set up an account. This means creating a username (or associating an email address) and a password for each account.

Although you can associate the same email address or username with many accounts, it's important that you use a different password with each account. Doing this helps keep all your accounts more secure, but the result is that you have to remember and keep track of many passwords.

The ideal password for each account you need to set up should be at least eight characters long, include upper- and lowercase letters, and include at least one number in the sequence. As you're creating your passwords, avoid using words that are common or easy to figure out.

For example, the word "password" is the most commonly used password among people using the Internet. Don't use it! Using your name, dog's name, child's name, spouse's name, maiden name, or birth date are all commonly used passwords that should also be avoided. In addition, avoid using ABCDEFGH, 12345678, 87654321, or ABCD1234 as your password.

To make your passwords easier to remember, use a seemingly random word that has some meaning to you, and include an unrelated number to it. For example, the word "superman" is an okay password, but when you add capital letters and a number to the password, making it "SuperMan572," "572SuperMan," or "Super572Man," you have a much more secure password.

>>>Go Further

WAYS TO REMEMBER YOUR PASSWORDS

There are many methods people use to remember all their account usernames and passwords. The most obvious is to write them all down in a notebook.

If you use this method, never allow that notebook to leave your home or office. When it's not in use, keep it locked in a drawer, and away from your computer. If that notebook gets lost or stolen, the person who finds (or steals) it will have complete access to all your online accounts, which is something you definitely want to avoid.

Another option is to allow your web browser to automatically store your usernames and passwords as they're created, and then automatically sign you back in to websites when you revisit them. All Apple computers and mobile devices offer a feature, called iCloud Keychain, that can be turned on to handle this task for you.

This option is perfect if you're the only person using your mobile device or computer. However, if others have access to your equipment, they can easily access your computer or mobile device's web browser, visit websites you've visited in the past, and then have the web browser sign in using your account information. The person using your equipment will then have access to your accounts.

A third option is to use a secure and encrypted password database application (also called a digital wallet application) that works with all your computers and mobile devices. Dashlane (www.dashlane.com) is an example of a digital wallet application that works with PCs, Macs, iPhones, iPads, and all Android smartphones and tablets. Dashlane allows you to create a single, password-protected database that includes all your account usernames and passwords. It then stores this information online and allows you to securely sync your database with your own computers and mobile devices.

Yes, you'll need to remember one username and password to access your Dashlane account, but all your other usernames and passwords are kept secure. Using Dashlane with one computer or mobile device is free. A Dashlane Premium account costs $39.99 per year. With a Premium account you can sync your password database with all your computers and mobile devices.

The drawback to using a digital wallet application on your computers and mobile devices is that it's your responsibility to update the database every time you create a new account or change an account password. This does not typically happen automatically. But, after the account information is stored within the database, it's readily accessible to you when you need it.

In addition to Dashlane, two other popular digital wallet/password database applications you can consider using with your mobile device and/or computer are Keeper Password Manager ($29.99/year, https://keepersecurity.com) and Password Manager Vault ($59.99, http://passwordvaultmanager.com).

Change Your Passwords Regularly

After you set up an online account, whether it's for email, online banking, online shopping, or something else that allows you to manage and store personal and potentially confidential information, it's important for you to get into the habit of changing your account passwords regularly, at least for your most frequently used and important accounts.

Manually changing your passwords every four to six weeks is a good strategy. It's also a good idea to change your password(s) immediately after you return from a vacation if you signed into your account(s) from public computers at Internet cafés, or if you believe your account(s) have been compromised for whatever reason.

Don't Follow Links to "Secure" Websites

If you receive an email that appears to be from your bank, credit card company, PayPal, an airline, or any financial institution, and that email is alerting you of a problem with your account, do not respond to that email or click any links or file attachments embedded within it.

It's very possible the email you've received is fake, and part of a *phishing* scheme. Criminals create and send emails that look like they come from legitimate banks or companies, and they try to scare you into responding immediately to the email by clicking a link or file attachment within the email.

These emails are typically fake and are designed to collect your personal information, passwords, as well as credit card or bank account numbers, so that the criminal who sent the fraudulent email can steal your identity or your money.

Most people receive at least several of these emails per week. Your best bet is to delete them without opening them, using your email management software. If you do open the email to read it, do not click any links or file attachments, because doing this will often result in you downloading and installing spyware or a virus onto your computer (or potentially your Android mobile device).

If you receive an email that you think might be legitimate, but you're not sure, instead of responding to that email in any way, pick up a phone and call the customer service phone number for the bank, credit card issuer, or company that's listed on the back of your credit card, debit card, or on your monthly statement. Do not call the phone number listed within the email.

Phishing Scheme Emails Often Look Legit

Emails that are part of a phishing scheme or online-based scan typically use the logo and name of a well-known business, such as a bank, credit card issuer, PayPal, or a major airline. The text within the email alerts you of some type of problem with your account and insists that you immediately click a link or attached file within that email. Don't be fooled by official-looking emails.

You can often tell if an email is fake by looking at the email address of the sender that's displayed within the From field. If the email says it's from Bank of America, for example, but the return address is from a random Gmail or Yahoo! email account, this is a clear indicator that it's fake.

Always Use a Credit Card When Shopping Online

Most of the time, shopping online, particularly with businesses you're already familiar with, is a safe, convenient, and fun way to shop. However, anytime you're making an online purchase, always use a major credit card, rather than a prepaid credit card or a debit card.

If you have a problem with the merchant, if the product you purchase is wrong or defective, or if you wind up placing an order with a disreputable company, you can contact your credit card issuer and pursue a chargeback or dispute.

However, if you paid using a debit card, the funds are immediately taken from your checking or savings account. If you ultimately need to have your bank intervene on your behalf, you will need to fill out a lot of forms, sign an affidavit, and in most cases, the bank will want to cancel your debit card and issue a replacement card (which could take up to seven business days). Then, if you do wind up getting your money back, the refund or funds recovery process could take 30 to 60 days.

Alternatively, Use a Secure Online Payment Service

Instead of using a major credit card when making online purchases, you have the option of using a secure online payment service, such as PayPal (www.paypal.com), Google Wallet (www.google.com/wallet), ApplePay (www.apple.com/apple-pay), Android Pay (www.android.com/pay), or MasterPass (https://masterpass.com).

However, be sure to link a major credit card—not your debit card, checking account, or savings account—to the account you set up with any of these services.

Manually Enter the Website URL That You Want to Visit

When surfing the Web, if you need to access the website for your bank, credit card issuer, a financial institution you do business with, or a company you plan to shop online with, always manually enter the correct website address (URL) you want to visit into the address bar of your web browser, so you know you wind up at the correct place.

If you click a link within an email or within another website, there's a chance you'll wind up visiting a spoof website, which is a website, created by a criminal, that's designed to look like a legitimate website for a bank, financial institution, or well-known business but that's actually designed to collect your personal and confidential information so it can be used for fraudulent purposes.

So, if you need to visit the website for Bank of America, for example, within the address bar of your web browser, type **http://www.bankofamerica.com**. This is particularly important to do if you receive a seemingly realistic email that brings to your attention a problem with your account, which according to the email, requires your immediate attention.

Don't Respond to Unusual Friend Requests on Social Media

The whole purpose of social media, and using services like Facebook, Twitter, Instagram, and other similar services, is to allow you to communicate with friends and family members via the Internet, and potentially meet new people who share similar interests.

More than one billion people from all over the world are active on Facebook. The service provides many ways to interact with other people. However, if you become active on any social media service and start receiving friend requests from total strangers who are not friends of friends or who have no connection to you whatsoever, it's a good idea to deny those friend requests.

One way online criminals and identity thieves seek out potential victims is by sending random friend requests on the various social media services. After you accept that friend request, the criminal will strike up seemingly casual online conversations, which over time will become more personal. At some point, the online friend will solicit information that will ultimately allow them to steal your identity or your money.

If an online friend (someone you've never met in real life), especially someone from another country, randomly asks you to send or wire them money so they can handle some type of personal emergency, don't do this, no matter how serious the request seems to be! This is a common ploy that many people fall victim to.

Avoid Sharing Your Social Security Number or Driver's License Number Online

In general, when you visit a website or communicate with someone online, you should never be asked to reveal your Social Security number, driver's license number, passport number, or an account password. These are all pieces of information that you should keep confidential because they can be used to more easily steal your identity.

There are a few exceptions to this rule, however. For example, if you're using a legitimate online travel-related website to book international travel, you will be required to supply your passport number. Likewise, if you're contacting the Department of Motor Vehicles in your state to renew your driver's license or car registration, or pay a ticket, you will likely be asked to provide your driver's license number.

Meanwhile, if you fill out a credit card, car loan, student loan, or mortgage application online, and you're visiting the website for a legitimate bank, credit card issuer, or financial institution, you will be asked for your Social Security number as part of the application process.

You'll also need to provide your Social Security number when you request copies of your credit reports from the www.AnnualCreditReport.com website, or contact the website for Experian, Equifax, and/or TransUnion, to request a copy of your credit report or credit score.

Every 12 months, as a consumer, you are entitled to one free copy of your credit report from each of the credit reporting agencies. It's an excellent strategy to request these credit reports and review them carefully for errors or for listings of accounts or loans that don't belong to you.

If you discover credit card accounts or loans on one or more of your credit reports that you did not authorize, or that don't belong to you, this is one of the ways to determine you've become a victim of identity theft.

>>>Go Further

HOW TO REQUEST COPIES OF YOUR CREDIT REPORTS

The easiest way to request a free copy of your credit report from Experian, TransUnion, and Equifax is to visit the www.AnnualCreditReport.com website and fill out the online request. This is the only website that's sanctioned by the federal government and all three credit reporting agencies. Many other similar-looking or -sounding websites exist, but these other sites charge you for your credit reports or require you to sign up for an independent credit-monitoring service that charges a hefty monthly or annual fee.

Another option is to contact each of the credit reporting agencies separately to request a copy of your free credit report, which you can do once every 12 months. To do this, visit www.experian.com, www.equifax.com, and www.transunion.com, and complete the online form, which will ask you for your name, address, date of birth, Social Security number, and other personal information.

When you request a free copy of your credit report from each credit reporting agency, it will not include your credit score. You can obtain a credit score for an additional fee, plus opt to pay for a three-in-one credit report that includes details from all three credit reporting agencies within one, easy-to-read report.

If you just want to see your credit score, there is a free service called Credit Karma (www.creditkarma.com) that will provide it, along with information on how to improve your credit score. In addition to the Credit Karma website, there's also a free Credit Karma mobile app available for the iPhone, iPad, and Android smartphones and tablets.

Alternatively, some credit card issuers, including Discover, now provide your credit score for free in conjunction with your monthly statement.

Avoid Doing Online Banking from Public Networks

Whenever possible, avoid doing tasks that involve sharing personal or financial information online when you're connecting to the Internet using a public Wi-Fi hotspot, or using a public computer within an Internet café, or one that's often found within the business center of hotels, for example.

There is a chance that a public Wi-Fi hotspot will not be secure, or that someone has loaded software onto the public computer you wind up using that records and shares personal information such as usernames, passwords, and account numbers.

Don't Respond to Emails from the Court or From an Airline You Did Not Book Travel With

One of the more popular online scams involves people receiving an official-looking email from a court stating that they've been summoned to appear. These emails are fraudulent and are designed to scare you into sharing your personal information. Ignore these emails, delete them, or mark them as spam within your Inbox.

In reality, if you have any business with any court within the United States, you will receive a notice in the mail (sent via Certified U.S. Mail), or you will be served (in person) by an officer of the court.

Likewise, if you receive an email from an airline that's confirming an expensive airline ticket for a trip you did not book, this too is part of a scheme to gather your personal information. You should ignore these emails, delete them, or mark them as spam within your Inbox.

It's Not All Good

No, You Did Not Just Win $1 Million Dollars

If you receive an email from a lottery, sweepstakes, or some other organization claiming you've won a massive cash prize or a free vacation, chances are this email message is part of a scam and should be ignored or immediately deleted.

Likewise, if you receive an unsolicited email talking about an inheritance or a request from a stranger located overseas who needs your help transferring money, these also are part of elaborate scams and should be ignored.

Another common scam involves you receiving an email from someone claiming to be a relative, who is "stuck" in a foreign country after having had their wallet stolen, for example. The request will be that you wire them money immediately. Do not do this! When you contact that relative by phone, you'll probably discover they're at home, perfectly safe, and have not sent you any emails.

>>>Go Further

CUTTING DOWN ON SPAM

You can do a few simple things to cut down on the amount of unsolicited email (spam messages) that you receive. First, when you receive one of these emails, do not respond to the offer. As soon as you do this, you'll find yourself added to many more email lists, and you'll receive even more unwanted spam messages.

Instead, send the message from your Inbox into your Spam or Junk folder. This should help your email management software prevent future emails from that same sender's address from reaching your Inbox.

Next, whenever you are asked by a website you visit to provide your email address, opt out of receiving promotional emails and select the option that prevents that company from sharing your email address with their "promotional partners" or selling your email address to other companies.

When you receive unsolicited emails, you can try clicking the Unsubscribe option that's often found at the bottom of the email message, but more often than not, this does not work. It simply informs that company that sent you the spam message that the email address it was sent to is legitimate and active.

There's a free service, called Unroll.me, that you can subscribe to by visiting the company's website, or by installing a free mobile app, that will help block unsolicited and unwanted emails from reaching your Inbox. For more information about this service, visit https://unroll.me.

Always Sign Off from Websites on Someone Else's Computer

Anytime you use someone else's computer or mobile device to sign in to any website—while you're at work, at an Internet café, or when visiting a friend's house, for example—always manually sign off from that website when you're done. Do not simply close the web browser window and then walk away from the computer.

To manually sign out from a website, click or tap the Sign Off, Sign Out, Log Off, or Log Out button, icon, or link. If this option is not prominently displayed on the website you're visiting, click your username or account name and look for this option.

Otherwise, if you simply walk away from the computer without signing off, someone else could potentially walk up to that computer or mobile device, reopen the browser window, and have full access to the account you were using.

>>>Go Further

ALWAYS USE COMMON SENSE WHEN SURFING THE INTERNET

The best way to protect yourself from online fraud, identity theft, or becoming the victim of any online crime is to use common sense whenever you're doing anything on the Internet. It's that simple! Even if you're not tech savvy, you should be able to determine when it's appropriate to share your personal information and when it's not.

In general, surfing the Internet, online shopping, managing your finances online, using social media, sending and receiving email, and most other online-based activities are perfectly safe—as long as you use common sense.

Always be careful about what information you share and whom you share information with. Avoid any websites that don't seem legitimate, as well as websites or email messages that contain offers that are too good to be true.

Glossary

The following is a summary of commonly used terminology that appears throughout this book:

Android The operating system created by Google that's used to run Android-based smartphones and tablets, including those manufactured by Samsung.

Apple OS X The operating system created by Apple that operates on all Mac desktop and notebook computers, including the iMac, Mac Pro, Mac mini, MacBook, and MacBook Air.

audiobook An audio version of a book that's read by a narrator and then listened to, in contrast to reading a physical book. Audiobooks are distributed in digital form, as well as on compact discs (CDs). Audible.com and Apple's iBook Store offer the world's largest collections of audiobooks.

cable/satellite TV receiver box The box that connects to a television set that enables it to receive programming from a cable or satellite television service provider, such as Comcast Xfinity, DirecTV, DishTV, or Time Warner Cable. A monthly fee is required to receive this programming, which typically includes more than 100 basic and premium cable channels, as well as all the major broadcast networks (ABC, CBS, FOX, NBC, and PBS).

cellular data connection How a smartphone or tablet connects to the Internet wirelessly, using a cellular signal, in contrast to a Wi-Fi signal. Based on the connection speed, it is referred to as a 3G, 4G, or 4G LTE connection.

cloud Online-based space where anyone can store data, documents, files, photos, and other content, in contrast to storing the content on a computer's internal hard drive or within a mobile device's internal storage. Cloud-based storage is accessed via the Internet.

digital entertainment Any form of entertainment, such as a television show, movie, music, audiobook, podcast, or eBook, that is distributed in digital form and that is accessible using a computer, mobile device, digital music player, eBook reader, or streaming device (that connects to a television set), for example.

digital music player This is either a dedicated device, such as an Apple iPod, that is designed to store and play digital audio files, or it's an app or software package that's used on a computer or mobile device to listen to digital audio files (including digital music files).

digital video recorder (DVR) A device that connects to a television set and allows programs to be recorded in a digital file format and stored within the hard drive that's build in to the DVR. This technology is built in to some cable or satellite television receiver boxes, or can be purchased as a standalone unit from a company such as TiVo.

download Content is sent via the Internet to a computer or mobile device, where it is saved as a digital file. After a file or content has been downloaded, it can then be accessed or utilized anytime later, without an Internet connection.

DVR *See digital video recorder.*

eBook The digital edition of a book that can be downloaded or transferred to an eBook reader, smartphone, tablet, or computer, and then read on a screen.

eBook reader A standalone device that is used specifically to download and read eBooks and digital editions of newspapers and magazines. It's a tablet with limited functionality. Amazon.com offers Kindle eBook readers, whereas Barnes and Noble offers Nook eBook readers. All full-function tablets, including the iPad and Android-based tablets, can function as an eBook reader when used with an appropriate app.

Facebook The world's most popular social networking service, with more than one billion active users. This is a popular way for people to communicate and exchange information online.

game app A mobile app that can transform a smartphone or tablet into a portable video game system. Some streaming devices, such as Apple TV, can also utilize game apps.

High-Definition Television (HD TV) A television set that's able to receive and display high-definition content that's offered in 720p, 1080p, or 4K resolution. An HD television set displays much more detailed and vibrant images than an older standard-definition television set. All the television networks and cable channels in the United States now broadcast their programming in HD.

in-app purchase A feature in an application or mobile app that requires an additional purchase to use it.

Internet radio *See streaming (Internet) radio.*

iOS An operating system designed by Apple that operates on all iPhones, iPads, and iPod touch mobile devices.

Mac A desktop or notebook computer manufactured and sold by Apple that runs the OS X operating system.

Microsoft Windows The operating system created by Microsoft that runs on PCs.

mobile app An application that is designed to run on a smartphone or tablet, and that's distributed by the Apple App Store (iPhone/iPad) or Google Play Store (Android), for example.

mobile device   Any smartphone or tablet that is capable of connecting to the Internet, running apps, and that can handle a wide range of tasks.

on-demand   The capability to access digital entertainment content, such as a television show, movie, or music, when and where the user wants to experience it on a computer, smartphone, tablet, or television set.

online shopping   The capability to use an Internet-connected computer or mobile device to shop for products and/or services online, in contrast to visiting a retail store.

parental controls   The tools offered by computers, smartphones, tablets, video game systems, digital music players, cable/satellite television service providers, and other devices that are used to access digital entertainment that allow adults to limit content that kids can experience or be exposed to. For example, parents or grandparents can prevent their kids or grandkids from accessing R-rated movies, music with explicit lyrics, or websites that showcase content that is not age appropriate.

playlist   A custom selection of songs that a user creates with a digital music player so that the user can access and enjoy music at any time. This is a modern equivalent to a cassette mix tape. A playlist can include any number of songs, from the same or different albums. Users can create as many separate playlists as they desire, each of which can include a different selection of handpicked songs.

podcast   An audio or video program that is distributed via the Internet, and that can be experienced on a computer or mobile device. Podcasts can be created and shared by anyone.

price comparison website   A website that allows you to quickly save money and find the best deal on any product by comparing what a handful of online-based stores and/or retailers are selling the desired product for.

satellite radio   Operated by Sirius/XM, this is a network of channels that are broadcast nationwide (and in Canada) via satellite. This programming can also be streamed to an Internet-enabled computer or mobile device.

search engine   An online-based directory of websites and content that's available on the World Wide Web. When you enter a keyword or search phrase into a search engine, a listing of related web pages is displayed, allowing you to quickly find what you're looking for on the Internet. Google.com, Yahoo.com, and Bing.com are examples of popular Internet search engines.

smartphone   A cellular telephone that's also able to handle a wide range of other tasks, such as sending/receiving text messages, managing email, contact management, scheduling, note taking, picture taking, and that can run many different apps.

social media   Online services that allow people to interact with one another by sharing messages, photos, video clips, and other content.

streaming The process of transferring video or audio-based content via the Internet to a compatible computer, mobile device, or streaming device. The content is sent to the equipment where it is displayed or played, but it does not get stored or saved. A continuous Internet connection is required to stream any type of audio or video programming.

streaming device A specialized device, such as Amazon Fire TV, Apple TV, or Google Chromecast, that connects to an HD television set and a home's Internet connection, allowing TV shows, movies, and music to be streamed from the Internet to the television set it's connected to. These devices work in conjunction with streaming video services (such as Netflix, Hulu, and/or Amazon Prime Video), as well as streaming music services (such as Apple Music, Pandora, or Spotify).

streaming music service A service that distributes music, on-demand via the Internet, to a computer, mobile device, or digital music player. In some cases, a paid subscription is required to access on-demand and commercial-free music, whereas other services are offered for free (but include commercials).

streaming (Internet) radio These are radio stations that broadcast their signal via the Internet, in addition to or instead of the AM or FM airwaves.

streaming video service These services provide access to TV shows, movies, music videos, and other content that gets streamed on-demand, from the Internet to a computer, smartphone, tablet, or streaming device that's connected to a television set. Amazon Prime Video, Hulu, Netflix, and YouTube are examples of popular streaming video services.

tablet A handheld, battery-operated device with a touchscreen that can run apps and handle a wide range of tasks. In terms of digital entertainment, TV shows, movies, music, audiobooks, podcasts, eBooks, digital editions of newspapers and magazines, games, and a wide range of apps can all be experienced using a tablet.

terrestrial radio A traditional radio station that transmits over the radio airwaves and that requires an AM or FM radio to listen to it. Many of these stations, however, now simultaneously stream their broadcasts over the Internet.

video game console A standalone device that connects to a television set and allows individual video games to be played. Nintendo Wii, Sony PlayStation 3, Sony PlayStation 4, Xbox 360, and Xbox One are all examples of popular video game systems. Each has a vast library of individual games (sold separately) available for them.

web browser The software or mobile app that's used to surf the Internet on a computer or mobile device.

Windows-based PC A desktop or notebook computer that runs the Microsoft Windows operating system.

Index